Run for the Border

CITIZENSHIP AND MIGRATION IN THE AMERICAS
General Editor: Ediberto Román

Run for the Border

Vice and Virtue in

U.S.-Mexico Border Crossings

Steven W. Bender

NEW YORK UNIVERSITY PRESS

New York and London

NEW YORK UNIVERSITY PRESS
New York and London
www.nyupress.org

References to Internet websites (URLs) were accurate at the time of writing.
Neither the author nor New York University Press is responsible for URLs
that may have expired or changed since the manuscript was prepared.

Library of Congress Cataloging-in-Publication Data
Bender, Steven.
Run for the border : vice and virtue in U.S.-Mexico border crossings / Steven W. Bender.
p. cm.
Includes bibliographical references and index.
ISBN 978-0-8147-8952-0 (cl : alk. paper)
ISBN 978-0-8147-8953-7 (ebook)
ISBN 978-0-8147-2322-7 (ebook)
1. Emigration and immigration law — United States.
2. Mexican-American Border Region — Emigration and immigration.
3. Fugitives from justice — Mexico. 4. Fugitives from justice — United States.
5. Emigration and immigration law — Mexico.
6. Border security — Mexican-American Border Region. 7. United States — Foreign
relations — Mexico. 8. Mexico — Foreign relations — United States. I.
Title.
KF4819.B46 2012
325'.2720973 — dc23   2011045432

New York University Press books are printed on acid-free paper,
and their binding materials are chosen for strength and durability.
We strive to use environmentally responsible suppliers and materials
to the greatest extent possible in publishing our books.

Manufactured in the United States of America
10 9 8 7 6 5 4 3 2 1

To my compañero, Gil Carrasco,
always game for a border run,
and to Keith Aoki, who taught me
how to cross borders in academia.

Contents

Acknowledgments

As always, I am grateful for those who invested their considerable time in reviewing this manuscript or in contributing ideas along the way, including Raquel Aldana, Keith Aoki, Ray Caballero, Gil Carrasco, Evelyn Cruz, and Ediberto Román.

The University of Oregon law school supported my research in several respects, from a 2010 summer research award to the usual invaluable help of our research librarian Angus Nesbit and, in 2010, from my secretary Jenn Peters Kepka, whose editorial expertise I enjoyed during her year with us. My former student Stefanie Herrington, former editor of the *Oregon Law Review*, contributed her own superb editing skills. My research assistants Charley Gee, Leticia Hernandez, Kara Palombo, and especially Daniel Prince submitted timely and helpful work. Seattle University School of Law, my new institutional home, supported this research as well.

Once again I had the privilege of working with the great NYU Press team, especially Deborah Gershenowitz and Despina Papazoglou Gimbel. I'm honored by this book's inclusion in the NYU Press series Citizenship and Migration in the Americas, and especially thank series editor Ediberto Román for his vision and dedication in creating the series.

Introduction

For years, Congress has been debating so-called comprehensive immigration reform proposals. Especially since the September 11 attacks, these proposals are grounded in U.S.-Mexico border security measures that include using walls, technology, and expanded border patrol fleets to exclude undocumented entrants and drug traffickers and to block terrorists who might someday enter through our southern border, along with increased internal enforcement to detect undocumented immigrants within the United States and deport them. Some of the more compassionate proposals address the fate of millions of undocumented immigrants already toiling in U.S. jobs by offering them a chance to legalize their status. Some aim to improve slightly the prospects for future temporary entry by immigrant laborers seeking economic opportunity in the United States in numbers that exceed the current stingy limits on lawful immigration.[1]

Comprehensive reform is exceedingly narrow in focus. Ignoring the conditions and history that have long drawn Mexican and other Latin American immigrants to the United States to supply U.S. labor needs, reform proposals emphasize border enforcement and interdiction of laborers. Derogatory characterizations of immigrants and their supposed motives for entry shape these restrictive proposals, as do misleading contentions of their negative economic impact and their reliance on social services as a lure. The United States tends to approach its immigration policies and proposals for reform unilaterally without engaging Mexico (and other feeder countries) in a mutual examination of the powerful economic factors that lure most immigrants north across a border that separates one of the world's richest countries from one wracked with poverty. Historically, we pay scant attention to these nameless migrants who cross our border to supply cut-rate labor and survive in the shadows of prosperity, unless they clamor for their own fair chance at the American dream.

The aim of this study is to suggest a more comprehensive and pragmatic border policy than one shaped only by restrictive immigration enforcement prerogatives. Instead, proposed below are protocols informed by the extensive history detailed herein and particularly by the motivations and effects, economic and otherwise, of U.S.-Mexico border crossings in both directions over the last century and a half. Viewed through this lens, a strong argument can be made that Mexican migrant laborers headed north, whether documented or not, are the most meritorious of border crossers in either direction and that their crossings should be celebrated for their positive contribution to U.S. labor markets and our economic well-being and for their renewal of the American dream that hard labor brings the hope of prosperity. Many Mexican migrants enter for the most compelling reason in the human experience—survival for themselves and their families. Seen against the other crossings detailed in this book, these immigrant laborer crossings stand out in virtue, as they will in history's eventual assessment of our current restrictive and oppressive border policies.

Not just the destitute come to the United States from Mexico. As will be examined, raging drug violence in Mexico is prompting wealthy residents fearing kidnapping and extortion to flee with their families to the United States, also in the vital interest of survival. There are other compelling motivations for migration north. Although not necessarily seeking to survive, Mexican family members coming to the United States to reunite with U.S. residents—a strong motive for immigration known as family reunification—pose no threat to our well-being.

At the other end of the spectrum of vice and virtue, certain crossings are harmful to both countries, particularly the trafficking of methamphetamine to supply U.S. users, the trafficking of children (and adults) into the United States for sexual slavery, and the entry of U.S. residents into Mexico as sex tourists to engage in illicit acts with minors. Both countries are also harmed when fugitives cross the border to escape authorities and justice—with the notable exception of the pre–Civil War fugitive slaves who entered Mexico to escape their U.S. owners in Texas. The comprehensive border policy envisioned below articulates a harm reduction agenda that targets those border crossings most damaging to the residents and ideals of the United States and Mexico after stripping away the stereotypes and myths that surround the immigration debate and border policy generally. This discussion urges reform as the product of bilateral negotiation and implementation by treaty and cross-border organizations—reform that honors the shared economic and cultural legacy of the United States and Mexico and the prospects for future integration of these countries.

Policymakers must accept the reality that whatever is needed or desired in one country historically will be supplied by the other, despite government efforts to the contrary. The overwhelming failure of supply-side enforcement measures in the histories of Mexican labor immigration, the illicit drug trade, and even Prohibition-era alcohol trafficking confirms this futility. Rather than blaming Mexico, reform must acknowledge the U.S. role in luring immigrant labor and drug traffickers over the last century, and more generally the insatiable U.S. lusts for narcotics, sex, alcohol, cheap labor, and economic prosperity for its retirees and entrepreneurs. As with the stereotypically unsavory Mexican undocumented immigrant and menacing drug dealer that pervade U.S. media and policy discussions that emphasize the supplier of unlawful goods and services, U.S. residents too might be seen as threats to morality and law and order, given their sustained history of inviting illicit deliveries from Mexico as customers as well as their own southbound crossings with illicit motivations. But the primary aim of this study is not to vilify either party. Rather, it looks broadly at the history of border crossings in both directions for guidance in developing a framework for comprehensive border reform that breaks old stereotypes and moves the Americas forward as a model of cross-border cooperation to address problems between wealthy and poor nations, particularly a wealthy nation addicted to cheap labor and narcotics.

Recognizing the inevitability and the value of our reliance on Mexican labor, this book argues for immigration policies consistent with our ongoing labor needs, primarily by returning to the approach that governed immigration through most of the last 150 years of border crossings where no fixed U.S. immigration limit controlled Mexican entry. For illicit drugs, as another example, the comprehensive framework stated here concentrates on reducing illicit trafficking through selective legalization and reduction of U.S. demand, in contrast to failed interdiction policies that leave Mexico tormented by drug cartel violence. Southbound crossings are relevant too in framing a truly comprehensive border policy, particularly given the consequence of free trade and U.S. agricultural supports that damaged Mexican agricultural markets and led to northbound migrations.

Before supplying its proposed border framework, this book details the history of border passages both north- and southbound by Mexican and U.S. residents. An understanding of history is vital to break from our pattern of impulsive border policy based on biases and prerogatives of the moment that tend to focus and exaggerate blame on entrants. Throughout this history, border crossings can be grouped into motivation-driven categories defined primarily by economic lures or the desire to elude stricter laws in one jurisdiction. Of course, oftentimes both motivations inspire the border run, as for example when a U.S. business heads south of the border to exploit cheaper labor markets while at the same time circumventing U.S. environmental and labor laws. Likewise, Mexican drug traffickers driven by the potential for enormous profits serving the unceasing demand of U.S. users enjoyed—until the last few years—the near de facto legality of drug production (in the case of opiates and marijuana) and distribution in and through Mexico, given the localized corruption those profits enable. Going well beyond just the few types of border crossings—drug traffickers and migrant laborers—that define U.S. border policy and debate, this study paints a broader picture of the complex push-pull factors that drive border crossings and that overwhelm the mostly interdiction-oriented strategies thus far employed to control them.

This study of border crossings also aims to separate the virtue of immigrant laborers from the murderous drug cartels. Rejecting their current conflation in U.S. media and among U.S. policymakers as a dangerous threat to the United States that justifies our restrictive border policy, this study contends that immigrant laborers and drug cartels warrant independent consideration of their impacts within the United States. Admittedly, it is easy to conflate these two entries since this climate of restrictive border enforcement has prompted drug cartels to operate highly profitable immigrant smuggling operations. Yet the immigrant laborer, once in the United States, is a virtuous entrant who can spark a renaissance of U.S. cities and our economy in ways that deserve separate consideration and credit. At the same time, much of the supposed harm of the Mexican drug smuggler can be attributed to the trappings of the U.S.-initiated war on drugs rather than to the inherent harm of drug use, particularly when measured against the now mostly legal drug of alcohol. While recognizing the linkage between drugs and immigrants because U.S. demand drives both these entries and their consequent inevitability, this study supplies a separate framework to resolve these vexing border issues of our time.

Setting the stage for these controversial proposals, Part I confronts a unique motivation for border crossings that stands in some contrast to the discussion below of economic and legal differences between Mexico and the United States. The flight to Mexico by fugitives to escape justice in the United States inspires the phrase "run for the border" and opens this study of border crossings. Despite the prevailing societal images of treacherous Mexican fugitives, this discussion also details the history of Anglo crossings into Mexico to escape authorities and illustrates the limits of the model for bilateral cross-border cooperation that our extradition treaty with Mexico provides.

Part II surveys the economic motivations for southbound border runs by U.S. residents and companies lured by the promise of cheaper costs of living and of doing business in Mexico. Particularly within the last 30 years, corporate entries into the Mexican borderlands and throughout the interior of Mexico increased dramatically on many fronts, including maquiladora factories, tourist facilities, retail outlets such as Wal-Mart, and residential developments. The latter are meant to draw U.S. retirees, as well as telecommuters and vacation home purchasers, to resort-like settings priced well below comparable resort enclaves in Southern California that share similar views and warm climates. This discussion demonstrates that corporate capital and trade in most goods are freely mobile within North America, particularly capital that moves to labor sources. In contrast, the reverse is not true, as U.S. immigration policy aims to severely restrict the movement of Mexican labor toward jobs in U.S. markets without regard to prevailing labor demand.

Augmenting this history of southbound border runs for economic gain is Part III's examination of vice tourism into Mexico motivated by cross-border differences in laws. Dating back to the early twentieth century, U.S. residents regularly traveled south of the border to partake in activities illicit in the United States but permitted, or at least more readily available, in Mexico. Alcohol has been a lure for U.S. residents both during the Prohibition era and more recently for underage U.S. visitors partying in border town Mexico on weekends and at coastal Mexico resorts over spring break. The seduction of illicit flesh brings U.S. youth across the border to lose their virginity in border town brothels, and the scourge of child prostitution continues to attract U.S. sex tourists to Mexico. Throughout the mid-twentieth century, the ready availability of no-fault divorces in Mexico, in contrast to strict standards then prevailing in many U.S. jurisdictions, drew spouses across the border to obtain a quickie Mexican divorce. Part III details the full range of these illicit lures, also encompassing gambling, pharmaceuticals, and medical procedures.

Part IV examines the core of today's border policy emphasis on the border-crossing Mexican immigrant laborer and the illicit drug trafficker, while establishing the connected but distinct economic motivations of these crossers. In brief, immigrant laborers come north for a mere chance at survival, while drug couriers more often seek the brass ring of riches. Part IV also discusses the history of Prohibition-era rumrunners who funneled liquor across the border to U.S. destinations, earning enormous profits and signaling the futility of supply-side enforcement against economically motivated crossings. Only the legalization of alcohol stymied liquor trafficking routes. This history demonstrates the intoxicating lure of U.S. demand in prompting border crossings north, which routinely overpowers legal policies aimed to restrict these entries.

In constructing a framework for comprehensive border reform, Part V first collects and examines such lessons from the 150 years of border crossings detailed in this study. Particularly, these experiences demonstrate the futility of supply-side enforcement that concentrates on interdiction, as well as illustrate the U.S. history of unilateral policymaking on subjects that spur border crossings and on the crossers themselves. In contrast to interdiction, reducing U.S. demand for cheap labor and illegal drugs may hold more promise for controlling border movement, as the Prohibition experience confirmed when legalization of alcohol mooted the Mexican trafficking market overnight. Further, the supply-side approach of launching economic vitalization in Mexico, in contrast to tactics of interdiction that have dominated the U.S. arsenal, holds promise for easing the migratory pressures that sometimes tear Mexican families apart. This could even alter the climate in which U.S. sexual predators readily find child victims in Mexico in the hubris of economic desperation.

Informed by these histories, Part V tackles the two dominant border issues today—undocumented immigration and the illicit drug trade—and proposes a legalization protocol supplemented by an economic stimulus to Mexico. Legalization is not desirable in some regulatory areas, though, particularly child sex trafficking and trafficking of some drugs that approach alcohol in societal harm, notably methamphetamine. For those areas where enforcement may lag in Mexico despite laws that on their face seem similar to those in the United States, Part V argues for cross-border cooperation in enforcement freed from the distractions of today's policy emphasis on targeting and villainizing meritorious immigrant laborers and chasing marijuana traffickers.

Part V also breaks the mold of our fixation on northbound crossings and suggests a comprehensive framework for Mexican (and U.S.) regulation of southbound entry. Finally, Part V deals more generally with the issue of synchronization—whether and when the laws of the two countries are best aligned in areas that induce border crossings. Today, despite the U.S. emphasis on border security and on enacting and enforcing draconian immigration laws, the United States and Mexico are increasingly interconnected in their economies and cultures. Culture, it seems, knows no boundaries. The compelling policy question for the United States is whether it desires to continue treating Mexican immigrant laborers as against the grain of the ongoing cross-border melding of economies and cultures, or whether we will accept the inevitability of border crossings as history implores. If we embrace our Mexican immigrant entrants, we might finally acknowledge that their virtuous dream of economic survival resonates with our own vision of the American dream. Indeed, we may come to see that their run for the border has enriched our lives as it often has theirs.

PART I

Running for the Border to Escape Justice

The phrase "run for the border" originated long before its use in Taco Bell fast food advertising. As examined herein, it represents the familiar image of the treacherous Mexican outlaw running south for the Mexican border to escape justice in the United States. In the last few decades, the phrase also came to connote border passages in the opposite direction—undocumented immigrant Mexicans headed for the United States to work in jobs across the lower-income spectrum in fields, factories, and at fast food restaurants that ironically include Taco Bell. Although U.S. residents tend to associate running for the border, in either direction, with Mexicans afoot, U.S. residents have made their own border runs for years, whether for vices such as alcohol or sex or for economic advantage. Chapter 1 addresses the statistically few southbound border runs by fugitives to escape justice, including the stereotypical Mexican fugitive fleeing U.S. authorities, while later chapters detail the more common motivations for border crossings in both directions.

Despite the media and societal focus on Mexicans, Anglo fugitives too have fled south for the Mexican border in fact as well as in fictional settings. Conversely, Anglos have run north for the safety of the U.S. side of the border in numerous slices of pop culture, as well as in real life. Before achieving fame on reality television (and then infamy for his racist tirades), bounty hunter Duane "Dog" Chapman fled prosecution in Mexico by racing for the U.S. border after he apprehended a wealthy U.S. fugitive in Puerto Vallarta, which Mexican authorities regard as a form of kidnapping. Fictional runs north for the U.S. border are a favorite of country music, including Bobby Bare's "Tequila Sheila" (1980) in which Bare beats a card dealer in Juárez and runs for the U.S. border after his lover Sheila betrays his location to the federales (Mexican federal police). On the literary side, best-selling author Robert James Waller's *Puerto Vallarta Squeeze: The Run for el Norte* (1995) follows the journey from that Mexican resort town of an Anglo writer hired by an Anglo killer to drive him north in what the publisher calls "a hair-raising run for the border."

The main contrast in conceptions of Mexicans and Anglos crossing the border is whose passage is cheered and whose is jeered. When fictional Anglos race north for the Mexican border pursued by authorities, or even a jealous husband,[1] and on many occasions when they flee south as outlaws, U.S. audiences applaud their flight to the finish line of sanctuary. In contrast, the image of the criminal Mexican that dominates media ensures that no one roots for the Mexican who flees U.S. authorities. In the current climate, some xenophobes can even justify killing innocent border crossers headed north in search of economic opportunity if they cross without authorization, as illustrated by a Kansas lawmaker who in 2011 suggested shooting undocumented immigrants from helicopters as he would feral hogs damaging Kansas farms. In these hostile eyes, a Mexican crossing south to escape justice in the United States deserves the same punishment.

While seemingly unique in motivation from the economic and legal differences that drive most other border runs, fugitive border runs nevertheless share some similarities to vice tourism which aims to escape more restrictive U.S. laws. Differences in death penalty laws between the two countries are little known among fugitives and therefore are not the primary motivation of border flights from justice. Yet the aim to elude capture by escaping from one legal regime to another no doubt plays a role in inspiring the border run. Although presumably subject to extradition if caught, most southbound border fugitives assume they can better elude their fate within the interconnected U.S. law enforcement network by fleeing to Mexican terrain that is less internally connected, and in any event mostly disconnected from the U.S. system. In this way, border fugitives share the ideal with the vice tourist of enjoying some pursuit—here freedom—that is less available within the United States.

The following chapter focuses on southbound border passages by fugitives rather than northbound crossings to escape justice in Mexico. Despite the perception that many Mexican immigrants flee to the United States as criminals, the reality in Mexico that only some 1 or 2 percent of crimes result in conviction and jail time[2] suggests there is little imperative for Mexican criminals to leave their country to elude justice and to continue a crime spree into the United States.

El Fugitivo

¿Que pasa, señorita? ¡I am el fugitivo!
  —Cartoon character Calvin practicing for a border
  run with his imaginary tiger Hobbes after doing
  something awful to his father's car[1]

Taco Bell's "Run for the Border" slogan tapped into a rich and long-standing vein of bandido imagery in U.S. media. The cinematic Mexican bandido dates to the silent "greaser" films of the early 1900s, depicting Mexicans as dirty, oily, and gap-toothed in appearance, and as treacherous and soulless in character.[2] They slung guns, swilled tequila, and terrorized gringo men, women, and children while prowling the borderlands terrain. As one writer put it, Mexican bandits "robbed, murdered, plundered, raped, cheated, gambled, lied, and displayed virtually every vice that could be shown on screen."[3] In the silent *Cowboy's Baby* (1910), for example, a Mexican villain tossed a child into the river to drown, while in 1910's *Broncho Billy's Redemption*, a Mexican stole money that was intended to save a dying man. Mexican bandidos became a staple of commercial advertisement, too, most notably the late 1960s' Frito Bandito (misspelled from bandido), who brandished a pistol and menaced anyone who had Fritos Corn Chips. This media construction of savage bandidos helped cultivate the image of Mexicans as crossing into the United States to commit violent crimes and then running back for the Mexican border with blood money or bloody hands.

Mexico is also perceived in media and by the U.S. public as a haven for any criminal escaping justice—el fugitivo. Whether in music, literature, or cinema, Mexico became the destination of choice for Anglos and Mexicans alike to flee authorities and elude capture. In music, examples of the lyrical run for the border include Johnny Cash's maniacal "Cocaine Blues" (1968), describing the cocaine-fueled killer of his U.S. lover who ran too slow, leading to his capture in border town Juárez, Mexico; Jimi Hendrix's murderous Joe ("Hey Joe," 1967) who killed his "old lady" and ran to Mexico where no one would find him; Billy Joe and Bobbie Sue who headed down south after Billy shot an El Paso man they robbed in the Steve Miller Band's "Take the Money and Run" (1976); and Christopher Cross's rousing anthem "Ride Like the Wind" (1980), where the son of a lawless man gunned down ten and rode for the Mexican border. Actor Jack Nicholson as a horse thief in *Goin' South* (1978) crossed the Rio Grande into Mexico on horseback with a Texas posse in pursuit, exclaiming: "Viva Mexico! This here's Mexican dirt, you can't touch me." In 2001's *Super Troopers*, a highway patrolman pretends to be an outlaw stealing a police car to scare three stoner youth in the back-seat, questioning, "You boys like Mex-ee-co?" At the conclusion of 1972's *The Getaway*, fugitive bank robbers Steve McQueen and Ali MacGraw cross the border from El Paso (Spanish for the pass) into the sanctuary of Mexico in a hijacked pickup truck. Beloved by audiences, the movie *Thelma & Louise* (1991) features the fated run for the border of two women who decide to "haul ass" to Mexico after one kills an attempted rapist.

A happier ending is 1994's critically acclaimed *The Shawshank Redemption*, in which a wrongly convicted inmate escapes and heads for coastal Zihuatanejo to open a hotel on the beach and operate a charter fishing boat. Drawn to the Mexican coastline, the escapee crosses the border at Fort Hancock, Texas, toward "a warm place with no memory." Another candidate for happiest ending in the cinematic run for the border sweepstakes is 1994's *The Chase*, with Charlie Sheen as a wrongly accused fugitive who kidnaps a politician's daughter and heads for the border by car with a convoy of police giving chase. Improbably escaping from authorities, the fugitive and his hostage-turned-lover share the closing scene sipping drinks on a sunny Mexican beach. Similarly, Martin Lawrence as an affable jewel thief in *Blue Streak* (1999) escapes to Mexico with a $17 million diamond.

Literary runs for the border include the Mexican fugitive detailed in the novel *Border Town* (which inspired the 1935 film *Bordertown* starring Bette Davis and Paul Muni). After killing his rancher employer and his foreman in California's Imperial Valley, fictional Juan "Johnny" Ramirez headed south of the border for Mexicali to launch a new career as a border smuggler of drugs and booze.[4] Although not without some anxiety, the fugitive Ramirez successfully crossed the border at California's Calexico: "[Ramirez] walked toward the International Boundary, calm save for a rapidly beating heart, excited rather than fearful. Had they heard of the murders? Were they waiting for Juan Ramirez to try to pass the border? Once across the border he was comparatively safe. But if they suspected him of the murders, the border was where they would look first."[5] In contrast to the cinematic tragedy of Thelma and Louise, no doubt readers cheered the demise of the Mexican Ramirez when his speeding car tumbled down a cliff as U.S. police gave chase on his final border run toward Mexico.

Media imagery of Mexicans running south for the Mexican border as desperados with the law in pursuit does not fully match history's lessons. The realities of U.S.-Mexico border crossings to escape authorities extend to other groups in addition to Mexicans. Moreover, as described below, some of the crossings by Mexicans were prompted by circumstances much different from the familiar media images of the marauding, heartless bandido driven by depraved greed and bloodthirsty savagery.

Some crossings even implicated the savagery of Anglos, as in the case of considerable numbers of runaway slaves escaping from their ruthless Anglo owners and crossing into Mexico from Texas before the Civil War. By the 1850s, more than 4,000 slaves were thought to have fled to Mexico.[6] Mexico abolished slavery in 1829, and once under U.S. control, Texans urged the U.S. government to adopt an extradition treaty with Mexico to require our neighbor country to surrender fugitive slaves back to their U.S. owners.[7] Encompassing murder, arson, rape, robbery, and other crimes, a treaty that Abraham Lincoln signed with Mexico in 1862 rejected extradition of runaway slaves caught in Mexico.[8] Because the Mexican government refused to cooperate with them, Texas slave owners turned to private means to apprehend their slaves, advertising in newspapers and offering rewards, as well as hiring the equivalent of today's bounty hunter to chase their former slaves inside Mexico. In 1857, Texas went as far as enacting a law (titled an "Act to Encourage the Reclamation of Slaves, Escaping Beyond the Limits of the Slave Territories of the United States") authorizing the Texas state treasury to reward persons capturing and returning runaway slaves to their U.S. owners.[9] The aftermath of the Civil War brought some sanity to the region with slavery constitutionally outlawed, but the legacy of fugitive slave crossings to escape the brutality and inhumanity of slavery in the United States was soon lost in the media construction of fugitive Mexican border crossings.

The flip side of the crossings by fugitive slaves came at or near the conclusion of the Civil War in 1865, when many Confederates from the U.S. South—an estimated 1,000 by summer 1865—fled to Mexico, some to avoid imprisonment.[10] As the *New York Daily News* summarized the exodus: "The unsatisfactory state of affairs in the South, added to the great bad feelings exhibited by the Northern men and [news]papers to Southerners, have made many of the latter conclude to leave the country. In several places whole families are assembling to emigrate to Mexico."[11] At the time, the French controlled much of Mexico and had appointed as Emperor of Mexico the Austrian Maximilian, who reigned from 1864 until he was executed in 1867 after the French were defeated. Maximilian welcomed the Confederates, whose short tenure in Mexico was doomed on several grounds, most notably for their affiliation with the vanquished Maximilian. Other perils the Confederates faced during their time in Mexico included the cessation of employment on the U.S.-Mexico railroad, uprisings from Mexicans whose cultivated land some of the Confederates had usurped, and attacks from Mexican bandits who perceived the settlers as wealthy despite their relative poverty. Within a few years, many of the Confederates had left Mexico, some for other countries such as England and Canada.[12]

A couple of decades later, another exodus from the United States brought Mormon polygamists to northern Mexico, particularly the state of Chihuahua. Fleeing potential prosecution in the United States after Congress passed the Edmunds Act of 1882 establishing polygamy as a felony, the Mormon immigrants formed productive colonies to farm Mexican land. Their practice of polygamy, however, alienated many Mexicans. At the same time, the prosperity of these colonists and their extensive landholdings in Mexico clashed with the principles of the Mexican Revolution in the early 1900s, prompting the flight of many colonists back to the United States.[13] According to one of the Mormon colonists, in the revolutionary atmosphere of the time, plundering Mexican bandits made it "uncomfortable and extremely dangerous for them to remain longer."[14]

The image of the Mexican bandido dates from the mid-nineteenth century, during which time cattle rustling, horse thievery, and other border banditry were rampant in the upheaval that followed the loss of considerable Mexican territory to the United States and the subsequent struggles for control of Mexico's government. Cavalries, posses, and the notorious Texas Rangers routinely pursued bandits into Mexico, sometimes with permission of the Mexican government, other times not.[15] Despite the dominant narrative of the bandits as lawless and menacing Mexicans, some commentators have documented how the border bandit emerged from the displacement—physical, cultural, political, and economic—that Mexicans faced in the southwestern United States and Mexico during and after the Mexican-American War. One sociologist questioned why Anglos viewed Mexican Robin Hoods of the time in such negative terms: "[I]f an Anglo took the law into his own hands, he was generally labeled a hero or revolutionary, but a Chicano who engaged in lawlessness was somehow a bandit."[16] Indeed, that sociologist suggests some of the alleged Mexican thieves were merely recovering their own livestock previously stolen from them by Anglos.[17]

Some Mexicans were transformed into outlaws by U.S. law enforcement, particularly the Texas Rangers who terrorized Mexicans, and who were said to have forced their sometimes innocent targets into the terrible choice of being killed if they failed to defend themselves, and arrested and hung if they did.[18] The subject of a famous corrido (a Mexican folk song), Gregorio Cortez well represented this legacy, having shot a Texas sheriff in 1901 while resisting the sheriff's attempt to arrest him on trumped up charges of stealing horses.[19] Cortez rode (no doubt like the wind) for the Mexico border some 500 miles away on a sorrel mare, chased by the Texas Rangers. Because his hundreds of pursuers expected Cortez to head toward the border, he changed direction and traveled on foot for more than 120 miles toward north Texas. Cortez was finally caught and convicted of second-degree murder, but the governor of Texas eventually pardoned him in 1913. Much like the fugitive slaves crossing into Mexico, Cortez's story is little known among Anglos today.

Probably the most notorious border incursion and flight across the border was Mexican General Francisco "Pancho" Villa's raid on the New Mexico town of Columbus in early 1916. Previously, Villa had earned a reputation as a Mexican Robin Hood, mostly for his redistributive exploits that laid the foundation for the Mexican Revolution. Villa's raiding party of hundreds of men killed some seventeen troops and civilians in Columbus, while stealing horses and guns.[20] Despite these appearances of banditry and even the recent labeling of Villa by some as a "terrorist,"[21] uncertainty still exists about whether Villa's raid was abhorrent or somehow justifiable in the climate of revolution. Some even believe the U.S. government orchestrated it by paying Villa in order to spark patriotism and military enlistment toward the U.S. efforts in World War I. Most commentators more plausibly suggest the raid was retaliation against a change in U.S. willingness to supply Villa's revolutionary campaign in Mexico with guns and arms from the Columbus stockpile after the United States chose to recognize Villa's rival, Venustiano Carranza de la Garza, in governing Mexico.[22] Allegedly, U.S. President Woodrow Wilson even allowed Carranza's Mexican troops to enter U.S. territory and travel by train from Texas to Arizona, where they reentered Mexico to deal Villa's forces a crucial blow.[23] Responding to the Columbus attack, President Wilson secured Carranza's agreement to permit U.S. troops to enter Mexico to pursue Villa.[24] Wilson sent surely the largest posse in history (until Osama bin Laden's time) after Villa, mobilizing as many as 150,000 U.S. troops in battalions using horses, tanks, trucks, and open cockpit planes in an ultimately fruitless search for Villa in the hill country of Chihuahua, Mexico. As one commentator described it, "The eleven-month Chihuahua campaign of U.S. [General] Pershing against Villa [was] the greatest wild goose chase in which the United States Army ever engaged."[25]

Running counter to the media construction of Mexican bandidos marauding north and racing south to escape authorities is the complicated nineteenth-century history of Indian raids in the borderlands (as the boundaries changed over time with war and treaties) to pillage Mexican livestock for sale in trafficking markets and to take captives of Mexican women and children. Examples of raids by tribes of Comanche, Kiowa, Navajo, and Apache origin include the Comanche raid in 1835 to torch a Mexican rancho and take 39 Mexicans captive.[26] An historian described the bloodshed and devastation of the raids: "In addition to plundering homes, taking captives, and seizing horses and mules, [Indian raiders] exerted great energy and took great risks to kill Mexicans, slaughter thousands of pigs, cows, goats, and sheep, and set fire to dwellings, barns, and granaries."[27] That historian blamed the toll these raids exacted on Mexico as contributing to Mexico's loss of territory in the Mexican-American War:

> Raids and counter raids claimed thousands of lives, ruined critical sectors of northern Mexico's economy, stalled the north's demographic growth, depopulated much of its vast countryside, and fueled divisive conflicts between Mexicans at nearly every level of political integration. Exhausted, impoverished, and divided by fifteen years of war, and facing ongoing and even intensifying Indians raids, northern Mexicans were singularly unprepared to resist the U.S. Army in 1846 or to sustain a significant insurgency against occupation forces.[28]

Although both European settlers in the United States and Mexicans in the Southwest and Mexico regarded the Indians and their raids as "savage," the reality was that settlements by both groups into territory previously occupied by tribes uprooted Indians,[29] particularly Comanches and Kiowas, and competed for game the Indians needed to survive. Moreover, raids were mutual operations, as European settlers and Mexicans raided Indian tribes too, although usually they claimed the justification of retaliating for Indian hostilities or the nationalistic need to pacify the tribes.[30] Mexicans pointed blame at the U.S. government for driving tribes south into the proximities of Mexico, prompting raids into Mexican territory. Mexicans also accused the United States of supplying tribes with arms in exchange for stolen Mexican livestock.[31] When Mexico ceded vast portions of its territory (ostensibly including tribal lands) to the United States by means of the 1848 Treaty of Guadalupe Hidalgo at the conclusion of the Mexican-American War, that treaty contained the following provision as its eleventh article to assuage Mexico's concerns of continued tribal raids:

> Considering that a great part of the territories, which, by the present treaty, are to be comprehended for the future within the limits of the United States, is now occupied by savage tribes, who will hereafter be under the exclusive control of the Government of the United States, and whose incursions within the territory of Mexico would be prejudicial in the extreme, it is solemnly agreed that all such incursions shall be forcibly restrained by the Government of the United States whensoever this may be necessary; and that when they cannot be prevented, they shall be punished by the said Government, and satisfaction for the same shall be exacted—all in the same way, and with equal diligence and energy, as if the same incursions were meditated or committed within its own territory, against its own citizens.[32]

The same treaty article addressed the capture of Mexicans in tribal raids and their transport north across the border, and enlisted the United States in efforts to help free them:

> And in the event of any person or persons, captured within Mexican territory by Indians, being carried into the territory of the United States, the Government of the latter engages and binds itself, in the most solemn manner, so soon as it shall know of such captives being within its territory, and shall be able so to do, through the faithful exercise of its influence and power, to rescue them and return them to their country, or deliver them to the agent or representative of the Mexican Government. The Mexican authorities will, as far as practicable, give to the Government of the United States notice of such captures; and its agents shall pay the expenses incurred in the maintenance and transmission of the rescued captives; who, in the mean time, shall be treated with the utmost hospitality by the American authorities at the place where they may be. But if the Government of the United States, before receiving such notice from Mexico, should obtain intelligence, through any other channel, of the existence of Mexican captives within its territory, it will proceed forthwith to effect their release and delivery to the Mexican agent, as above stipulated.[33]

Despite these assurances, tribal raiding into Mexico increased after the treaty, prompting Mexicans to assert restitutionary claims against the United States in the millions of dollars. When the United States purchased parts of Southern Arizona and New Mexico in the Gadsden Purchase for $10 million in 1854, it bought its way out of these anti-raiding obligations: "The government of Mexico hereby releases the United States from all liability on account of the obligations contained in the eleventh article of the treaty of Guadalupe Hidalgo; and the said article . . . [is] hereby abrogated."[34] Cross-border raids continued into the 1880s, a time of displacement of tribal lands for Mexican railroad development,[35] prompting an 1882 agreement between Mexico and the United States allowing troops of either country to cross the border "when they are in close pursuit of a band of savage Indians."[36] Today, some 26 federally recognized tribes occupy the immediate U.S. borderlands and, overall, 149 tribes populate the four southwestern U.S. border states.[37] In many instances, today's enforcement against unlawful entries along the U.S.-Mexico border interrupts historical passages by these tribes across the border, requiring the tribes to honor the artificial separation of nations and cultures that border fencing represents.

As evident in the discussion above and particularly the history of the Indian raids and the legacy of counter raids, there is no simple narrative of banditry and lawlessness in the borderlands that implicates a single group such as the iconic Mexican bandido. Rather, the southwestern United States and northern Mexico, as physical boundaries changed over the years, hosted bandidos of all backgrounds. European settlers, Indians, and Mexicans (themselves a mix of Euro and indigenous cultures) ignored national boundaries to murder, rob, rape, and kidnap, and then ride to the sanctuary of their home base, sometimes in a different country.[38] Nevertheless, with an assist from Hollywood and the television western, the image of the Mexican bandido (or of Indian tribes in the southwestern United States attacking European settlers rather than Mexicans) defines that era of fugitive border crossing.

A modern isolated example of the Mexican bandido sourced in fact rather than media invention arose in the 1990s along the Southern Pacific train tracks connecting New Orleans to Los Angeles. The tracks follow the Mexican border just west of El Paso along the southern reaches of the New Mexico city of Sunland Park. Across from Sunland Park on the Mexican side of the border lies the desperately poor settlement of Colonia Anapra. Using an ingenious technique, Mexican bandits boarded stopped trains earlier on their route and once under way would pry open railcars looking for valuable cargo, even while traveling at high speed. Upon reaching the Colonia, the bandits would trigger the emergency brakes, often by tampering with the air hoses or putting scrap metal on the tracks. Youths recruited from the Colonia would rush pre-selected railcars to remove easily fenced items such as televisions, tennis shoes, and the like, loading them into vehicles on the Mexican side of the border.[39]

Despite the historic and modern images of marauding Mexicans running for the Mexican border, the reality of modern fugitive crossings also implicates Anglo residents of the United States. Child sex tourists, detailed in chapter 5, are the best example of modern-day outlaws who head to Mexico to commit heinous crimes and then return to the relative sanctuary of their homes and jobs in the United States. Alternatively, some Anglo fugitives commit their crimes in the United States and then flee to Mexico in order to better escape authorities. The ease of travel by air, combined with the now Anglo-cized resorts on Mexican beaches, make flights from justice seem like an extended vacation in comfortable surroundings with plenty of gringos for company. Although Mexicans in the United States, including U.S.-born, documented, and undocumented Mexicans, have fled justice into Mexico, Anglos, too, both prominent and obscure, have fled to Mexico with the law in pursuit. Yet the dominant narrative of a fugitive running to the border remains the Mexican bandido heading south.

Probably the most publicized run for the border in recent years by a Mexican is the flight of 21-year-old Marine Corporal Cesar Laurean from North Carolina to the Mexican interior. Born in Guadalajara, Laurean gained citizenship in the United States and married. Suspected in the disappearance of a pregnant Marine lance corporal who had earlier accused him of rape, Laurean became the target of a highly publicized three-month manhunt after police found the lance corporal's charred remains buried in Laurean's yard. Police arrested him in April 2008 as he walked down the main street of a small Mexican town. Laurean spent his months as a fugitive in Mexico living in a three-room cabin, sleeping on crushed cardboard boxes. For food he ate avocados from a nearby orchard, and the shelves of the cabin stored his supplies of canned tuna, soup, and candy. Laurean walked to town each day, spending hours in an Internet café. Locals thought he was a drug trafficker hiding in the mountains.[40]

Another widely publicized flight to the border followed the murder of an 18-year-old community college student in Kansas in 2007. Twenty-four-year-old Israel Mireles, a Mexican immigrant, was suspected after he left behind a blood-splattered hotel room and that hotel's floral bedspread was found near the victim's body along a highway. Mireles headed south for Texas, abandoning his rental car in northern Texas where he had relatives. Mireles fled to Melchor Muzquiz, a Mexican mining city near the Rio Grande, with his pregnant 16-year-old girlfriend who reportedly thought the trip was a vacation. Authorities apprehended Mireles there less than a month after the murder. Sparking international interest in the case was the revelation that the Anglo murder victim, Emily Sander, was actually a barely legal Internet porn model who used the pseudonym Zoey Zane.

Although Laurean and Mireles were both born in Mexico, they are a U.S. citizen and a documented immigrant, respectively. The most prominent example of an undocumented Mexican immigrant committing heinous crimes in the United States and fleeing south is probably serial murderer Ángel Maturino Reséndiz, the so-called Railway Killer, who routinely rode the rails from Mexico into the United States in the 1980s and 1990s. Reséndiz killed at least 16 people in the United States, many of them along or near the railroad tracks, before he surrendered on foot in 1999 to a Texas Ranger, accompanied by Reséndiz's sister, on a bridge connecting El Paso, Texas with Mexico's Ciudad Juárez. He was executed by lethal injection in Huntsville, Texas, in June 2006 after a judge ruled him mentally competent for execution.[41]

Anglos too have crossed the Mexican border to escape authorities in the United States. Likely the most high-profile fugitive is Andrew Luster, the heir to the Max Factor cosmetic fortune who grew up surfing and partying on the Southern California beaches. Freed on a $1 million bond in 2003 during his trial in California for drugging and raping three women that led to his conviction and a 124-year sentence, Luster fled for the border. His fondness for beaches drew him to the shores of Puerto Vallarta, Mexico, where he blended with the surfers and tourists under the assumed name of David Carrera. Tipped by a phone call that Luster was living in Puerto Vallarta, U.S. bounty hunter Duane "Dog" Chapman captured him in June 2003. Although in the United States bounty hunters operate legally in pursuing fugitives, mostly as agents of bail bond companies otherwise forfeiting bail, in Mexico (and Canada) bounty hunting is illegal.[42] So while Luster was returned to authorities in California to serve his lifetime prison term, Dog Chapman languished in a Mexican jail charged with deprivation of liberty, a lesser species of kidnapping. Once released on bail in Mexico, Chapman made a run for the U.S. border, driving to Guadalajara and boarding a plane for Tijuana, where a van took him across the border. As Chapman describes it, a U.S. immigration officer greeted him at the border: "Welcome home. We've been waiting for you. I'm with Homeland Security. You are safe. You're free."[43] But the Mexican government declared Chapman a fugitive from justice and prevailed on U.S. marshals to arrest him in Hawaii. Chapman fought extradition, and in 2008 a Mexican appeals court ultimately ruled Mexican prosecutors were barred from extraditing and prosecuting him, as the statute of limitations had lapsed.

Fugitives run for the Mexico border for many reasons. Some may be Mexican-born documented or undocumented immigrants who know the terrain of Mexico better than the United States. Internal flight within the United States is particularly risky for undocumented immigrants, because they are just one traffic stop away from arrest and capture in most U.S. jurisdictions for driving without a license or for possessing false identification. Some fleeing to Mexico may hope to take advantage of the difference in legal systems and of freedom from increasingly interconnected police and computer networks in the United States. Mexico offers the perception of an outlaw haven, although the author of a book on surviving as a fugitive disabused Anglos, particularly, of plans to escape to Mexico, warning that gringos are too conspicuous there, and that abject poverty opens too wide a possibility of snitching: "A country full of easily bribed informants isn't an outstanding place to hide, generally speaking."[44] As noted above, however, the presence of large numbers of Anglo tourists in beach destinations no doubt beckons some Anglo fugitives to blend in with the revelers.

For perpetrators of heinous crimes no matter their nationality, Mexico offers an additional lure for a fugitive run—Mexico's abolition of its death penalty and its refusal to extradite anyone who might face the death penalty. Mexico's last execution was in 1961. Although capital punishment remained legally possible in Mexico for subsequent decades, particularly within the military judicial system, it was not used.[45] In December 2005, Mexico abolished the death penalty across its legal system, joining the growing list of more than 100 countries to have done so, including Canada in 1976. Mexico's abolition evidences strong Roman Catholic influence and the widely shared global view that capital punishment violates human rights.[46] Sparked by raging drug trade murders and cartel kidnappings for ransom terrorizing Mexico, calls for reinstating the death penalty reflect widespread public opinion there (between 70 and 80 percent) that kidnappers who murder their victims should be executed.[47] Responding in 2008 to the demand to reinstate capital punishment, the president of the College of Catholic Lawyers in Mexico articulated the moral grounds against reinstatement: "[W]e would be falling into vengeance, and when will it end? If you kill a criminal, there will be a sense of hatred and vengeance and it will be a circle that never ends."[48] That president questioned the deterrence effect of the death penalty, pointing to 14-year-olds killing their peers in the United States, and called for reducing crime through the alternative means of education and establishing respect for the rule of law.

Although subject to some constitutional constraints, capital punishment remains embedded in the U.S. criminal justice system.[49] In 2008, only China (estimated 1,718), Iran (346), and Saudi Arabia (102) executed more persons than the United States (37).[50] Still, with the recent addition of New Jersey (2007), New Mexico (2009), and Illinois (2011) banning executions, almost one-third of U.S. states (16) have abolished the death penalty. Capital punishment is increasingly confined to the Southern states, where 80 percent of U.S. executions occur.[51] Because 34 U.S. states still permit execution—including the border states of California, Arizona, and Texas—the potential for conflict exists with Mexico's ban on capital punishment. Mexico's extradition treaty with the United States resolves the conflict against the death penalty, providing:

> When the offense for which extradition is requested is punishable by death under the laws of the requesting Party and the laws of the requested Party do not permit such punishment for that offense, extradition may be refused, unless the requesting Party furnishes such assurances as the requested Party considers sufficient that the death penalty shall not be imposed, or, if imposed, shall not be executed.[52]

As a condition to extradition for capital crimes, Mexico routinely insists on local assurances that the death penalty will not be sought, as do Canadian officials. U.S. prosecutors of accused killers Israel Mireles and Cesar Laurean, for example, had to deliver these assurances to gain the extradition of these two fugitives. Both ultimately were convicted and sentenced to life terms without parole. Pursuant to a 2001 decision of its Supreme Court, Mexico once viewed life sentences without the possibility of parole in the same category as death sentences—both precluded extradition unless U.S. prosecutors committed to a lesser sentence. Among the outcry prompted from the United States was a letter to Mexico's president from Senator Dianne Feinstein, who contended the interpretation stymied criminal justice in California, which punishes more than 40 different crimes with possible life sentences. She suggested that "Mexico's policy encourages people committing serious crimes in

California to flee to Mexico and escape just punishment."[53] Four years later in 2005, Mexico's Supreme Court reversed itself, allowing extradition despite the suspect facing life in prison in the requesting country.[54]

Because local district attorneys are not a party to the extradition treaty with Mexico, in theory they might renege on the agreement to waive the death sentence once the fugitive is back on U.S. soil. Prosecutors so far have not crossed this line.[55] Presumably, the U.S. government would pressure the local prosecutor, and prosecutors surely realize that their continued ability to gain the return of fugitives from the Mexican government depends on whether prosecutors across the United States play by the rules. Still, prosecutors rail at losing the death sentence. The district attorney prosecuting Cesar Laurean lamented that the case "should have been tried as a capital case [because] . . . there were aggravating factors but, unfortunately, we can't because of the [treaty] agreement we entered with Mexico many years ago."[56] An assistant prosecutor in Phoenix, Arizona, even characterized Mexico's stand as interfering with U.S. authorities:

We find it extremely disturbing that the Mexican government would dictate to us, in Arizona, how we would enforce our laws at the same time they are complaining about our immigration laws. Even in the most egregious cases, the Mexican authorities say, "No way," and that's not justice. That's an interference of Mexican authorities in our judicial process in Arizona.[57]

At the same time, Mexico apparently feels similarly about the U.S. criminal justice system that had 51 Mexican citizens awaiting execution in 2003, prompting Mexico to seek relief that year with the World Court in Hague. The Court responded by calling on the United States to review all pending death sentences given the widespread failures of U.S. authorities to adhere to the Vienna Convention. That Convention requires informing foreign detainees in the United States of their right to contact their government's consulate for legal advice.[58]

Although not a Mexican citizen and therefore outside the World Court's ruling, convicted mass murderer Christian Longo's story illustrates a similar disregard for the Vienna Convention on the other side of the border when U.S. officials removed a U.S. citizen fugitive from Mexico without involvement of the U.S. consulate. Prosecutors in the Oregon coastal community of Newport managed to elude the Mexican extradition constraints on capital crimes in retrieving Longo. An Anglo U.S. citizen and Jehovah's Witness,

Longo murdered his wife and three small children in 2001 and dumped their bodies in Oregon's coastal waters. Longo fled first to San Francisco in a stolen car, and flew from there to Cancún using a stolen credit card number. Earlier in his marriage, Longo and his wife had made several vacation trips to Mexico, where Longo had learned to scuba dive,[59] and Cancún must have seemed familiar to him. Longo spent his first few days as a fugitive in a Cancún hostel. After being accused of stealing from other guests, Longo joined a group of tourists headed for a campground near Tulum, a coastal town south of Cancún. There, Longo assumed the identity of a *New York Times* journalist while romancing a German photojournalist. By day, Longo pretended to research a travel story, while by night he smoked marijuana, drank, danced, and romanced his hut-mate. Featured on the television show *America's Most Wanted*, Longo was captured almost a month after the murders by an FBI agent accompanied by Mexican police. Ordinarily such an egregious case would require a death penalty assurance to Mexican officials, but the FBI agent apparently convinced Longo to voluntarily leave Mexico with him without informing Longo of the cross-border differences in death penalty laws or of Longo's right to see the U.S. consulate in Cancún, who likely would have informed Longo of the extradition protections.[60] Fearful of staying in a Mexican jail while awaiting the lengthy process of formal extradition, Longo opted instead to return to the United States, where he signed an acknowledgment of his voluntary return and ultimately was convicted of murder and sentenced to death by lethal injection. As of fall 2009, Longo was prisoner number twenty-seven on Oregon's death row, facing years in limbo while exhausting a federal and state appeals process in which Longo's lawyers will contend the FBI agent misled him to return voluntarily to the United States.[61]

U.S. officials have used a more blunt tactic than silence to elude Mexico's extradition laws—kidnapping. In 1989, Texas police officers kidnapped two Mexican nationals within Mexico and brought them to face capital murder charges in Port Arthur, Texas.[62] The next year, U.S. officials arranged the forcible kidnap of a Mexican national murder suspect in Guadalajara, who was flown by private plane to El Paso where U.S. Drug Enforcement Administration officials waited.[63] In the case of Mexican nationals such as this suspect, extradition to the United States under its treaty with Mexico is discretionary:

> 1. Neither Contracting Party shall be bound to deliver up its own nationals, but the executive authority of the requested Party shall, if not prevented by the laws of that Party, have the power to deliver them up if, in its discretion, it be deemed proper to do so.

2. If extradition is not granted pursuant to paragraph 1 of this Article, the requested Party shall submit the case to its competent authorities for the purpose of prosecution, provided that Party has jurisdiction over the offense.[64]

Under this provision, the United States must request extradition, and Mexico may in its discretion deny the request, in which event Mexico would prosecute its own citizen internally under its own laws. In an opinion authored by then-Chief Justice Rehnquist, the U.S. Supreme Court refused to read the treaty as frustrated if the United States abducted a Mexican citizen in order to circumvent Mexico's discretion to extradite him.[65] Following denouncement of the case by Mexico's government as "invalid and unacceptable" and threats to oust U.S. drug agents working in Mexico, in 1994 the two governments signed a treaty to prohibit transborder abductions, but the treaty was never sent to the U.S. Senate for ratification.

Historically, Mexico had been reluctant to extradite its citizens except in "extraordinary circumstances."[66] Moreover, in many cases Mexico failed to prosecute these accused citizens itself under Mexican law. In recent years, however, Mexico has been more willing to honor extradition requests.[67] Most U.S. extradition requests are related to drug trafficking charges,[68] the remainder for murder charges. U.S. officials are particularly concerned over Mexico's historical reluctance to extradite drug traffickers, contending the Mexican prison system is so corrupt that traffickers can continue their operations from behind bars. Former Mexican President Vicente Fox recognized this climate of corruption in ramping up extraditions of drug cartel leaders during his tenure, stating:

> To me [Fox] it simply made good sense to rid Mexico of a cartel leader who could offer a million-dollar bribe to our underpaid prison wardens. . . . Bush and I, together with our legal experts and our diplomats, worked out a deal in which the United States agreed to forgo the death penalty and give life sentences to cartel leaders who had committed crimes in both countries. We were able to extradite sixty-three drug lords to safer U.S. prisons. Immediately after taking office, President Calderón [Fox's successor] used these legal tools to extradite fifteen more drug kingpins.[69]

Despite the appearance of cooperation in extraditing suspected drug traffickers to the United States, the history of U.S.-Mexico relations reveals that the United States often acts unilaterally in areas of mutual interest such as drug enforcement. Further, as discussed in chapter 8, this recent Mexican imperative to ramp up internal drug enforcement, while earning praise from U.S. officials, has devastated Mexico with resultant drug violence. The current enforcement approach that relies on the arrest and in many cases deportation of drug traffickers to the United States is part of the deeply flawed emphasis on supply-side enforcement that the United States has advocated for decades. This enforcement prerogative cares little for its effects on Mexico, elevating law and order principles in the United States over the security and survival of Mexico's borderland communities, despite the root cause of trafficking attributable to U.S. drug use. Chapter 12 poses an alternative strategy to effectively end the drug war and the staggering violence Mexico has endured in the interest of supplying the resilient U.S. habit.

The dominant stereotype of Mexicans has shifted over time from the rural bandido portrayed above to the equally treacherous urban gangbanger or drug dealer. As explained in chapter 8, mainstream Anglo users in the United States anchor the drug trade, yet the overwhelming media and societal focus on drug trafficking is on Mexican and other Latino/a suppliers. Similarly, people of all backgrounds commit crimes in the United States, but anyone listening to hate radio and media outlets such as Fox News might assume that Mexican undocumented immigrants are solely to blame for most illegal activities.[70] This modern construction of the urban undocumented Mexican immigrant as a marauder responsible for most lawlessness in U.S. cityscapes connects directly to the historic image of the Mexican fugitive running south to the Mexican border to escape justice in the United States.

PART II

Economic Motivations for
Southbound Border Runs

U.S. citizens retiring in Mexico or purchasing a vacation residence on its sandy beaches, and U.S. corporations headed south of the border, tend to share the economic motivation of maximizing wealth or profit. Yet even more striking economic imperatives propel most Mexican immigrants headed north. The Mexican immigrant often has lived hand to mouth in Mexico and aims to make a better life for his or her family, and in many cases simply to survive. By contrast, retirees, second-home owners, and U.S. companies intend to enhance wealth, not grasp a chance at survival.

Mexican immigration north defines the relationship today between the United States and Mexico. Increasingly, Mexican immigrants are stigmatized and challenged as poisoning the well from which the U.S. economy and culture spring. Contrasting with this derogatory framing of northbound crossings, U.S. residents regard retirees and second-home purchasers abroad in wistful, romanticized terms. These entrants are admired for their initiative and envied as pioneers on Mexican soil and sand. Although some U.S. politicians might voice objections about lost jobs, U.S. companies headed south of the border in turn are seen in financial circles as merely fulfilling their corporate raison d'être—to earn the most possible wealth for their shareholders. Yet when Mexicans cross a line in the dirt toward a better chance at survival, their northbound run for the border in the eyes of many observers imperils the United States.

This hostile attitude surrounds the immigration debate despite strong evidence of the economic contribution of immigrants, even undocumented immigrants, to the United States. Economists have demonstrated that immigrant entrepreneurship creates jobs in the United States, and that undocumented labor particularly is a boon to the U.S. social security system.[1] Despite ending the current windfall in social security revenues from undocumented immigrants now ineligible for benefits, immigration reform loosening restrictions would boost the economy overall by generating new tax revenue currently lost in the underground labor economy.[2] Although xenophobes can point to contrary studies on the economic costs of immigration, these are normally focused on costs for public services that immigrants may need for their families, particularly education, without considering the economic benefit these families deliver to the local community through their hard work, entrepreneurship, and even their payment of property taxes through rents that directly support the school systems. It is deceptively easy to suggest that school budgets have increased to accommodate immigrant students, but far more accurate to account for the myriad ways in which these immigrants have boosted the local economy through their presence and their hard work. Even to the extent that local costs might be shown to outweigh the benefits from immigrant families in a particular jurisdiction, this is often because local employers aren't paying a fair living wage (or providing medical benefits) to their immigrant employees, forcing them into overcrowded housing that may strain local resources while wealthy investors outside the community enjoy the corporate profits from underpaid labor.

In contrast to the hostility toward Mexican immigrants in the United States, Mexico currently regards its emigrants in compellingly laudable terms. Rather than being seen as traitors, they are now viewed as "courageous, hard-working individuals who sacrifice for their families."[3] At the same time, Mexicans generally think well of U.S. retirees and U.S. corporate entries—for the latter, Mexicans flock to the border maquiladora factories seeking employment and to Mexican Wal-Mart stores to shop. Discounting possible concerns of drug violence in retirement enclaves, Mexico's President Felipe Calderón expressed his country's zeal for hosting U.S. retirees in telling the AARP that "Mexico is a great place to live and enjoy, so, come with peace of mind, feel safe."[4] Sadly, U.S. residents fail to similarly regard Mexican workers who have contributed so steadily and significantly over the last century in building the U.S. economy through their hard labor. Whether in the agricultural fields during World War II or later, or in countless other workplaces from factories to their domestic service in U.S. homes, Mexican laborers have served U.S. interests. But too often in the United States, the American dream excludes newcomers from its promise that hard labor will bring economic reward and social acceptance. If the laborers are undocumented immigrants, no degree of hard work can earn them favor. Rather, California's 2010 gubernatorial candidate Meg Whitman channeled the prevailing U.S. attitude toward the undocumented when she allegedly discovered that her longtime Mexican housekeeper was an undocumented immigrant and rebuked her, "From now on you don't know me, and I don't know you."[5]

In contrast to the restrictive U.S. policies for entry of Mexican immigrant laborers discussed in chapter 9, the materials below consider the relative ease with which U.S. retirees and vacation home purchasers, and U.S. corporate interests, can gain entry into Mexican terrain in their pursuit of economic prosperity. As with our travel as tourists, we tend to take these entries for granted as the prerogative of residents of a wealthy country to enjoy and exploit the opportunities that a poorer neighboring country offers. Yet when Mexican laborers head north for survival, our formal, lawful avenues of entry for most such low-wage laborers stand closed, in effect with signs reading: "You don't know us, and we don't know you."

Gringos in Paradise

What few people—at least, outside of Mexico—have bothered
to notice is that while all the nannies, cooks, and maids have
been heading north to tend the luxury lifestyles of irate Repub-
licans, the Gringo hordes have been rushing south to enjoy glo-
rious budget retirements and affordable second homes under
the Mexican sun. Yes, in former California Governor Pete
Wilson's immortal words, "They just keep coming." . . . Many
wealthy Southern Californians evidently see no contradiction
between fuming over the "alien invasion" with one's conservative friends at the Newport Marina one day, and flying down to
Cabos the next for some sea-kayaking or celebrity golf.
—Mike Davis, "The Baby Boomer Border Invasion"[1]

Addressed in chapter 4 is the lure of Mexico as a tourist destination.
Related to that impetus for transitory south-of-the-border runs is Mexico's
more permanent attraction to retirees and second-home buyers, as well as
telecommuters and others with the flexibility to conduct their business in the
United States from Mexican turf. In 2005, the *Dallas Morning News* reported
that more than one million U.S. citizens were living in Mexico at least part of
the time, a fivefold increase over the decade.[2] The largest group of this migration is retirees. Published by *International Living* magazine, albeit before drug
violence gripped the country, the 2008 Global Retirement Index rated Mexico
as its top location for retirees. Although they are also motivated by the rich
cultural history of Mexico, its sunny climate, and its white sand beaches, no
doubt the cheaper cost of living is the primary attraction of a Mexican retirement. For example, in the Mexican seaside town of San Carlos, about a four-
hour drive from the Arizona border, houses sold in 2005 at the peak of the
international real estate market for between $300,000 and $500,000. For that
money, "you get a three-bedroom, three-bath, 2,000 square foot house with a
sea view and a swimming pool. That's perhaps a third the price of comparable,
sea-side real estate in Southern California."[3] A few years later, in the deflated

U.S. market, Southern California's Laguna Beach still boasted an average Zillow[4] value in May 2009 of $1,440,400 for its housing stock, some of it without views. Nevertheless, homes are cheaper in many inland U.S. retirement communities, especially in comparison to the resort enclaves in Mexico that tend to best attract U.S. retirees, many of whom prefer gate-guarded communities with resort-style amenities and U.S. citizen neighbors to living within traditional Mexican neighborhoods. Often situated in the most picturesque locations, these enclaves carry a considerable price premium, in part to compensate for their resort amenities. Before the international real estate crisis arrived, a 2004 article chronicled the dynamic and frenzied growth of these privileged housing markets in Mexican beach resorts intended for U.S. buyers, observing the condominium and other housing developments often sold out before construction was complete.[5]

Even where home acquisition costs equal or exceed options available in the United States, the cost of operating a home tends to be far cheaper in Mexico. Insurance rates are lower and real estate taxes can be dramatically less—as little as $30 a year on a $200,000 property.[6] Of course, those lower tax rates reflect the lesser government services the retirees and transplants receive in Mexico, owing to minimal infrastructure outside the gated walls and fewer government safety nets, from health care to unemployment. Repair and maintenance costs tend to be less in Mexico, as are the costs of hiring maids and landscapers. Other costs of living, such as medical and dental care, may be less, aside from the potentially greater expense in Mexico of certain luxury goods.[7]

With its lower cost of living, Mexico is also drawing residents from the far end of the retirement spectrum with its nursing homes staffed with bilingual workers in a warm climate. One source announced recently that Mexico had displaced Florida and California as the most popular North American location for nursing homes, and suggested that while initially these nursing homes attracted third-generation Latinos/as who had no family in the United States to care for them, now U.S. residents of all backgrounds were coming to Mexican nursing homes.[8] Although most of the remittances sent to Mexico from the United States are from immigrants in the north sending money to their needy families who stayed behind south, no doubt a sizeable portion of the remittances that immigration foes decry as bleeding the United States of resources is in fact being sent to Mexico by retirees from their U.S. bank and investment accounts.

Adding to the appeal of Mexico to U.S. residents is the increasing access in Mexico to U.S. goods and media. For example, satellite television can bring any English language programs and movies into the Mexican retiree's living room, and the Internet allows them to read their favorite U.S. morning paper. Retirees can bring a one-time duty-free load of a reasonable amount of their household goods from the United States, including their computers and televisions to tap into this U.S. programming.[9] Food stores increasingly stock brands found in the United States. Wal-Mart, Costco, and Home Depot supply household items. In resort areas, particularly, familiar U.S. restaurants abound. A recently opened shopping mall in Puerto Vallarta offered U.S. and Mexican patrons the eateries of Hooters, Chili's, Burger King, and Subway, and a Starbucks coffee shop.[10]

In contrast to the numerically limited potential for retirees from other countries to retire in the United States, Mexico generally welcomes U.S. retirees with immigration categories many retirees can satisfy. Retirees generally opt for FM2 status, an immigrant visa for one year that can be renewed four times. At the end of the five-year period, the visa holder can request residency status in a subjective decision made by Mexican government authorities.[11] Those granted full residency status in Mexico need not give up their U.S. citizenship, and are entitled to all rights of Mexican nationals aside from the right to vote in elections.

Some have argued that the United States should similarly encourage foreigners of means to retire on its shores by issuing an unlimited number of retirement-friendly visas.[12] Such a retirement visa would allow a no-hassle entry for those retirees meeting verifiable income or asset requirements, presumably boosting the fractured real estate markets in traditional retirement states such as Florida, California, Arizona, and Nevada. Instead, today's foreign retiree in the United States probably needs a familial connection already here and the patience for a long wait toward obtaining permanent resident status the applicant may never live to see.

Mexico's FM2 immigrant visa may also be suited for U.S. citizens with flexible work locations such as artists, writers, and telecommuters. For example, in 2008 the HGTV network show *House Hunters International* showcased the quest of a U.S. family of four looking to relocate from their cramped two-bedroom condo in coastal Carlsbad, California, to a home in the sustainable master-planned development of Baja's Loreto Bay. Both parents were telecommuters, one in international sales, the other a nursing consultant, and the family was looking for a larger home with office space, for around $300,000 to $400,000, in a much less expensive market than Carlsbad. Even after the U.S. real estate implosion, the Zillow website specified the average home value in Carlsbad in September 2009 as $549,900. The U.S.

family found their dream home in Loreto, which they raved about as a "very safe" community—a three-bedroom home known as Casa Aquarius, with a roof deck and viewing tower offering ocean and mountain views, for only $420,000, amounting to $185 per square foot and only slightly over their budget. *House Hunters International* also featured a Seattle real estate broker searching for a home in the Cabo San Lucas area from which she could continue to run her U.S. business. She purchased a 3,000-square-foot residence near Cabo, just a short walk to the ocean, with a swimming pool, an ocean view, and a freestanding circular office with a 360-degree view, for only $300,000.

Second-home owners are increasingly drawn to Mexico for the same reasons as retirees and telecommuters, with many of them looking toward an eventual retirement in Mexico. For years, wealthy U.S. residents have purchased residences in Mexican beach and resort towns, flocking south for winter as early as October. Even less wealthy U.S. residents, with the aid of a home equity loan on their primary U.S. residence, might purchase a relatively inexpensive Mexican second home as close as a nonstop flight from most major U.S. cities. For those with fewer resources, fractional time-shares in Mexican resort hotels and condominiums in locations such as Cabo San Lucas and Puerto Vallarta offer an alternative form of sustained tourist occupancy. In 1974, *Los Angeles Times* columnist Jack Smith published *God and Mr. Gomez*, his ode of hiring Romulo Gomez, a Mexican contractor, to build a second home on leased land on Baja's Pacific coast, south of Ensenada.[13] Despite delays and cost overruns, Smith acknowledged his vacation home would have cost at least twice and very likely three times as much to build in Los Angeles, without the Mexican craftsmanship. Reflecting that dreams of Mexican vacation home ownership still exist, HGTV's *House Hunters International* recently documented a U.S. family with a modest home in Utah that purchased a dramatic three-bedroom vacation home in coastal Puerto Escondido (in the Mexican state of Oaxaca). Perched on a seaside cliff with an ocean-view swimming pool, the residence cost only $430,000—perhaps 15 percent of what a similar home would cost in Southern California. The couple—a doctor and her husband, a college men's golf coach—planned to spend all their vacations at the house. Many of these vacation home owners rent out their Mexican residences while away, often taking advantage of professionally managed rental pool arrangements available in some of the resort condominium developments.

Mexico provides a visa designed for these second-home owners (or for those retirees who prefer its flexibility)—the FM3—permitting residency in Mexico up to one year, renewable for an additional four years, following which a new FM3 can be sought.[14] Well suited for vacation-home owners who may spend only a few total months or even weeks annually in Mexico, this visa allows unlimited entries into and exits from Mexico. The FM3 visa does not include the FM2's restriction that permits that visa holder to be absent from Mexico only up to a specified number of months during a five-year period.

Whether as retirees, telecommuters, or vacation-home owners, U.S. residents have changed the complexion of many Mexican towns and cities. Four Mexican waterfront regions have emerged as the primary corridors of U.S. migration: southern Baja in the Cabo San Lucas area, the Puerto Vallarta region, Sonora on the northern Sea of Cortez from San Felipe to Puerto Penasco, and the Cancún area.[15] Some who purchased early in the Mexican market in scenic locations such as Cancún (which was populated in the early 1970s only by a few fishermen) earned fantastic returns on their housing investment.[16] Developments in the Cabo area experienced as much as 300 percent appreciation in the boom years between 2000 and 2005.[17] Emerging coastal regions for expatriates include Loreto Bay, on the Sea of Cortez about 360 miles northeast of Cabo, and the Ensenada beach area south of Tijuana, only a 90-minute drive from San Diego. In the Loreto region, recently the Mexican government's national trust fund for tourism development, FONATUR, poured $200 million into infrastructure improvements in transportation, sewage, and the like, hoping to position Loreto for tourism on par with similar targeted improvements years ago in Cancún that created an international destination. With the arrival of the global real estate crisis beginning around 2007, however, developments in these blossoming regions have suffered the most. For example, developers planned to construct three 26-story condominium towers just 30 minutes south of San Diego on the Baja coast. Carrying the prestigious Trump name, the Trump Ocean Resort fell victim to the credit crisis that stripped potential condominium buyers and the developer of financing, and construction was cancelled in early 2009. Similarly, a 6,000-unit residential community developed by a Scottsdale, Arizona-based company for U.S. buyers, located near the picturesque Baja coastal village of Loreto, was suspended in mid-2009. Featured in the above-described HGTV episode before its failure, this Loreto Bay development, with prices once ranging from $375,000 for a small two-bedroom attached home to the mid-$900s for four-bedroom models, was conceived as a sustainable community with density and environmental restrictions. Surviving the crisis thus far is a U.S.-based condominium project in Loreto, JW Marriott Residences, offering ultra-luxurious waterfront view units starting from the $700,000s, with a 2,251-square-foot unit currently advertised for $1,178,000.[18]

As it has done in slowing tourism, the drug war in Mexico has helped dampen residential interest from U.S. buyers. Particularly affected are markets proximate to the border, such as the Baja coastline south of Tijuana, where prices are falling. Moreover, the border crackdown on drug smuggling, as well as the enforcement prerogatives against undocumented immigration, have slowed border travel north and thus strain the once convenient weekender use of these Baja vacation homes only a few hours by freeway from most Southern California residences.[19]

In the early 1900s, U.S. residents controlled vast and valuable Mexican terrain, punctuated by the massive ranches in Northern Mexico owned by publishing magnate William Randolph Hearst. Crafted by the bloody Mexican Revolution, the 1917 Constitution embodied ideals of land reform by outlawing foreign ownership of border and coastline property: "Within a zone of one hundred kilometers [sixty-two miles] along the borders and fifty [thirty-one miles] of the shores, for no reason may foreigners acquire legal title to the lands and waters."[20] This so-called restricted zone encompasses the entirety of Mexico's almost 6,000 miles of coastline, as well as the borderlands territory, and overall comprises most of the Baja peninsula and some 40 percent of Mexico's total land area. Despite the apparent ban on any form of U.S. ownership in the zone, Mexico enacted creative legislation in 1973 to allow U.S. residents and other foreigners to acquire the beneficial interest in coastal and border property through trusts (known as fideicomisos) created with Mexican banks. For a fee (now averaging between $200 and $1,000 annually), these banks hold the legal title to the property, and designate the U.S. resident as the trust beneficiary entitled to possess the property as an owner would. The fideicomiso owner may transfer the remaining beneficial interest in the trust to any buyer of the property, whether a Mexican national or a foreigner. Aside from their ongoing fees, the downside of these trusts initially was their expiration after 30 years. Even for retirees, 30 years might pass too quickly for the investment to pencil out. But in 1989, the Mexican government liberalized the land trust procedure to authorize a 50-year initial term, with an automatic renewal for another 50 years. Shortly thereafter, in the 1993 Federal Investment Act, the Mexican government sparked commercial development in the restricted zone, such as resorts and retail, by allowing foreign investors to form a Mexican corporation to own direct title to the real estate when used for nonresidential purposes.[21]

For real estate in the Mexican interior outside the restricted zone, known as the permitted zone, the 1917 Constitution allows foreign ownership conditioned only on the foreigner signing what is known as a Calvo clause agreement with the Ministry of Foreign Affairs whereby the U.S. citizen agrees to be treated as a Mexican national with respect to the interior property and to refrain from invoking protection of the U.S. government in matters relating to the property. Any fears that Mexico might nationalize foreign-owned real estate, however, are mostly unrealistic today, given the North American Free Trade Agreement (NAFTA) provision that neither the United States nor Mexico may "nationalize or expropriate an investment of an investor of another Party [nation] in its territory . . . except (a) for a public purpose . . . (c) in accordance with due process of law . . . [and on payment of fair market value]."[22]

With these immigration and ownership allowances, there are no fundamental legal impediments to U.S. citizens entering Mexico and acquiring a retirement residence or vacation home. Practical constraints may come into play, however, primarily the higher interest rates (albeit at a huge drop from the staggering 65 percent interest rates prevailing in the mid-1990s)[23] and down payment requirements that Mexican mortgage loans tend to carry given the greater uncertainties lenders face south of the border, as well as the sporadic availability of title insurance insuring that the U.S. owner (or the bank holding in trust) has good title to the underlying real estate. Many U.S. enclave areas in Mexican resort towns offer both financing arrangements with U.S.-based lenders and the prospect of title insurance, contributing to segregation within Mexico of U.S. transplants in resort settings and native Mexicans outside the gates.

Given the relatively high prices of these enclave communities, few U.S. transplants will be mingling with the Mexican locals. The signs promoting one representative development in Cancún—the Residencial Bay View Grand condominiums—signaled this message by featuring "a blue-eyed family of Nordic appearance frolicking in the sands of the world-famous resort."[24] Instead, their neighbors will be other U.S. retirees, telecommuters, and vacationers, and the wealthy from other countries. All have made the economic decision that owning or renting property in Mexico is financially wise given the higher costs of resort real estate in the United States.

In contrast to the U.S. immigration system that stymies the dreams of many desperate Mexican families to seek greater financial opportunities in the United States, Mexico contemplates and in many instances encourages these U.S. resident entries, illustrated most vividly by the aforementioned

$200 million of infrastructure improvements the Mexican government invested in Loreto to lure U.S. transplants. Rather than building border walls, then, Mexico is building bridges to foreign investment and opportunity.

Despite the temporary impediment of the global real estate crisis and the deterrent of drug violence, the long-term demographic writing on the wall for Mexico is continued immigration from U.S. retirees, as tens of millions of baby boomers reach retirement age and, as many experts predict, look for warmer climates and cheaper homes.[25] The current economic crisis may prove a boon for Mexican resort communities as retirees with devalued retirement accounts opt for cheaper venues abroad in lieu of working longer in the United States. These U.S. arrivals tend to inflate local property values, presumably displacing local residents no longer able to afford areas proximate to the gated enclaves of U.S. expatriates. One writer described the dichotomy between wealth (or relative wealth) and poverty, and the mixed bag of economic and other benefits, that accompany U.S. residents moving onto the Baja coast:

> Largely retirees, they dominate a seventy-mile stretch of beachfront settlements that range from cheap trailer parks to tony condominiums and red-tiled homes. Their owners or renters provide jobs for Mexican housemaids and handymen, but these residents also monopolize the beaches, now closed to Mexicans. The contrast between their abodes and the shacks of poor Mexicans who live on hillsides across the way is startling.[26]

Although Mexicans living in Mexico have a much higher rate of homeownership (exceeding 80 percent) than Mexicans living in the United States (about 50 percent), Mexico's housing stock is often self-built, dilapidated, and overcrowded,[27] supplying this stark contrast between Mexican citizens in shacks and U.S. transplants in stylish homes.

In the United States, however, Mexican immigrants with their limited financial resources face de facto restricted zones in many U.S. communities, particularly those along the California coastline and near New York City, that are too expensive to enable immigrants in their prime working years to dream of comfortable living, much less of retirement. Arrivals of immigrants into crowded U.S. urban communities sent real estate values soaring in the 1990s and early 2000s and contributed to the challenging economics of Mexican immigrants seeking prosperity while laboring in low-paying jobs in the shadows of the American dream. Many of these Mexican immigrants, some refugees from NAFTA's devastation of rural economies in Mexico, came from outside the coastal and borderlands restricted zone. U.S. settlements in Mexico will do little to boost the struggling economy in Mexico's interior, as most retiree and tourist enclaves are in the Mexican coastal regions. Discussed in chapters 10 and 13, meaningful economic assistance to these rural interior zones is needed to relieve the undue pressures on immigration north.

Winning critical acclaim, the film *Sleep Dealer* (2008) assumes a future with a fully sealed border, requiring the outsourcing to Mexico of control over U.S. robots that perform the grueling labor Mexican immigrants currently undertake. Given the scant likelihood of a truly sealed border, should today's trends prevail, Mexican immigrants facing an absence of opportunity in rural Mexico will venture to the United States at the same time the aging U.S. Anglo population migrates southward to their retirement havens in coastal Margaritavilles. The irony is that, through their labor contributions, the Mexican immigrants will sustain the U.S. social security system these retirees rely upon, yet the retirees themselves will have departed for cheaper Mexico. Although the Mexican coastal regions may flourish with the construction and service jobs these U.S. arrivals create, this model holds no promise for the rest of Mexico, stripped of its most determined and industrious youthful workers in return for an aged gringo population hugging its coastlines. In this vision, the gringo influx may exacerbate rather than solve Mexico's economic woes.

3

A Giant Sucking Sound

You implement NAFTA, the Mexican trade agreement, where they pay people a dollar an hour, have no health care, no retirement, no pollution controls, et cetera, et cetera, et cetera, and you're going to hear a giant sucking sound of jobs being pulled out of this country right at a time when we need the tax base to pay the debt and pay down the interest on the debt and get our house back in order.

—Ross Perot, October 19, 1992 presidential debate

Just as U.S. retirees and second-home owners have journeyed south of the border for economic advantage, so too have U.S. entrepreneurs and corporations run for the Mexican border for decades to profit from Mexican business and labor markets. Around the start of the twentieth century, U.S. entrepreneurs amassed controlling stakes in crucial Mexican economic sectors such as railroads, mining, and petroleum that could serve U.S. markets by extracting Mexican resources. More recently, U.S. entrepreneurs entered Mexico by means of the maquiladora structure (from the Spanish word maquilar, meaning to perform a task for another) to produce goods in Mexico meant for U.S. consumers, while taking advantage of cheaper Mexican labor. In similar fashion, U.S. home buyers in Mexico reap the benefit of cheaper labor costs in the construction of their Mexican homes.

Typically, economic motives drove these foreign entries and investments. Closely linked to and augmenting the economic reasons for entry of U.S. entrepreneurs is the motive of differences in laws or legal treatment in Mexico. As discussed below, although Mexican law ostensibly protects labor and the environment in similar fashion to laws in the United States, a relative absence of enforcement, both due to a lack of resources and to well-entrenched bribes of government officials, essentially strips these protections of teeth. In this regulatory void, U.S. entrepreneurs can flee rigorous and, in economic terms, expensive environmental and labor laws in the United States by setting up shop in Mexico.

U.S. entrepreneurial inroads in Mexico are clustered roughly into the two significant time periods mentioned above—the turn of the twentieth century accumulations of corporate controlling interests, and the modern era of corporate entry through maquiladoras since the 1970s. Still, the interim period after the Mexican Revolution of the 1910s to the 1970s was active for U.S. corporate entry on many fronts. Among the notable entries during that period were those of taverns, liquor producers, and brothels, discussed in chapters 4 and 5, that entered Mexico during the Prohibition era to take economic advantage of prevailing differences in laws.

Near the turn of the twentieth century, U.S. entrepreneurs were motivated in their Mexican acquisitions by the potential for great economic returns and the amassing of power. U.S. residents built railroads connecting Mexico to the United States, a network covering 11,500 kilometers in Mexico by 1896. Elite U.S. entrepreneurs ultimately owned 80 percent of Mexican railroad stocks and bonds.[1] These rail lines extended into Mexican terrain with extensive deposits of silver, coal, oil, copper, and iron,[2] all of considerable value in the U.S. industrial-based economy. In addition to their controlling stake in the Mexican railroads, by the early 1900s, U.S. interests owned 81 percent of the Mexican mining industry and 61 percent of the total investment in its oil fields.[3] Names still familiar today controlled significant sectors of the Mexican economy, including John D. Rockefeller's Standard Oil, J.P. Morgan in the financial sector, and the Guggenheim family in the smelter business. U.S. land barons amassed vast property holdings in Mexico that stretched from cattle ranches to sugar plantations and farmland. Publishing magnate William Randolph Hearst acquired enormous tracts of ranch and forestland in northern Mexico. One of Hearst's ranches in Chihuahua alone totaled some 1,192,000 acres. Hearst apparently assumed that Northern Mexico, like the southwestern United States, would eventually succumb to U.S. governance or perhaps would fall under the thumb of U.S. interests without any formal takeover. Reflecting his arrogance, Hearst boasted, "I really don't see what is to prevent us [U.S. entrepreneurs] from owning all of Mexico and running it to suit ourselves."[4]

The Mexican Revolution, however, ushered in a period of hostility to many forms of foreign investment. Among other things, as described in chapter 2, the 1917 Mexican Constitution that emerged from the uprising restricted foreign ownership of lands proximate to the border and the desirable Mexican coastlines. That Constitution also placed petroleum exclusively in state ownership and control and restricted concessions for exploitation of mines only to Mexicans by birth or naturalization, or to Mexican companies. In 1938, the Mexican government expropriated existing foreign-owned petroleum companies, paying some compensation, though far less than the companies sought.[5] The Mexican government also nationalized its railroads. Agrarian reform transferred massive agricultural estates, such as Hearst's ranchland, into collective (ejido) farm ownership and small individual landholdings, in both cases by Mexicans. During the heyday of land redistribution from 1927 to 1940, U.S. property owners, including Hearst, lost about 6.2 million acres in Mexico to redistribution, some of those takings without compensation.[6] In 1944, the Mexican government further diminished foreign control by restricting foreign corporate ownership of Mexican companies to a minority (49 percent) stake.[7]

Eventually, however, the policy of encouraging foreign investment in Mexico gained favor. As examined in chapter 9, from 1942 to 1964, the Bracero labor pact supplied U.S. industries with Mexican labor. When Congress bowed to pressure from labor and humanitarian groups to allow this guest worker program to lapse in December 1964, Mexico aimed to replace the considerable employment opportunities Mexican citizens had enjoyed under that labor program. Instead of sending Mexican laborers to the United States, why not bring U.S. employers across the border to Mexico? What emerged on the heels of that expiration was the 1965 Border Industrialization Program. On the Mexican side, Mexico agreed to allow imports from the United States of raw materials (such as fabrics) and parts free of any trade duties. Located proximate to the border, maquiladora plants would then use Mexican labor to process and assemble the materials into finished goods. Once completed, the goods could be shipped into the United States upon paying the U.S. government an import tax only on the value added (primarily the labor) in Mexico.[8] Mexico boosted the program by exempting the maquiladora industry from the ceiling of 49 percent foreign ownership, allowing maquiladoras to be wholly foreign-owned.[9] In contrast to the mostly extractive industries of U.S. investment in Mexico during the early twentieth century, the maquiladora ushered in a new phase of foreign investment in labor-intensive industry in Mexico.[10]

The maquiladora sector started slowly. Beginning in the late 1970s, however, as the peso lost value during economic distress in Mexico, the economic advantages of the now even cheaper Mexican workforce became irresistible, prompting several U.S. companies to adopt the maquiladora structure. Early maquiladoras produced textiles such as clothing. Eventually, maquiladoras evolved to manufacture other products such as electronics and automobiles. Most maquiladoras took root in the three major border towns of Tijuana,

Mexicali, and Ciudad Juárez,[11] and many were either U.S. investor-owned or owned jointly by U.S. and Mexican investors. Japanese, Korean, Taiwanese, and European companies also operated a considerable number of Mexican maquiladoras to assemble products destined for U.S. consumers, including foreign companies such as Sony, Panasonic, Samsung, Toshiba, and Toyota.[12] In the decade from the early 1980s to the early 1990s, the number of maquiladora factories jumped from about 600 to more than 2,000, employing about half a million Mexican workers by 1992.[13]

Critics of the maquiladora structure point to the oppressive economics of its wages and to the avoidance of environmental and labor laws otherwise applicable in the United States. As a Nogales maquiladora manager admitted, "I don't think the companies came down here to benefit Mexico. They came down . . . to benefit themselves."[14] Throughout its history, the maquiladora has paid wages at a fraction of prevailing wages in the United States for similar employment, explaining the appeal to entrepreneurs of this production structure. Mexican workers earn about one-tenth of the salaries of comparable U.S. workers. For example, one study in 1996 found that Mexican auto parts workers earned $2.75 an hour, a high wage for Mexican laborers, but small in relation to the $21.93 U.S. hourly average then for such workers, who also enjoyed considerable fringe benefits the Mexican workers did not receive.[15] More representative of the miserly wages paid maquila workers was the hourly wage of fifty-five cents that Sears employees in Mexico earned manufacturing doors in 1997, about 5 percent of their U.S. counterparts' earnings, and the seventy cents an hour earned in 1998 by Mexican employees of a Levi Strauss operation, the same year that Levi announced plant closures in the United States where workers then received, on average, $10–$15 an hour.[16]

Mexican law sets a minimum wage that varies by region. The highest wages are mandated in the border states of northern Mexico where maquiladora factories predominate, but these wages are inadequate to support the higher cost of living in that region. In Juárez, the cost of living runs 80–90 percent of the cost in its U.S. sister city, El Paso, but the maquiladora wages for a full day's work start below U.S. minimum wage for an hour's work.[17] Between 1980 and 1989, the real value of the Mexican minimum wage dropped by more than 50 percent as the Mexican government devalued the peso to allow Mexican labor to better compete with foreign competition.[18] The result was that many maquiladora workers could not afford basic necessities despite in many instances earning more than the applicable Mexican minimum wage. Using the then-prevailing factory wage of $3.57 a day for a hypothetical Tijuana assembly line worker, one study found it would take 2 hours and 25 minutes of labor to purchase a bottle of 20 aspirin, 4 hours and 17 minutes to purchase a gallon of milk, 11 hours and 30 minutes to purchase a box of 30 diapers, and 57–86 hours to purchase a child's elementary school uniform.[19] Further illustrating the dismal economics of these factory jobs is the reality that some female maquiladora workers, in order to provide for their families, prostitute themselves on weekends.[20] The shantytowns that sprouted outside the Mexican border cities evidence the inadequate living wages paid by the factories and the meager contribution to local infrastructure by the maquiladoras recruited by government officials with lures of tax breaks. As one writer describes it colorfully: "[O]n a maquiladora salary, no worker could afford much rent. So shantytowns leaped into the desert. They were without drinking water, sewers, parks, lighting or paved streets. An apocalyptic folk craft—shack-building—developed using plastic tarps and barrels, wood pallets, cardboard, wire cord, all that was maquiladora detritus. Bottle caps were used for bolts."[21] In contrast to the impoverished living conditions of Mexican laborers, U.S. citizen managers and plant engineers at the Mexican maquiladoras tend to live on the U.S. side of the border, such as in San Diego or El Paso, and commute across the border daily for their well-compensated jobs, returning each evening to luxurious homes in the United States.

Illustrating the differences in legal protection enjoyed by comparable U.S. workers over maquiladora workers are Mexico labor laws ostensibly protecting the maquiladora workers that in practice are not enforced. In the aggregate, these differences augment the already attractive economics for U.S. companies of relocating jobs south of the border. As one commentator charged, "[T]o cultivate foreign manufacturing operations, Mexican labor authorities . . . ignore or even condone violations of labor law."[22] For example, Mexican law purports to protect pregnant laborers with paid maternity leave. Maquiladora employers, however, are notorious for screening for pregnancy upon hiring and monthly thereafter, and for firing pregnant employees.[23] Sexual harassment is commonplace, as is child labor. Given children's vulnerable position, child labor invites complacency on workplace rights and salary, thus driving down wage costs. Labor in the maquiladoras by those younger than age 14 is illegal in Mexico, and workers younger than 16 are restricted in their daily hours, causing most maquiladoras to require workers to be at least 16. Nevertheless, cheaply acquired false documents of age, and employers who look the other way, are common.[24] Employers flout overtime laws.[25] Workers absent a day might be docked three days' pay.[26] Mexican law gives workers the right to organize labor unions, but union leaders in the maquiladoras are often corrupt and beholden to management prerogatives,[27] earning maquiladora unions the moniker "ghost unions."[28] Moreover, firing of union organizers is commonplace despite Mexican law that runs counter to these prevailing industry practices.[29] To encourage maquiladoras, the Mexican government acceded to industry demands to cut employer social security contributions and to lengthen the probationary period for new employees.[30] Through its lack of enforcement of existing laws, as well as through its earlier devaluing of the peso, the Mexican government succeeded in its goal of attracting U.S. companies to invest in Mexico. Still, the maquiladora model as a means of economic growth is deeply flawed and reflects instead the ongoing exploitation of the Mexican labor force, whether in Mexico or in the United States.

The experience of female workers illustrates the nature of abuse in the maquiladora operations. Despite the initial intent that maquiladoras would employ the mostly male bracero workers returning from the United States, in practice maquiladora workers overwhelmingly have been women, many of them drawn to the borderlands from the Mexican interior. Scholar Elvia Arriola explains the preference among border factories for female workers from the outset:

> Women were seen as ideal workers because their smaller hands and fingers could better assemble tiny parts of export goods, such as light bulbs, cassette tapes, and recorders. The ideal maquiladora worker that emerged was thus a hybrid of stereotypes based on sex, race and class—she was not only more docile and passive than Mexican men, but submissive, easily trainable, and unlikely to pose problems with union organizing.[31]

Arriola lays blame for the staggering ongoing femicide in Ciudad Juárez—at least 300–400 women confirmed killed between 1994 and 2000 alone—at the door of the maquiladora industry. Many of these women were raped, beaten, mutilated, and dumped or buried in the desert, and most of their murders remain unsolved as the slayings continue and disappearances mount into the thousands. Many were abducted while commuting to work in the maquiladoras, often walking unlit roads in the dark, given the prohibitive cost for some laborers of buses, taxis, or other transportation.[32]Arriola contends the "Ciudad Juárez murders are an extreme manifestation of the systemic patterns of abuse, harassment, and violence against women who work in the maquiladoras—treatment that is an attributable by-product of the privileges and lack of regulation enjoyed by the [mostly U.S.] investors who employ them under the North American Free Trade Agreement."[33]

Many scholars and studies attest to the perils of working in the maquiladora factories, where production speed and cost efficiencies trump worker safety in this labor environment, in part because young replacement workers are plentiful as existing workers are injured or lose their efficiency. A Tijuana border rights advocate summarized:

> The maquiladoras are risky and unhealthy labor places. Most of the companies force the workers to deal with dangerous chemicals with no training and no appropriate protection. As a result, labor diseases and accidents are common in Tijuana. Workers ruin their eyes, lungs, hands, backs, and nervous systems after a few years of work in a maquiladora. In addition, workers without fingers and hands are not rare, but worker's negligence is always used to explain recurrent "accidents."[34]

Maquiladoras also exact a toll on the surrounding border town residents and families by hogging scarce water supplies and causing neighborhoods to go dry for residential uses during summer months.[35] Moreover, the factories pollute the air and water with lead and other hazardous substances. As with other regulatory areas associated with the maquiladora industry, despite ostensibly stringent environmental laws in Mexico that resemble those in the United States,[36] the Mexican government fails to enforce these requirements either due to inadequate resources or bribes. A Tijuana community activist charged that "companies have made under-the-table payments to environmental and health and safety investigators for years."[37] Tijuana maquiladoras poured lead, copper, zinc, arsenic, and other toxic chemicals into drainage ditches. Infrastructure in border towns could not keep pace with the maquiladora worker boom, leading to deficient sewage systems. In Mexicali, the New River has been described as a "swirling, olive-green soup of chemicals and bacteria, reeking of dead animals, industrial waste and human excrement."[38] Maquiladoras have also been blamed for increased birth defects and disease along the border,[39] as well as cancers.[40] Producing 164 tons of hazardous waste daily, U.S.-owned maquiladoras are compelled by Border Environmental Agreements (known as the La Paz Agreements and signed by the United States and Mexico in 1983) to return industrial wastes to their country of origin,[41] but inadequate enforcement has turned Mexico into a dumping ground. In 1988, only 1 percent of maquiladora owners sent their hazardous wastes to the United States for treatment.[42] By 1992, a U.S. government study found every U.S. border town plant was violating Mexico's environmental laws,[43] validating those who claimed the maquiladora model was a race to the bottom—in this case the border—on the regulation front.[44] Although the mid-1990s brought NAFTA and its side agreement, the North American Agreement on Environmental Cooperation, environmental enforcement in Mexico remains deficient.[45] President Obama's campaign promise to amend NAFTA to supply enforceable environmental (and labor) standards, in contrast to unenforceable side agreements,[46] floundered in the ensuing global economic crisis.

Overall, the maquiladora experience has delivered mixed economic and other benefits to Mexico. Maquiladoras brought new jobs but abused their workers and the host communities on several fronts. Moreover, some Mexican critics invoke national concerns to decry the maquiladora policy "that shamefully kowtows to the whims of foreigners, allows total outside control over a major industry, alienates the land, and endorses a quirky transformation of the border and ultimately the national economy into an export platform."[47] At the same time, if the maquiladoras pulled up stakes, Mexico's economy would suffer from this massive job loss.

On the U.S. side of the economic equation, presidential candidate Ross Perot warned in his 1992 campaign of a "giant sucking sound" in the wake of NAFTA as U.S. companies ran for the border.[48] NAFTA's actual impact on corporate border traffic proved far more complicated. NAFTA eclipsed the maquiladora structure by removing duties on goods moving north or south across the border, in contrast to the previous imposition of duties on the value added by the Mexican maquiladora.[49] At the same time, NAFTA imperiled Asian-owned maquiladoras by eliminating duty-free imports into Mexico of component parts not comprised of a majority of North American materials.[50] Against the backdrop of a complex post-NAFTA mix of legal, tax, environmental, investment, international, and economic factors, the maquiladora industry initially boomed.[51] From 1993 to 1998, maquiladoras, and the workers they employed, nearly doubled in number from 2,405 to 4,234 maquiladoras, and from 542,000 to 1,008,000 jobs.[52] Maquiladora employment peaked in 2000 at 1.35 million Mexican laborers.[53] By 2001, however, maquiladoras began to wither from the forces of the early 2000s recession in the United States, along with emerging competition from China, India, and developing countries in Latin America and the Caribbean that offered an even cheaper labor force.[54] China's manufacturing wages, for example, are only 3 percent of U.S. manufacturing wages.[55] Particularly hard hit were textile and apparel maquiladoras that do not enjoy the same advantages of transportation proximity to the United States as do factories producing more bulky and costly items to transport such as automobiles and televisions. The recession that began in 2007 dealt another blow to the borderland maquiladoras, as U.S. sales of consumer goods plummeted, evidenced by Chrysler suspending production in May 2009 at all five of its Mexican auto plants.

Although initially some U.S. entrepreneurs and companies ran for the Mexican border, bringing jobs previously held by U.S. residents, NAFTA's impacts on border crossing were multi-fold and ran in both directions. Ultimately, there was no unilateral "giant sucking sound" heard from southbound crossings. Among the post-NAFTA impacts were those felt by U.S. border towns that lost jobs not by companies leaving for Mexico, but by residents of Mexico border towns choosing to shop in Mexico. Previously, the unavailability of certain U.S. consumer goods in Mexico, or the imposition by Mexico of significant trade duties, led residents of Mexico border towns to do much of their shopping in U.S. stores and when necessary to smuggle those items back across the border. Entering with tourist visas or other means of entry over the years, these Mexico residents routinely frequented stores in El Paso and San Diego. Studies once found 70 percent of Juárez residents visited El Paso regularly to shop.[56] By the 1960s, there was a profitable industry in smuggling televisions, radios, and other consumer items into Mexico.[57] In the 1970s, "[l]ight planes loaded with television sets, microwave ovens, and small refrigerators made virtually daily flights to small airstrips in [Mexico]."[58] In 1978 alone, smugglers brought an estimated $2.8 million in televisions from Laredo, Texas, into Mexico. Even food items such as powdered milk were commonly purchased by Mexicans from U.S. grocers and smuggled across the border to avoid Mexico's protectionist policies that survived until NAFTA.[59] Among the most popular items to cross the border over the years are stolen cars taken from owners in the southwestern United States and sold across the border to Mexican residents. According to one calculation, annually one million used cars cross the border for sale in Mexico, some of them stolen vehicles.[60]

U.S. border town sales had already begun to slide with the devaluation of the Mexican peso in the 1980s and 1990s.[61] The ability to purchase identical goods in Mexico under NAFTA sealed the decline of the U.S. border town retail markets, as did the post–September 11 tightening of the border. In Arizona, the enactment in 2010 of Senate Bill 1070 further stifled business in border town Nogales, Arizona, as Mexico warned its citizens about travel into such a rogue state.[62]

Before NAFTA, foreign investment in Mexico outside of the maquiladora assembly plants generally was restricted to a minority (49 percent) interest.

NAFTA swept in liberalization of Mexican law on foreign investment, which now allows foreigners to wholly own companies in Mexico outside of certain sectors reserved in whole or in part for government or Mexican national control, such as petroleum, for which the Mexican Constitution mandates state control, and retail sale of gasoline, which is reserved for Mexican nationals.[63] With the green light to enter Mexico, U.S. retail and hospitality companies ran for the border, not to serve consumers in the United States with Mexican labor as the maquiladora model offers, but to subvert Mexican retailers and businesses in serving Mexico residents as well as U.S. tourists and transplants.

So began the Wal-Martization of Mexico. As it did in the United States, Wal-Mart trampled Mexican merchants operating on smaller economies of scale, and soon became Mexico's largest private-sector employer, with more than 150,000 employees and 1,000 stores on Mexican soil.[64] Although notoriously underpaid in the United States, Wal-Mart employees fare worse in Mexico, earning about $1.50 an hour as a cashier near the top of the wage structure. Joining Wal-Mart in Mexico were Home Depot, with some 60 locations,[65] and a host of U.S. retail outlets, restaurants, and hotels, together with U.S. insurance companies, banks, and long-distance carriers that entered the Mexican consumer marketplace. U.S. beer giant Anheuser-Busch expanded its ownership stake in Grupo Modelo, the Mexican brewer of Corona beer, to a 50.2 percent interest.[66]

Along with U.S. companies tapping Mexican markets came subsidized exports from U.S. markets, particularly agricultural crops such as corn that walloped Mexican farmers who do not enjoy similar government largess. The impact of these artificially cheap goods crossing the border and flooding the Mexican market contributed to another post-NAFTA dynamic that Ross Perot failed to anticipate. Rather than sucking U.S. jobs into Mexico, the upheaval of the rural Mexican poor who bore the pain of the post-NAFTA trade markets drew many rural Mexicans toward the U.S. border.[67] As U.S. employers tried to remain competitive on labor fronts in the increasingly globalized race to the salaried bottom, and as the Mexican maquiladora market began to decline, Mexican immigration into the United States soared as these migrants merely lengthened their northern journey toward jobs. With the opposite effect on undocumented immigration than was anticipated under NAFTA, one commentator remarked, "It was as if Ross Perot's warning of a 'giant sucking sound' finally took place, except the jobs were created in the United States [for undocumented immigrants] and not in Mexico."[68] Moreover, of late with global competition from even cheaper foreign labor markets, Mexico has experienced a further rupture of its once burgeoning maquiladora sector, described as "'the giant sucking sound' in stereo these days—from China in one ear and India in the other."[69] Adding to the borderlands misery, the escalating drug violence in Ciudad Juárez and other Mexican border towns has spooked U.S. companies and investors,[70] with little likelihood of south-of-the-border plant expansions or new enterprises. A 2010 survey of private U.S. companies found 15 percent had already postponed investment or expansion plans in Mexico because of drug violence.[71]

U.S. entrepreneurs flocked to the maquiladora structure to enjoy the economic advantages of a cheaper labor force outside the United States and also to exploit the lax labor and environmental regulation in Mexico. A motley group of U.S. entrepreneurs and hucksters had earlier established a foothold in the Mexican border town business community through the phenomenon of border radio on the AM dial. These borderblasters were motivated predominantly by the increasing U.S. regulation of the airwaves that allocated transmission frequencies and of advertising through the Food and Drug Administration that began targeting unsafe or falsely advertised products. The ingenious solution was to set up shop on the Mexican side of the border with enormous broadcasting wattage (as much as 1,000 times the wattage of many U.S. stations) to encompass the United States and even much of the world, as airwaves readily cross national boundaries. Although Mexico occasionally cracked down on the border pitchmen, the mordida (bribe) and the many tourists and entertainers that frequented the stations and the surrounding community helped keep the Mexican regulators at bay. Huge profits garnered from mail-order products hawked on border radio supplied any payoffs needed to keep the airwaves crackling.

One notable borderblaster illustrates the legal and financial motivations of border radio. John R. Brinkley broadcast medical "advice" from his Kansas-based radio station in the late 1920s. Famously, he touted a rejuvenation operation for men that entailed implanting goat glands into a man's testicles, with the claims it lowered blood pressure, enhanced health and activity, and also improved performance in the bedroom. Eventually, Brinkley attracted the ire of regulatory authorities, losing his medical license to the Kansas State Medical Board and his U.S. radio station to the forerunner of today's FCC, the Federal Radio Commission.[72] Rather than hang up his scalpel, Brinkley founded a Mexican border radio station, remarking, "Radio waves pay no attention to lines on a map."[73] Although the Mexican government eventually shut him down in 1941 and he died bankrupt, during the 1930s Brinkley amassed a fortune from his border station and medical clinics that he spent on ranches, farms, an airplane, yachts, and automobiles.

Perhaps border radio's most famous deejay was U.S.-born Wolfman Jack, an Anglo broadcaster who howled over the airwaves for a few decades into the rock 'n' roll era playing soul music. The Wolfman pitched everything from diet pills to baby chickens actually delivered inside boxes to mail-order customers.[74] He even sold Wolfman Jack roach clips and glow-in-the-dark Wolfman photos.[75] In the 1960s, his most lucrative returns came from selling airtime to preachers who were prohibited from soliciting donations over the U.S. airwaves.[76] As the Wolfman put it, "[T]hey was sellin' Jesus all day and I was sellin' sin all night."[77] Wolfman's banter likely would not have survived U.S. standards: "This is Wolfman Jack down here with the donkeys. Gonna get you some soul, man. . . . Get naked—Blow the evil weed."[78]

Mexican border radio followed a familiar pattern of U.S. citizen announcers at U.S.-financed radio stations hawking products in English on behalf of mostly U.S. companies, and playing music of mostly U.S. artists,[79] their formats intended primarily for U.S. audiences. Later in his career, Wolfman lived in the United States, as did some of the other border announcers, prerecording his radio shows for the Mexico station and sending tapes regularly.[80] For Mexico's part, it "supplied land for the studios and broadcast towers, some technicians, and the call letters."[81] Border radio declined as the AM dial lost popularity beginning in the 1970s; for FM broadcasts, the United States and Mexico eventually agreed to mutually assign power and frequencies.

While active, border radio embodied the familiar model of U.S. entrepreneurs crossing the border as they desired for economic gain, and to avoid more restrictive U.S. law. The materials presented next address border crossings driven more by legal differences than by profit-seeking motives.

Illicit Motivations for
Southbound Border Runs

For at least a century, U.S. residents have crossed the border into Mexico to engage in activities otherwise illicit[1] in the United States. In contrast, in Mexico these pursuits were legal or, if not, at least more readily available. This history demonstrates that differences in law can prompt border crossings, particularly transitory crossings, whether for lust, addiction, or other aims. Although additional factors spur border crossings, especially economic advantage, there is no question about the role of law as a motivation of the first order.

Prohibition best illustrates this assertion. Starting with the ban of alcohol in Texas in 1918 and followed by the approval of the Eighteenth Amendment in 1919 and the federal Volstead Act enforcing it in 1920, vast numbers of U.S. residents quenched their thirst for booze in Mexican border towns. As illustrated in chapter 7, some of the U.S. demand was met by delivering booze across the border to underground U.S. markets. But as explained in chapter 4, many U.S. residents ventured south of the border to slake their thirsts as well as their passion for other activities largely illicit in the United States. When Prohibition ended in 1933 and the north once again was wet, vice tourism dried up. Of course, other factors unrelated to differences in laws, primarily the Great Depression, played a role in staunching southbound border travel.

Vice nonetheless proved resilient. By the time of World War II, many U.S. servicemen arriving at bases near the Mexico border (particularly in San Diego and El Paso) were limited by the drinking age of 21 in California and Texas at the time. For them and also for servicemen of legal drinking age, the lure of flesh drew many across the Mexican border and revived the border vice industry. Eventually the maquiladora industry discussed in chapter 3 helped give Mexican border towns a less lurid identity, as industry arrived along with a considerable workforce drawn from the far reaches of Mexico, and the bars and bordellos catering to the vice tourist became more of a sideshow.[2]

Given the changes over time of laws and of taste, the vice impetus for border crossing is fluid. For example, many U.S. residents desiring to gamble can now find a myriad of legal outlets in the United States. Divorces are readily available in the United States without proof of fault, eliminating the need for the quickie "Mexican divorce" of the past. Abortions are constitutionally authorized since 1973, enabling women to obtain safe and legal terminations of pregnancy within the United States rather than venturing to unlawful but once widespread abortion "emporiums" in Mexico. Developing mores against animal cruelty have lessened interest in borderlands spectacles such as bullfighting that previously drew large crowds of U.S. residents.

Today, although the ascendency of the U.S. porn industry and the advent of illicit sexual hookups over the Internet appeased some of the lustful would-be tourists, differences in legality still prompt a significant sector of tourism across borders. The difference between the federally induced drinking age of 21 in the United States and Mexico's less enforced and lower drinking age of 18 lures spring-breakers to Mexican beach resorts as well as weekender youth coming from U.S. border cities such as San Diego and El Paso.

Vice tourism over the years sparked a question as to the source of the immorality—was it an immoral and hedonistic Mexico corrupting U.S. residents, or were U.S. residents and their illicit desires to blame for the vice industry south of the border? The answer is that, despite the stereotypical views of many in the United States who blame Mexico as a haven for illicit acts and even a substandard culture, there is blame in most cases that reaches well into the United States. Acknowledging this mutual responsibility must precede development of a border strategy that honors the interests of both countries.

Some may wonder whether the economic fruits of vice tourism caused Mexico to intentionally deviate from the laws of the United States. This accusation was hurled most recently when Mexico decriminalized personal use amounts of drugs in 2009. But history demonstrates that undercutting U.S. law is rarely, if ever, the impetus for Mexican law. For example, U.S. Prohibition did not prompt Mexico to loosen its drinking laws—they remained the same after the launch of Prohibition. As described in chapter 4, despite its lure of U.S. residents, gambling was under constant attack from Mexican authorities at a time when vice tourism was flourishing. Mexico's current legal drinking age of 18 does not seem manipulative given the reality that only three countries join the United States in specifying a drinking age as high as 21—Indonesia, Mongolia, and Palau.[3] Many U.S. states set their minimum drinking age below 21 until Congress in 1984 compelled states to raise their drinking age. Moreover, Mexicans and Mexico historically have not profited from vice as much as it might seem. As with today's often foreign-controlled hotels and restaurants in Mexican tourist zones, most of the border town entertainment venues of the early twentieth century were owned by U.S. residents who in many cases merely relocated their business operations across the border with the advent of Prohibition. Vice dealers, along with their U.S. customers, ran for the border.

Margaritaville

The Lure of Alcohol

The strong breath of Prohibition blew life into many bordertowns. Dry *americanos* descended upon the bars in droves
and cash registers rang with joy from noon to noon. *Señoritas*
danced and *mariachis* sang and cocks fought and bulls died and
gringos guzzled.
—Ovid Demaris, *Poso del Mundo: Inside the Mexican-American Border, from Tijuana to Matamoros* (1970), 28

[A]ll bordertowns bring out the worst in a country.
—Charlton Heston as agent Vargas in *Touch of Evil* (1958)

Before Prohibition, Mexico's border region had already begun to
draw vice tourists based on differences in laws. For example, the state of California, like many U.S. cities, forced out prostitution in the early 1900s.[1] California banned betting on horse racing in 1915, and two years later banned
professional boxing.[2] In Tijuana, horse racing and organized boxing dated
to the late nineteenth century, attracting some tourists,[3] and Baja California
authorized gambling more broadly in 1908.[4] Similarly, reform efforts against
vice in El Paso on the threshold of Prohibition led gamblers, and johns seeking prostitutes, to travel south of the border to Ciudad Juárez, a move reinforced by the advent of Prohibition.

Prohibition took hold in border states when Texas outlawed alcohol and
closed its saloons in April 1918, and when Congress enforced the Eighteenth
Amendment in 1920 under the Volstead Act to reach all the states.[5] The law
exempted alcohol for sacramental, industrial, and medicinal purposes, but
its ban of beverages with more than 0.5 percent alcohol prompted closures
of saloons across the United States. Although reform efforts spilled south
across the border as Mexican state legislatures took up the issue of barring

alcohol during the U.S. Prohibition years, the licensing revenues from liquor stores and taverns proved too lucrative and prohibition never reached the Mexican border towns. In turn, U.S. Prohibition sparked border town tourism across the reaches of the Mexican border with the United States, from Tijuana on the Pacific Ocean to Matamoros on the Gulf of Mexico. Tourism jumped dramatically during the early stages of Prohibition, with the number of tourists crossing the border into Mexico at just El Paso from July 1918 to July 1919—14,130—increasing to 418,735 in the following year.[6] The discussion below focuses on the three largest border towns today—Tijuana, Mexicali, and Ciudad Juárez—all of them once boosted by Prohibition-era vice business.

In 1915, at the cusp of Prohibition, Tijuana was still a small town of only 1,000 residents. As one tourist described it then, Tijuana consisted of "a number of wooden stores, restaurants, and saloons, mostly one-story, with a scattering of wooden bungalows. . . . [Its streets are] dusty and often rutty and, in wet weather very muddy."[7] By the end of the Roaring Twenties, however, Tijuana's population had surged to 8,384 residents.[8] Tijuana benefited from its proximity to populous Southern California and to Hollywood when the advent of talking motion pictures coincided with the Prohibition era. During the dry years, Tijuana became Hollywood's playground, with stars flying in from Los Angeles aboard Ford trimotor airplanes.[9] European gamblers arrived by ship from Monte Carlo to frolic in the Mexican desert. Tijuana's crown jewel of chic decadence, the Casino de Agua Caliente (hot water), opened in 1928 and was a magnet for celebrities. Combining the lures of gambling and alcohol, Agua Caliente offered vice entertainment such as gambling rooms, bars, and greyhound and horse tracks, as well as other entertainment including a golf course, a theater for floor shows, hot spring baths, swimming pools, and restaurants.[10] One of its gambling rooms, the Salon de Oro, allowed high-stakes gambling only with gold coins. Stars seen at Agua Caliente in its brief heyday included Clark Gable, Charlie Chaplin, Gilbert Roland, John Barrymore, Tom Mix, Douglas Fairbanks, Jean Harlow, the Marx brothers, Jimmy Durante, Buster Keaton, and Bing Crosby.[11] Some of these stars performed at the resort, along with such entertainers as Rita Hayworth and Laurel and Hardy. Gangster celebrities at the resort included Al Capone (said by local lore to have lost half a million dollars gambling one night). Sports icons Jack Dempsey (who boxed in Mexicali and Ciudad Juárez) and Babe Ruth were seen there too. Gamblers in Mexican border towns such as Tijuana had an array of choices: horse and greyhound racing, playing cards and slots and dice in the casinos, and even cockfights in less formal settings.

Liquor flowed freely in wet Mexican border towns. In downtown Tijuana, one establishment, La Ballena, advertised the world's longest bar, stretching 510 feet.[12] A Methodist Church Board of Temperance condescendingly described Tijuana in 1920 as having "scores of gambling devices, long drinking bars, dance halls, hop joints, cribs for prostitutes, cock fights, dog fights, [and] bullfights." Further, "the town is a Mecca of prostitutes, booze sellers, gamblers, and other American vermin."[13]

Bordering Calexico on the California side, Mexicali attracted smaller crowds of U.S. tourists and Imperial Valley ranchers, given its distance from population centers. Nevertheless, Mexicali offered the diversity of opium dens in its thriving Chinatown, gambling in casinos, and prostitution in its brothels, notably in the Owl brothel that also claimed to be the largest gambling house in the Americas.[14] A U.S. traveler described the confines of one Mexicali casino in unflattering terms:

> A dozen or so gambling-tables at which you lose your money at faro, monte, roulette, or what you please; a thriving bar; an incessant racket of "ragtime" from a quartette of tenth-rate musicians at the rear; three painted girls, or rather children, in dirty pink, who now and then ceased their crude blandishments of the men near them to shout the words of a ribald song.[15]

Hollywood's Paul Muni, co-star of the 1935 film *Bordertown* with Bette Davis, described how he prepared for the role of playing a border town casino owner by going "swimming in tequila" in Mexicali.[16] The novel on which the film was loosely based described a seedy Mexicali of the late 1920s and early 1930s: "The principal street, which runs at right angles to the border, is a street of bars, gambling palaces, houses of prostitution, and combinations of all three. . . . With the coming of night, gamblers, dope-peddlers, smugglers, pimps, cutthroats, fugitive criminals, pickpockets, rum-runners, all the easy-money boys, will come out of their holes. In Mexicali it is noon at midnight."[17]

Billed as the "Monte Carlo of America"[18] during Prohibition, Ciudad Juárez delivered its blend of border town vice to hordes of tourists crossing from its U.S. sister city, El Paso. As an American Consul described it in 1921: "Juárez is the most immoral, degenerate, and utterly wicked place I have ever seen or heard of in my travels. Murder and robbery are everyday occurrences and gambling, dope selling and using, drinking to excess and sexual vices are continuous. It is a Mecca for criminals and degenerates from both sides of

the border."[19] Gambling options were plentiful in Juárez, including horserac-
ing, and cockfighting at a ring erected in 1926.[20]

South-of-the-border vice in this era may have attracted degenerates from
both sides of the border, but its clientele came decidedly from the United
States, and vice purveyors were mostly U.S. residents as well. As discussed
in chapter 5, even many of the prostitutes working the border town brothels of the era came from the United States. Throughout the terrain of the
Mexican border, U.S. residents and companies owned entertainment venues
and the transportation infrastructure to reach them. For example, in Ciudad Juárez, saloon owners from dry Texas simply moved their operations
south of the border. As one writer summarized, "When the gates of Ciudad
Juárez were thrown open [upon Prohibition], in marched the saloon-keep-
ers [of El Paso], arm-in-arm with the less socially acceptable prostitutes and
gamblers."[21] Hoteliers and other businesses that remained in El Paso profited
from the adjoining vice, as advertisements promoting El Paso as the "Wet-
test Spot on the Rio Grande" drew convention crowds and tourists.[22] Other
U.S. entrepreneurs came from distant reaches—for example, two prominent distilleries moved from Kentucky to Juárez during Prohibition[23] and, as
described in chapter 7, some of their product found its way into the United
States. Three U.S. resident Anglos owned Tijuana's prestigious Agua Caliente
casino complex,[24] and U.S. residents owned the horse track in Juárez and
controlled bullfighting there. Breweries, distilleries, wineries, saloons, gambling halls, and other Mexican venues of entertainment and vice were controlled mostly by U.S. residents. Related to the U.S. control of much of the
vice was rampant discrimination against Mexicans. U.S.-owned casinos and
bars hired Anglos from the United States as bartenders, waiters, and dealers,
while rejecting Mexican help. Some of the clubs even asked Mexicans, particularly those with darker skin, to leave, thus reserving patronage to Anglos
from the United States.[25]

Despite pervasive U.S. financial interests anchoring the Mexican vice
industry, the U.S. government faced pressures from reformers upset at the
blatant borderlands evasion of moral standards during Prohibition times.
Yielding to these pressures, in 1924 the U.S. government closed its border
stations daily at 9 p.m. and even earlier. The primary effect was to spur the
expansion of lodging facilities in Tijuana.[26] When the border curfew resur-
faced in 1931, U.S. tourists eluded it on their late night return trips by slipping
through holes in the border fence in an early version of the journey to el
Norte of undocumented immigrants from Tijuana into Southern California
during the 1980s and early 1990s.[27]

The Great Depression that followed the stock market crash in late 1929, which curbed travel and excess, combined with the return of legal alcohol to the United States in 1933, stifled border crossings. The 27 million border crossings in 1928, including those of tourists, fell to 21 million by 1934, and traffic did not recover to 1928 levels until the wartime economy and U.S. soldier traffic revived crossings in 1944.[28] At the end of Prohibition, many saloon owners and prostitutes departed north for El Paso and other U.S. locations. By 1933, 110 taverns and liquor stores had opened across the border in El Paso, displacing the Juárez booze industry.[29]

Gambling in Mexico has been under constant attack at the local, state, and federal levels for years, occasionally leading to its prohibition, as when then-President Francisco Madero banned gambling in 1911, a ban that survived until his ouster in 1913.[30] Through the issuance of licenses, gambling supplied critical revenues for Mexican government infrastructure such as public works projects and highways. Therefore, gambling prohibitions in the early twentieth century tended to be short-lived. Casino operators often survived periods of illegality by paying bribes to the appropriate Mexican government officials. But a strong blow to border town vice business came when Mexico's President Lázaro Cárdenas banned gambling in 1935, leading to the closure of Tijuana's Agua Caliente casino and racetrack in July of that year.[31] Juárez saw its vice industry shrink as forces of the bleak U.S. economy and of law reform in both the United States and Mexico combined to pull businesses back to the United States and keep U.S. residents at home. As one writer described the exodus of vice:

> Gone are the hundred-odd saloons, the downtown honky-tonks and brothels, and the open gambling. In the Tívoli Casino the visitor no longer can hear the click of dice, the riffle of cards, and the sing-song of croupiers at the roulette tables. The place is closed by presidential decree. The Moulin Rouge, once the home of nude dancers, is closed. . . . A few cabarets remain open . . . but most of the girls have moved to El Paso's restricted zone.[32]

The lure of fiscal revenue and bribes of officials meant that some less visible forms of illegal gambling thrived in Mexico's many underground casinos, or in its illegal cockfights, as did some limited forms of legal betting such as jai alai, dog racing, and eventually the national lottery. Officially, Mexico's 1947 Federal Gaming and Raffles Law reinforced the 1935 presidential ban, and the legal prohibition survived for the rest of the twentieth century. Sports betting was allowed in 1989, but the ban on casinos was not lifted until 2004 when the federal government began issuing limited permits, one of which allowed Tijuana's (Agua) Caliente casino to reopen its doors in 2008 with bingo-based electronic games and a greyhound track. By now, more than fifteen legal gambling casinos on tribal reservations operated on the U.S. side of the border near San Diego. In a reverse flow from earlier days, some of these casinos offered free transportation to draw Mexico's residents across the border to gamble. One U.S. casino earns 40 percent of its business from residents of the Mexican cities of Tijuana, Tecate, and Mexicali, illustrating that vice tourism flows in both directions.[33] The Caliente casino is expected to keep some of these residents home, particularly with the increasing regulatory hassles of northbound border travel. The issuance of gambling licenses also comes at a time when Tijuana and other border towns, most suffering the decline of the maquiladora industry due to international competition and the decline of tourism from raging drug cartel violence, need the lift.

Nearly coinciding with the 1930s demise of legal gambling in Mexico was the rebirth of the U.S. gambling economy in Reno and Las Vegas (Spanish for "the meadows"). Previously allowing gambling from 1869 to 1910, the Nevada legislature revived legal gambling for those age 21 and older with "The Wide Open Gambling Bill of 1931." Starting that same year with a casino in Las Vegas, the desert city grew to become the West Coast magnet for gamblers, offering the additional attractions of liquor upon the lifting of Prohibition and even legalized prostitution in brothels permitted in many rural Nevadan counties outside of Clark County that encompasses Las Vegas and Washoe County that contains Reno.[34] Vegas eventually replaced Mexico as the Hollywood celebrity destination of choice and a hub for international vice tourism. Movies such as *Knocked Up* (2007), with a psychedelic mushroom-stoked excursion to Las Vegas, *Get Him to the Greek's* (2010) "drug neapolitan" enjoyed on a Las Vegas sojourn, and *The Hangover's* (2009) drug-, alcohol-, and stripper-infused night of debauchery accurately depict this U.S. "Sin City" as a lawless frontier and morality-free zone, akin to the prevailing vision of Mexico, in which U.S. residents can misbehave yet leave their transgressions behind. Trademarked as the official Las Vegas slogan, "What happens in Vegas, stays in Vegas," captures our longstanding need for a run across the borders of vice.

Following the decline in vice tourism during the Great Depression, some Mexican border towns returned to glory with the economic stimulus of World War II and the proximity of Mexican border towns to large military bases in San Diego and El Paso. In the early 1950s, the Korean War would provide a similar boost. Although federal Prohibition ended in late 1933, Texas outlawed sales of hard liquor by the drink in 1935, effectively barring saloons where liquor (other than beer) was consumed on the premises.[35] Thus, U.S. servicemen stationed in Texas crossed the border nightly to drink in the saloons of Juárez, enabling the city to fund civic improvement projects.[36] Although California did not similarly prohibit liquor saloons, Tijuana offered servicemen the additional lure of sex and smut for sale. As one writer described wartime Tijuana: "To many who visited during the 1940s, it was a city of vice where prostitution, pornographic movies, live sex demonstrations, and drug traffic were unequalled. It was said to be a city where sailors could get roaring drunk, take over the bars, and fight in the streets with the marines."[37] By World War II, Mexican owners had taken control of the Mexican border town vice industry of bars and brothels, mostly by replacing the ritzier Prohibition-era establishments owned by U.S. residents with cheaper establishments.[38]

Since the 1960s, Tijuana and the other border towns have needed to reinvent themselves more than once as the legal landscape changed. Tijuana's smut trade of sex shows and dirty pictures, detailed in chapter 5, was eclipsed by the growing pornography industry in the United States. By the early 1970s, widely released U.S. pornographic movies, notably *Deep Throat* (1972) and *Behind the Green Door* (1972), were a vogue source of entertainment, and topless bars were widespread. Tijuana responded by catering more to family tourism. A 1972 *Time* magazine article titled "Respectable Tijuana" described its reinvention in response to "[t]ougher Mexican laws and more liberal U.S. attitudes [that] shrank the market for 'attractions' such as divorces, abortions, prostitution and sex shows."[39] Rather, Tijuana emphasized the exotic to sell itself as "So near but yet so foreign,"[40] lodging its visitors in newly opened resort hotels and catering to buyers of Mexican handicrafts, furniture, and other goods not readily found in the United States. As addressed in chapter 3, maquiladora assembly plants before and after NAFTA brought an explosion in population among border towns—in Tijuana the population increased from 65,346 in 1950 to more than 700,000 residents by 1980[41]—helping transform Mexican border towns into bustling trade centers where vice was no longer center stage. Aspirations of family tourism in border towns, however, were eventually dashed by rampant drug violence, as detailed in chapter 8.

Modern developments in alcohol law prompted another shift in border crossings toward border towns as well as to Mexico's beach resorts. When Texas law changed in 1971 to give local government the option to allow hard liquor sales by the glass, the El Paso area swiftly opted wet to the detriment of Juárez. Prompted by concerns over drunk driving by U.S. youth, Congress reshaped the landscape of vice tourism when the 1984 National Minimum Drinking Age Act raised the U.S. drinking age to 21 under penalty of withholding federal highway funds from recalcitrant states. Texas was among the states compelled to raise the minimum drinking age, many of these having previously lowered that age during the Vietnam War era. The federal law quickly spurred weekend border town blitzes by underage U.S. youth from nearby cities, particularly San Diego and Los Angeles, as well as spring break excursions by U.S. college students traveling deeper into Mexico. Mexico's drinking age of 18, itself rarely enforced with vigor, lured the new youthful face of south-of-the-border vice tourism.

The resulting crush of young weekend partiers to Juárez, Tijuana, and other Mexico border towns perhaps exceeded decadence during the Prohibition era. Even those of U.S. drinking age joined in the fun to cavort with the underage drinkers and to circumvent the state and local laws that close many U.S. bars by 2 a.m. By contrast, in Tijuana booze flows, music plays, and prostitutes beckon at all hours of the night. In Tijuana alone, by 1986 as many as 12,000 youths crossed the border each weekend night, many of them from San Diego and most of them leaving cars behind and crossing as pedestrians to drink in Tijuana's bars, where the party never stopped.[42] One survey of youths entering Mexico from California found half intended to get "a little" or "very" drunk, and another found that upon reentry to the United States, 31 percent of pedestrians aged 18–20 had a blood alcohol content above 0.08 (California's legal limit).[43] With this youthful infusion, by the 1990s more U.S. tourists traveled to Tijuana than internally to Disneyland.[44] As with Disneyland, most were short-term visitors who stayed in Tijuana briefly—the average tourist stay in both Tijuana and Juárez ranges from about six to eight hours.[45] A Tijuana police captain lamented in 1988 during the early days of the crush: "We get two kinds of tourists here. The good families; and kids who only want to fight and drink and make trouble."[46] Fueling the debauchery are "tequila poppers," a drinking experience in which whistle-blowing and sometimes costumed bartenders pour huge quantities of tequila mixed with juice or soda into a customer's mouth.[47] A journalist at one Mexican border town club found that youth as young as 14 were served alcohol in the dance clubs: "There are 14- and 15-year-old girls all dressed up. They look mature and sophisticated, but they're just pups."[48] Some of the bars offer all-night drinking on the house for an admission charge, serving free drinks until 4 a.m.[49] To stem the throng of teens headed for Mexico, in 1998

California police began invoking state law that required parental consent for youth under 18 to cross the border.[50]

As it did for family tourism in borderland regions, increasing drug cartel violence in the 2000s eventually dampened the weekend party crowds in Tijuana and particularly in Juárez. As one border dweller lamented on the downturn: "There used to be so much mixing. Young people in San Diego would go for the night to Mexico. As a young boy in Tijuana, a night out in San Diego was something I did all the time. You got to know people on the other side."[51]

Dating at least to the 1950s, flights to Mexican coastal resorts away from the borderlands brought tourists looking more for oceanside relaxation than for vice. Among the earliest chic destinations was Acapulco, memorialized in a 1963 Elvis Presley film *Fun in Acapulco*, and, for the romantic set, in Frank Sinatra's hit "Come Fly with Me" (1957) which touted Acapulco as a perfect honeymoon spot. Probably the most famous Acapulco honeymoon occurred in September 1953, when then-Senator John Kennedy and his new wife Jackie spent two weeks in paradise. In the 1950s, stars such as John Wayne, Hedy Lamarr, and Susan Hayward frolicked in Acapulco.[52] *Night of the Iguana* (1964), starring Richard Burton, launched Puerto Vallarta as another hip destination, joined later by such coastal resort cities as Cabo San Lucas.

Apart from those cementing a marital union, Mexico also lured tourists seeking what the convict in *The Shawshank Redemption* (1994) desired: "a warm place with no memory." This escapist side of Mexican tourism, particularly where memory of lost love is drowned in tequila south of the border, animates U.S. pop culture, particularly music. In "Margaritaville" (1977), for example, country singer Jimmy Buffet found refuge as a Mexican tourist in the frozen drink, while country singer Johnny Duncan drank tequila in bed and romanced Mexican señoritas to forget his U.S. lover in "Hello Mexico" (1978).

Vice, however, eventually returned to the spotlight in Mexican tourism. Spring breakers of the MTV generation forged a new hedonistic identity for Mexican beach resorts, eventually helping crown Cancún as the king of the beach party. Cultural icon MTV confirmed Cancún's royal status by choosing it in 2009 for the fourth international location (after London, Paris, and Sydney) of the popular reality TV show *The Real World* that follows the adventures of young housemates, most of legal U.S. drinking age. Previously, a motion picture titled *The Real Cancun* (2003) borrowed that MTV formula to situate an unscripted reality movie on Cancún's sandy beaches and inside its seamy nightlife.

Aside from its renowned beaches, Cancún's main attraction is its drinking scene. One of the cast members of MTV's *The Real World*, kicked out of a Cancún hotel suite for hurling a fire extinguisher from the balcony while drunk, embodied the alcohol-fueled chaos of U.S. youth partying in Mexico. Previously, MTV hosted spring break parties in Cancún, promising "Beaches, bikinis, bands and babes galore."[53] Alcohol is the lifeblood of the ritualistic festivities—one study of spring breakers found the average man downed 18 drinks while the average woman consumed 10 drinks per day.[54] Booze companies are always on hand on Mexican beaches—Bacardi Rum marketers in Cancún sponsored a Bacardi shower in which youthful drinkers climbed into a shower to guzzle rum and coke from a showerhead.[55] Beer trucks supplant the neighborhood ice cream truck, selling cases of Corona and picking up empties. Nightclubs and tour operators offer "all you can drink" cover charges that promote excess. In a throwback to the discriminatory days of the Prohibition-era border town taverns, clubs favor U.S. tourists over locals: "At the entrance to [Cancún] discos, they first admit foreigners and only later do they admit Mexicans."[56] Those students desiring drugs such as marijuana or Ecstasy usually can obtain them more cheaply than in the United States. Although lacking the overt prostitution scene of Tijuana and other border towns, in Cancún there is less need for prostitution or organized sex shows when promiscuous youth from the United States are thrown into a bowl and marinated in booze. As a CNN report described the Cancún scene:

> Young Americans fill dozens of bars every night to drink, dance, and watch a variety of contests, almost all of which involve women getting naked. "Three words: debauchery, drunkenness, and nakedness," [said one 23-year-old]. . . . The drinking age is 18, and is hardly enforced. Most clubs offer open bars with the cover charge. For college kids who can't legally drink in the United States, the attraction is obvious. . . . With all that alcohol, normally reserved college students leave all inhibitions at the door. The mostly teen-age students jump atop bars to show their breasts to hooting crowds, compete for prizes by showing their creativity in inventing sexual positions[,] and slide into strangers' beds.[57]

One Houston television station in 2005 used hidden cameras to capture Cancún's carnal jubilee, finding teenagers having sex in clubs, on the beach, and even on the street.[58] Much sexual contact, however, is not consensual. Women are routinely groped on the Cancún dance floor.[59] Tijuana weekenders are equally at risk for victimization, mostly at the hands of their U.S. cohorts—a 2005–2006 study of women crossing the border into Tijuana to party found that more than half (53 percent) reported some form of verbal, physical, or sexual victimization. More than half also witnessed removals of clothing and some 30 percent saw fights.[60]

Starting in 2002, the tourist industry in Cancún took measures to restore some civility among the rowdiest U.S. visitors by withholding alcohol from visibly intoxicated students and even handing out leaflets to arriving tourists on unacceptable behavior,[61] likely deterring a few hardcore partiers. Other forces set in motion by U.S. residents desiring home delivery of their illicit-substance-of-choice eventually rocked the Mexican tourism industry from Cancún to Ciudad Juárez.

The drug violence threat, combined with the economic crisis, took its toll on alcohol-motivated border runs, both for spring break on beach resorts and weekends in the border towns. In 2009, especially, cartel violence escalated, particularly in Mexican border towns but also in its beach resorts. Bloodshed and beheadings in and near Acapulco scared U.S. tourists away from that once legendary romantic hideaway. U.S. officials alerted travelers in Mexico to exercise caution, and the Justice Department warned U.S. spring-breakers to stay away from Tijuana and nearby Rosarito Beach. Fox News' Bill O'Reilly opined in 2009, "I would not allow my children to go to Mexico on spring break, particularly when you have Florida and the Caribbean and other alternatives."[62] The Texas Department of Public Safety joined the chorus of warnings in 2010, urging college students to avoid Mexican border cities on their spring break. Even U.S. Marines stationed at San Diego County's Camp Pendleton and other Southwest bases were restricted in 2009 in their travel to Tijuana and adjoining beaches by an order conditioning border crossing on written approval from specified officers and satisfaction of other conditions such as completion of anti-terror training, presumably to ward off drug violence.[63]

At the same time, the weak dollar in Europe led some to vacation in the Americas rather than abroad. As with U.S. retirees choosing to live in the cheaper terrain of Mexico, tourists are to some extent making a similar economic choice of destination given the greater value for their tourist dollars in Mexico. Overall, Mexico has remained popular as a tourist destination—although down from the 28 million who visited in 2007, Mexico still drew 22.6 million tourists in 2008, 18 million of them from the United States,[64] to constitute the most popular destination in Latin America that year. Although 2009 numbers were down even more, by 2010 tourism to Mexico from the

United States and internationally began a recovery. Overall, without considering the lucrative illicit drug trade, tourism ranks third in revenues for Mexico behind oil exports and remittances from emigrants, most of them working in the United States.[65] One in every 6.6 Mexican jobs is in its vital tourism industry.[66]

One potential growth area for tourism south of the border is gay tourism. Although Mexico as a whole remains hostile to same-sex marriage and homosexuality generally, Mexico City now authorizes gay marriage and aims to be a destination for gay travelers.[67] Evidence of that emphasis is Mexico City's new gay tourism office that opened with the hope of establishing Mexico City as an international honeymoon destination for same-sex couples, akin to the heyday of coastal Mexico for heterosexual honeymooners. Gay tourism, of course, is not vice tourism. Yet the recognition of gay marriage, in contrast to most U.S. states, offers a special attraction for gay couples to visit Mexico City either to marry or to celebrate their union.

Although changes in law have altered the landscape of south-of-the-border travels over the years, one constant is the stake of U.S. financial interests in the tourism industry. In addition to U.S.-based ownership today of nightclubs and hotels (including Hilton, Hyatt Regency, Marriott, and Ritz-Carlton resorts in Cancún),[68] tourists in beach resorts, particularly Cancún, can expect to find a proliferation of familiar restaurants—Outback Steakhouse, Planet Hollywood, Hard Rock Cafe, Subway, McDonald's, Burger King, Hooters, Pizza Hut, and T.G.I. Friday's. Nightclub DJs spin U.S. rap records and beachgoers are more likely to hear popular songs from the United States in English blaring from pool bar speakers than the sounds of salsa or cumbia. Taxi and shuttle drivers speak passable English, as do most restaurant servers. A Mexican tourism official joked once about the difference between Cancún and Miami—"in Cancún, everybody speaks English!"[69] As one author put it, "the raison d'être of Cancún is all about making the American vacationer feel as though he has never left the U.S. of A."[70]

As described in chapter 2, gated enclaves in Mexico lure U.S. retirees and vacation-home owners. U.S. residents, it seems, prefer to replicate their familiar surroundings, whether in Mexico for vice or relaxation. In the reverse flow of Mexican labor to the United States, we prefer that Mexican laborers remain invisible in our cityscapes while we rely on them for our most basic needs of food and, through the construction and home maintenance industries, shelter. In this dynamic, Mexicans exist to serve the U.S. public whether in the United States or on a Mexican beach. As one Cancún hotel worker remarked, "The gringos expect to be treated like kings and queens when they travel to Mexico on vacation."[71] In contrast, the average Cancún tourism worker earns less than $200 a month.[72] We hold Mexicans culpable for serving our vices, yet fail to acknowledge their labor contribution toward our life necessities. As examined below, a comprehensive border policy would recognize this virtuous contribution that merits a fresh and enlightened cross-border relationship.

Losin' It

Prostitution and the Child Sex Trade

Night arrives; boys from Amarillo and Texas A&M pile out of vehicles, urinate on the bumper, emit war whoops, and stagger off toward Papagallo's [Brothel in Mexico's Nuevo Laredo]. . . . [A]ll along the border, Mexican women are receiving American men and their dollars in their bed.

—Alan Weisman,
La Frontera: The United States Border with Mexico (1986), 42

Hot in and out of bed! Serena is a wild girl who loves to have a good time, and enjoys life to the fullest AND love[s] to do [a] Lesbian Show with her Marcela. Good for a night out to dinner or to a nightclub, full of sensuality and Latin flavor! Let's enjoy a night or two on the town in Baja, a sunset walk on the beach and an extended fantasy vacation.[1]

Eclectic international rocker Manu Chao's signature ode to Tijuana—"Welcome to Tijuana"—includes in its chorus the three vices U.S. residents tend to associate with the Mexican border town—tequila, sex, and marijuana. Constituting a wide range of indulgences, the south-of-the-border sex industry prompts border crossings to view sex shows and strippers, as well as to solicit prostitutes, including abhorrent child sex tourism. Over the years, the availability in Mexico of sex for sale and sex shows for voyeurs has drawn mostly men across the border to quench their sexual thirsts and in some cases their depravity.

Our unflattering attitudes toward Mexicans suggest a dynamic in which the perversions of Mexico and its supposed cultural traditions lure and entrap innocent U.S. residents beyond their inhibitions. Elsewhere I detailed the construction of Latinos/as in the U.S. imagination to include, on the male side, the Latin lover, and for females, the derogatory conceptions of the easy Latina, the fertile Latina, and the Latina whore, the latter conveyed by an oft-told "joke": "What did the Mexican do with his first 50 cent piece? He married her."[2] For both genders, the image of the dirty Mexican encompasses living conditions as well as sexual encounters. These derogatory conceptions allow U.S. residents the excuse that what happens in Mexico must have been prompted by Mexican culture, rather than by any perverse predisposition or premeditation of their own in crossing the border. Although Mexicans share some blame for their role in facilitating illicit sexual experiences, it is striking how the United States tends to unilaterally point the finger at Mexico in arenas of mutual responsibility. This same failure to share responsibility pervades border crossings from the drug trade to undocumented immigration. As with other areas, a mutual acceptance of responsibility and a mutual engagement toward solutions are necessary to address the illicit and in some instances the economic lures of border crossings.

Prostitution was part of the Wild West legacy in the southwestern United States. Eventually, the same morals movement that tackled saloon drinking drove many Southwest bordellos out of business during the Prohibition era and earlier, pushing both prostitutes and their johns across the border into Mexico. As with drinking, Mexico offered greater legal acceptance of the sex trade. Although prostitutes were required to obtain licenses and to undergo weekly medical examinations for sexually transmitted diseases, they were otherwise free in many Mexican towns to solicit customers seeking pleasure. In the Prohibition era in particular, many Mexican border town prostitutes were U.S. citizens, reflecting the flight of illicit business owners, employees, and their customers south of the border in response to changes and variations in laws. As discussed in chapter 4, saloon owners and gambling enterprises similarly operated in Mexico under the prevailing model of U.S.-owned businesses serving U.S. residents through U.S. citizen employees. So, too, it was in Mexican border towns for the world's oldest profession.

From 1900 to 1917, more than 2,000 towns across the United States closed their red-light districts in the prevailing morals attack on prostitution.[3] The border city of El Paso fell under this imperative. Prostitution flourished early in the city's history, but in 1882 El Paso began fining prostitutes weekly or monthly in what amounted to a de facto license to engage in prostitution, as the fines were collected outside the court system.[4] By 1913, El Paso authorities enforced the vice ordinance more rigorously, requiring the arrest and appearance in court of prostitutes as a condition to paying the fine. When increased enforcement prerogatives combined with the Prohibition-era flight of saloons south of the border to Juárez, the prostitution trade followed. Previously, prostitutes in Juárez catered to Mexican customers, and El Paso prostitutes serviced U.S. resident johns. The shift in legality brought U.S. customers across the border, and red-light districts sprang up in Mexico throughout its northern boundary. In a tradition that continues today, women solicited expensive drinks from customers in the bars of Juárez and elsewhere, earning a commission for the drink sale and some of the proceeds of the sexual encounter should the customer wish to fortify his drinking with carnal pleasure.[5] By 1918, Mexicali's famous brothel The Owl supplied 104 rooms into which customers might retreat with the prostitute of their choice. Mexicali registered its prostitutes by licensure, tracking the women by their demographic profile and with front and side photographs. Most of Mexicali's licensed prostitutes of that era were U.S.-born, presumably to reflect the preferences of their Anglo customers, and most of these women were from the Western United States.[6] Similarly, in Tijuana most of the prostitutes of the time hailed from the United States, Europe, or Asia, and almost all of them resided across the border in the United States when they weren't working.[7]

When the customer base for border town decadence rebounded after the Prohibition era to include U.S. servicemen during World War II, prostitution serving U.S. customers thrived again in Mexico's cities proximate to military bases, particularly in Tijuana and Juárez. In his autobiography, astronaut "Buzz" Aldrin wrote of his rite of manhood in a Juárez brothel as a 19-year-old in 1949: "While at Fort Bliss in El Paso, a group of us [West Point cadets] slipped across the border to Juarez, Mexico, where for a reasonable fee we were relieved of our virginity. . . . At nineteen, I finally learned about 'doing it.'"[8] A rise in gonorrhea and syphilis cases eventually prompted military officials at El Paso's Fort Bliss and nearby Biggs Field to forbid soldiers from crossing the border for their nightly release.[9]

Not just servicemen frequented the border town prostitutes in the second half of the twentieth century. Reflected in the lore of the border states, particularly in Texas, and depicted in several novels and movies, is the saying, "I lost my virginity and had my first drink in a Mexican border town."[10] Larry McMurtry's 1966 novel *The Last Picture Show* sent two small-town Texas boys to Matamoros, Mexico, where their younger guide escorted them to the screening of a pornographic movie featuring a couple in a ménage à trois with a German shepherd dog. Later, the Texan youth bargained for an all-night party with Juanita, a prostitute pregnant with her third child. Jack Kerouac's quasi-autobiographical *On the Road* recounts his south-of-the-border visit to a whorehouse where he and his friends chose from girls as young as age 15, then "made the bed bounce a half-hour."[11] In the 1983 film *Losin' It*,

Tom Cruise and his three high school cohorts traveled to "the nastiest, raunchiest . . . place in the whole world, Tijuana." Tijuana circa 1965 didn't disappoint the boys, offering its smorgasbord of illicit delights including drinking, illegal fireworks, a Mexican divorce (see chapter 6), strippers, a donkey show, and a brothel in which two of the boys huffed and puffed away their virginity.

Over the years, Mexican border towns lost some of their notorious status as bastions of illicit sexual pleasure. On the Mexican side, cities concerned with attracting family tourism pushed brothels and prostitutes away from the most visible sectors of town, and the introduction of maquiladora factories offered alternate employment to Mexican women drawn to the borderlands, although not without its own perils, as detailed in chapter 3. On the U.S. side, the tawdry appeal of Mexican border towns faded some as pornography in the form of strip shows, adult films, and magazines became more visible in U.S. culture and communities, particularly with the development of Internet pornography and the use of the Internet as a means of soliciting johns and prostitutes within U.S. cities. The United States is now home to some 2,500 to 5,000 strip clubs, and over a million and a half adult websites attract Internet customers.[12] Prostitution in Mexico's border towns and beach resorts hangs on, though, in places such as Mexico's Nuevo Laredo, the sister city to Laredo, Texas, where U.S. youth still venture on weekends to one of the border's largest red-light districts.[13]

Prostitution in Mexico continues to follow the model of Prohibition-era regulation, with many areas allowing licensed prostitution conditioned on regular health exams for the sex workers. Tijuana, for example, registered 13,340 sex workers in 2003.[14] As one researcher put it, "illicit sex still abounds in Juárez, just as it does in all bordertowns, but in most cases, one must look for it."[15] Tijuana's red-light district, known as Zona Norte, however, remains just three blocks from the main street of its tourist core, Avenida Revolución.

Today's border town prostitution blends old practices with new technologies. Traditional venues of prostitution are massage parlors, as well as nightclubs and strip joints where sex workers solicit men to accompany them to adjoining rooms for private dances and sexual acts. For example, Tijuana's popular Adelita Bar advertises on its website: "Adelita Bar opened its doors in 1962 and is the #1 tourist bar in Tijuana. The beer is cold and cheap and there are plenty of available women. Rooms upstairs at the Hotel Coahuila are $11 for half an hour."[16] Most prostitutes there charge between $40 and $60, plus the cost of the tiny room.[17] Often an older woman supplies items such as condoms for purchase, and is tipped.[18] Older prostitutes resort to attracting customers on street-level, escorting them to nearby one-room flats. Technology-based solicitations, as in the United States, are delivered in Mexico by means of escort service websites and advertisements, and erotic services listings on Craigslist[19] such as this ad posted in November 2009 aimed at Anglo tourists: "A real fun time is waiting for you here [in Mexico] with Luna! She is a University student who speaks and understands English. Take her out to dinner, enjoy her company, take her back to your hotel for an hour or evening of wild adventure."

A study of prostitution in 2006 in the small Mexican border towns of San Luis Rio Colorado and Algodones found that its prostitutes overwhelmingly were single mothers, many coming from poverty-stricken regions of Mexico.[20] A significant number of border town prostitutes work for just a couple of years, and many of them only on weekends, commuting weekly by bus from their homes in Mexico's interior, where jobs and opportunities are scarce. Although since 1965 the development of border town maquiladoras offered alternate employment to women, prostitution retains its lure as one of the highest paid occupations in Mexican border towns, even as a sideline for some maquiladora workers.

A study published in 2009 found that many men who regularly have sex with Tijuana prostitutes engaged in risky behavior, such as being under the influence of drugs while having sex with a prostitute, or failing to wear a condom, putting both parties at risk for AIDS transmission.[21] Overall, however, a study of prostitutes in border town Mexico and in Southern California found Mexico's sex workers comparatively less at risk for AIDS because fewer were alcoholics and drug users themselves and most used their job for survival rather than as a gateway for drugs.[22] Moreover, the legality of prostitution by licensed sex workers who undergo regular health examinations supplied an incentive for the licensed Mexican sex workers to insist on condom use, although the prohibitive cost of regular health exams caused many to forgo registration with authorities.[23]

In addition to prostitution, border town sex workers often stage live sex shows, both lesbian and heterosexual, for customers in private flats or in brothels.[24] Imbedded in U.S. pop culture, the so-called donkey show is increasingly rare in border town Mexico despite its hype in television shows such as *The O.C.* and *House* and comedic films such as 1983's *Losin' It*. In *The Heartbreak Kid* (2007), two Anglos purchasing tickets to "Traditional Mexican Folk Dancing" to their horror gained admittance to the spectacle of an erect donkey trying to mount a Mexican woman. In a variation of the media fixation with donkey bestiality, actor Seth Rogen's character in *The 40-Year-Old Virgin* (2005) described a weekend jaunt to Mexico to see "a woman fucking a horse."

As with other motivations for border crossing, U.S. sexual perversions are not limited to southbound runs for the border. In the case of pedophiles, for example, some are inclined to travel to Mexico as sex tourists to exploit children, while others prefer to frequent secret houses in the United States for child sex. For the latter, Mexico serves as a human smuggling gateway to deliver Mexican children, and those of other national origins, across the border to operators of these despicable U.S. enterprises.

Pedophiles aren't drawn to Mexico by differences in laws, as for the most part Mexican law purports to protect children from sexual exploitation. Although the Mexican age of consent is generally younger than in most U.S. states and can be as young as age 12 in some areas, Mexican law protects, among other things, against sex obtained through deceit and the corruption of minors. Mexico has criminalized the promotion of child sex tourism and joined United Nations protocols against child prostitution and trafficking.[25] Rather, what draws pedophiles to Mexican border towns and beach resorts is a more complicated backdrop that combines abject poverty with the permissiveness of prostitution among those of legal age, and pervasive official corruption allowing child prostitution in some areas. In this environment, street children are especially vulnerable. Here, economic compulsion may lead pimps and even relatives to betray a child's humanity.

The legacy of child prostitution in Mexico includes the early twentieth-century border town bordellos where underage prostitutes serviced U.S. customers.[26] Today, despite the restriction of legalized prostitution to those who are at least 18 years old, both boys and girls are still available for purchase in some border town red-light zones that are even used as a macabre "training ground" for later trafficking of the now-experienced children to the United States.[27] Beach resorts such as Acapulco, Cancún, and Puerto Vallarta also are popular destinations for child sex tourism that predominantly draw men from the United States, Canada, and Western Europe. A 2004 article described the abuses prevalent in Acapulco on "a small section of beach where wealthy foreign men use cold drinks and snacks to bait underage boys for sex."[28] As the director of an international charity for street children lamented about Mexico's other coast: "In Cancún, you have the precise mix that pedophiles are looking for. You have poverty, which means you have a lot of desperate kids. You have weak laws, and then you have corruption."[29] Pedophiles from the United States sometimes justify their south-of-the-border perversions with twisted logic—one retired U.S. schoolteacher explained: "On this trip, I've had sex with a 14-year-old girl in Mexico and a 15-year-old in Colombia. I'm helping them financially. If they don't have sex with me, they may not have enough food."[30] Although the United States in 2003 made child sex tourism abroad by U.S. citizens a severe federal crime, men from the United States still drive the engine of child prostitution in Mexican resorts and border towns. Tijuana alone has at least 900 minor prostitutes.[31]

Offering a different type of day labor, some young Mexican male prostitutes found they could more easily serve their U.S. clientele by journeying from Mexico and other Central American countries to San Diego. Earning more money than in Tijuana, these undocumented boys are solicited by drivers of BMWs in business suits: "Monstrous as it seems, they are supply for San Diego's demand: adults solicit their services in broad daylight, even take them on trips." When asked whether he worried about the risk of AIDS, one immigrant boy servicing U.S. men replied: "Of course. But the money comes first."[32]

In addition to U.S. pedophiles arriving south of the border to assault Mexican children, an active sexual trafficking network delivers Mexican children to destinations in the United States. These victims are both male and female, and human trafficking extends to adults and also to victims throughout the world, particularly women from Eastern Europe (such as Russia and the Ukraine), Mexico, and Latin America, who are trafficked into the United States through the gateway of Mexico:

> [There are] dozens of active stash houses and apartments in the New York metropolitan area—mirroring hundreds more in other major cities like Los Angeles, Atlanta, and Chicago—where under-age girls and young women from dozens of countries are trafficked and held captive. Most of them—whether they started out in Eastern Europe or Latin America— are taken to the United States through Mexico. Some of them have been baited by promises of legitimate jobs and a better life in America; many have been abducted; others have been bought from or abandoned by their impoverished families.[33]

An extensive 2004 *New York Times* report detailed the stark realities of child sexual slavery in the United States, focusing on a raid of a New Jersey residence that revealed four undocumented Mexican girls aged between 14 and 17 who were being held captive as sex slaves in a prostitution house with putrid bare mattresses, bathrooms without doors, and stashes of penicillin and morning after pills.[34] Overall, the director of a U.S. anti-slavery organization estimated that between 30,000 and 50,000 sex slaves are being held captive in the United States.[35] Many work the casinos and streets of Las Vegas, described by a police sergeant as: "[T]he Mecca for child prostitution. They all come here."[36] Mexican sex slaves are particularly vulnerable to trafficking into the United States, given their geographic proximity and the establishment of networks to coerce, kidnap, and deliver them across the border by car, boat, and even by foot on migrant trails. Adult victims are held captive by means of the coercive threat of harm to their families abroad should they fail to cooperate. Moreover, as a *New York Times* reporter lamented, "Who can expect a young woman trafficked into the U.S., trapped in a foreign culture, perhaps unable to speak English, physically and emotionally abused and perhaps drug-addicted, to ask for help from a police officer, who more likely than not will look at her as a criminal and an illegal alien?"[37]

Obviously, border crossings of trafficked sexual victims are the most vile imaginable. Yet the conflation of Mexican immigrants to include drug traffickers, undocumented immigrant laborers, and trafficked sex slaves, all as posing a threat to the United States as unlawful entrants, prevents appropriate focus on the most dangerous entrants, here the traffickers of these sexual victims. The proposal for liberalizing entry of immigrant laborers discussed below in chapter 11, in addition to removing the stigma of migrant labor crossing into the United States, will enable undocumented victims of sexual trafficking to more readily seek help within the United States without fearing the shameful legal treatment that the undocumented receive now.

As explained in chapter 9, trafficking of Mexican children and adults extends beyond the sex industry to encompass those trafficked for forced labor in U.S. agriculture and industrial sweatshops.[38] Horrifically, Mexican babies have also been the targets of illegal human trafficking. Stolen from hospitals or elsewhere, or purchased from mothers in prostitution, these babies, and those from other countries, are trafficked through Mexico for illegal adoptions in the United States. In the 1980s, for example, babies smuggled out of Mexico in the illegal adoption trade drew $5,000 each.[39] Equally macabre are accusations of trafficking of human organs such as livers and kidneys from Mexicans who are literally murdered and cut into valuable pieces for transport to the organ markets of the United States.[40]

Related to the trafficking of children as sex slaves is the demand for child pornography in the United States, which in turn drives porn production in Mexico in order to help feed the estimated 100,000 child porn websites in existence. By 1996, the U.S. Postal Service had announced that Mexico City was a leading producer of child pornography videos that can virtually cross the border to any U.S. recipient. As detailed above, before the advent of the Internet and ready availability of adult pornography in the United States,

Tijuana, among other Mexican cities, was a hub for the sale of adult pornography. Unlike adult pornography, it is unthinkable that child pornography will become acceptable in the United States, meaning that its production in Mexico to serve U.S. users will continue until authorities prioritize its eradication.

Going Southbound

Mexican Divorces and Medical Border Runs

Differences in laws throughout history have drawn U.S. residents south of the border. As with travel southward for illicit entertainment and the pleasures of drinking, gambling, and sex described in earlier chapters, U.S. and Mexican residents crossed the border in both directions for a variety of other aims that took advantage of permissiveness in one country, or at least the more ready availability of goods and services. As laws change from time to time between the two bordering countries, border crossings are reshaped too. The following examples of mostly southbound crossings demonstrate the connectedness between Mexican and U.S. law, and consequent border crossings.

A vivid example is the so-called Mexican divorce once offered in Juárez as well as in other border town locations such as Tijuana. State divorce laws in the United States used to more rigidly articulate specified grounds of fault as a condition to divorce. New York was the strictest, recognizing only one ground for divorce into the 1960s—adultery proven by third-party testimony. Couples wishing to divorce there had to resort to staged infidelity, or travel to another state to obtain a divorce.[1] Other states allowed additional grounds for divorce such as proof of cruelty or desertion, but granted divorce only to the victimized spouse.[2] A few states were more lenient, but they required residency to seek divorce. Although states such as Idaho and Nevada authorized divorce after only six weeks' residence, establishing residency for such an extended period was burdensome, particularly for Hollywood stars and other celebrities who seemed to change spouses as often as they did clothes. Mexico, however, offered a more convenient and cheaper alternative.

Beginning in the Depression times of 1931 when the Mexican state of Chihuahua liberalized its divorce laws, its largest city, Juárez, became the world's divorce capital.[3] Between 1940 and 1960 alone, more than half a million married U.S. residents crossed the border to return single.[4] Although variations existed, the most common technique involved mutual consent of the spouses, with one traveling across the border and the other appearing through a Mexican lawyer by proxy. El Paso travel agencies lured U.S. residents, particularly New Yorkers, to fly south aboard so-called Divorce Runs or Freedom Riders' Specials. Once in El Paso, the traveling spouse would cross the border by cab to meet a Mexican lawyer, all part of the travel package, and to sign the Official Registry of Residence of the Juárez City Hall certifying he or she was in Juárez. Three divorce courts waited downstairs to complete the process of this bilateral proxy divorce for the traveling spouse.[5] Another Mexican lawyer represented the absent spouse by proxy (a power of attorney signed by that spouse). The divorce was complete the same day for legal fees in the early 1960s that amounted to as little as $500.[6] Hordes of celebrities obtained the Mexican quickie divorce. Notably, Richard Burton divorced his then-wife Sybil Burton using this proxy procedure in Puerto Vallarta while filming *Night of the Iguana* and courting Elizabeth Taylor. Johnny Carson, Katharine Hepburn, Ingrid Bergman, Marilyn Monroe, Bette Davis, Charlie Chaplin, Mia Farrow, Tony Curtis, Jane Mansfield, Norman Mailer, Shelley Winters, and Gloria Vanderbilt were among the celebrities who headed south of the border married and returned single.[7]

Legal uncertainties dogged the Mexican divorce throughout its history, especially the possibility of a divorce without two willing parties. Actress Shelley Long crossed the border to Tijuana with Tom Cruise in the film *Losin' It* and emerged with a cinematic Mexican divorce without her spouse's knowledge. Similarly, the vocal group The Drifters released a Burt Bacharach song, "Mexican Divorce," in 1962, calling a Juárez divorce a sin and begging the border-bound spouse not to go. New York courts, in fact, would not honor such an ex parte divorce without both parties' agreement, nor would they recognize a "mail order" divorce in which both parties executed powers of attorney to Mexican lawyers, but neither spouse traveled across the border.[8] New York's highest court did honor a Juárez bilateral proxy divorce in a 1965 decision, thereby giving its residents who could afford to fly to Mexico the opportunity to elude its rigid divorce laws if both spouses agreed to the divorce and at least one appeared in Mexico.[9] At the same time, courts in some other states such as New Jersey, New Mexico, and Ohio refused to honor these bilateral proxy divorces.[10] Moreover, although permitted under the law of some Mexican states and recognized by the New York courts, bilateral proxy divorces arguably ran contrary to Mexican federal law.[11]

Carrying this cloud of legal uncertainty, developments on both sides of the border eventually ended divorce runs to Mexico. U.S. states began to relax their standards for divorce. California enacted no-fault divorce in 1969 and eventually all states did so, with New York the last in 2010.[12] At the same time, Mexican federal law, passed in March 1971, imposed a six-month residency requirement as a condition to filing for divorce.

Exploiting differences in economic standing rather than laws, the burgeoning business of "Cowboy Cupid" Ivan Thompson is a fascinating counter to the Mexican divorce runs. As portrayed in the documentary *Cowboys del Amor* (2005), the U.S.-born Thompson helps desperate U.S. men find Mexican brides south of the border who aim to improve their financial status. Thompson's services include leading his clients on journeys into the Mexican heartland to interview potential brides. If all goes as planned, the U.S. resident men return north with a prospective Mexican bride following him on a so-called fiancé visa.[13]

Abortions present another compelling example of the lures of cross-border differences in laws and practices. Until the 1973 decision of *Roe v. Wade*, abortions were severely restricted in most U.S. states. Although the Catholic influence in Mexico resulted in similarly strict abortion laws there—indeed, until 2002 Mexico failed to even permit abortion for rape victims[14]—the U.S. demand for abortions produced a surreptitious market. Particularly in the 1960s, Tijuana and nearby Ensenada served as an "abortion emporium"[15] for U.S. women who faced the alternative in the United States of back-alley abortions or safer but cost-prohibitive abortions by U.S. doctors acting illegally. Tijuana was a cheaper option. As one writer in 1970 described the barely underground procedures in Tijuana: "For years, the Paris Clinic . . . was the biggest and classiest abortion mill in Tijuana. It provided a whole coterie of movie stars with well-publicized 'miscarriages.'"[16] Mexican abortions entered the cultural mainstream, serving as the storyline for author/poet Richard Brautigan's *The Abortion: An Historical Romance 1966.*[17] Alternatively, some Mexican doctors with travel visas were willing to perform an abortion inside the United States at the U.S. patient's home if the price was right.[18] As for most illicit activities and goods encompassing underage sex, narcotics, and Prohibition-era booze, Mexicans have been willing to home-deliver the illicit service or cargo to U.S. residents for a sizable profit.

When U.S. abortion law was liberalized in the 1970s, the underground Tijuana abortion industry declined significantly. Instead, transient border crossing by women seeking to terminate their pregnancies shifted direction, as the expanded availability of abortion in the United States contrasted with its continued prohibition in Mexico. Now, Mexican women who can afford to do so cross the border to obtain a safe and legal abortion. In 1996, a study found that one-fifth of women seeking abortions at San Diego's largest clinic reported a Mexican address.[19] The availability of safe and legal abortions in one of two bordering countries serves as a discussion model in chapter 14 that considers the extent to which laws that motivate border crossings should be aligned.

Another lure for southbound border travelers is Mexico's border town medical clinics that offer nontraditional cancer treatment, particularly those that combine holistic approaches using large doses of herbs and dietary supplements with low doses of chemotherapy. Some of the herbs and supplements used may be untested and thus unavailable for cancer patients who remain within the United States. By some reports, hundreds of cancer patients cross the border into Mexico each year to receive nontraditional cancer care.[20] Others come for cheaper medical treatments and procedures at the hands of lesser trained and less regulated doctors and plastic surgeons.

Connected in many ways to the flow of illegal drugs headed north, described in chapter 8, is Mexico's burgeoning border town pharmaceutical industry. Pharmaceuticals increasingly are among the drugs trafficked through Mexico and sold illegally to users in the United States. Illicit demand for prescription painkillers in particular is skyrocketing in U.S. markets, especially among youth, as nearly one in ten U.S. high school seniors admits to abusing prescription painkillers.[21] In addition to trafficking into the U.S. interior, Mexico also serves the drug needs of U.S. residents with the take-out model of border town pharmacies. Tijuana, for example, has ten times as many pharmacies as San Diego despite their similar population.[22] Tijuana's 1,400 pharmacies employ 7,000 workers annually and sell more than $100 million of product, much of that to U.S. residents.[23] Adult tourists on average spend $300 on medicines in Tijuana, and some 70 percent of those drugs and medicines are sold without a prescription.[24] As one writer described Tijuana's confluence of pharmacies and cheap medical procedures:

> Tijuana has the greatest concentration of pharmacies on the planet. That says two things about Americans: either they're very sick people or very self-indulgent hypochondriacs. Prescription drugs so vigilantly controlled in the U.S. can be bought here without a prescription.
>
> Dentists, dermatologists and plastic surgeons are the biggest beneficiaries of the border's cheap unregulated medicine. On a good day, you'll bump into a pack of clinical tourists. And if you're lucky, you'll see these humanoids with cherry-red faces fresh off the plastic surgeon's table.[25]

The film *Losin' It* captured the lore of Tijuana pharmacies when one of the horny teenagers, with the aid of a cabdriver, sought a pharmacy to purchase the legendary aphrodisiac "Spanish fly," which turned out to be overpriced aspirin.

Lower prices (10–50 percent cheaper)[26] draw some U.S. tourists, including busloads of seniors, into Mexico to purchase pharmaceuticals. Further, some experimental drugs may only be available in Mexico while they are mired in the lengthy U.S. testing process. Most border crossings for pharmaceuticals, however, are likely undertaken by U.S. residents addicted to prescription painkillers and sedatives. Popular and widely abused drugs in the United States such as Valium and Vicodin may require a prescription from a Mexican physician before they are dispensed, and in addition U.S. travelers would need to possess a U.S. doctor's prescription to bring the drugs across the border. Nevertheless, lax Mexican pharmacies, a lively illegal market in Tijuana,[27] and the undetectability of most prescription drugs on their journey north across the border effectively mean U.S. tourists can elude these legal constraints in their illicit border run for pharmaceuticals.

Widely and notoriously used by athletes in a variety of sports, steroids are readily available in border town pharmacies. A *Boston Globe* reporter in 2005 located steroids in Nogales, Mexico, after just a six-minute search. Although ostensibly meant for animal use, the Mexican pharmacist instructed the reporter to simply adjust the dosage for humans by taking a half-dose.[28] Over the years, numerous U.S. bodybuilders and other athletes have made their own run to the border for a stash of anabolic steroids.

Another pharmaceutical, abortion pills to induce miscarriages, can be obtained over the counter in Mexico for between $87 and $167 a bottle. For some poor women living on the U.S. side of our southern border, these pills are a desirable alternative to the more expensive and more public abortions in embattled and geographically inaccessible U.S. abortion clinics.[29]

PART IV

Economic Motivations for Northbound Border Runs

The variety of border crossings by U.S. residents into Mexico, some of them detailed above, run into the many millions annually. Border politics today nevertheless are shaped by the numerically much smaller reverse flow from Mexico of undocumented immigrants and drug runners annually into the United States. For example, during the recession years of 2007 through 2009, only about 150,000 undocumented immigrants came to the United States annually from Mexico.[1] Despite the smaller numbers of these northbound entrants, this policy influence warrants the detailed emphasis below on the history of these controversial northbound crossings.

In the minds of many U.S. residents and policymakers, Mexican undocumented immigrants and drug runners congeal into a single nefarious foreign threat, akin to terrorism, invading the United States with the intent of harming its economic, moral, and social fabric. As then-California Governor Pete Wilson warned in television advertisements during his 1994 reelection campaign, "They keep coming." Channeling these threatening images into policy has meant armoring the border with walls and fences, technology, border fleets, and citizen militia forces, along with resisting proposals to confer permanent resident status or citizenship on existing undocumented immigrants, and racially profiling Mexican-appearing persons deep into the interior of the United States on the assumption they are either undocumented or transporting drugs, or both.

The discussion that follows aims to examine the motivations of border crossers headed north and establishes that today, as in the past, economic motives drive these migrations. Financial opportunity propels both Mexican immigrants and drug traffickers northward. The reality of a rich nation with capitalist needs for cheap labor and a vast hedonistic drug habit situated next to a relatively poor nation creates the unique recipe for an extensive traffic in human labor and illicit drugs to feed those demands. As numerous commentators have pointed out, nowhere on earth does such a sharp contrast exist in per capita national income between two border countries.[2] And no other country matches the U.S. appetite for illicit drugs.

The same potential for tremendous profits once fueled alcohol trafficking during the Prohibition era, as discussed in chapter 7. In contrast to the drug trade today, U.S. citizens were both the primary beneficiaries of and the participants in that trafficking, as U.S. distilleries and wineries simply relocated south of the border, and U.S. residents controlled most of the illicit trade north. Driven by considerable profits, today's illicit drug network stretches from delivery points in the United States down to Mexico and to other global locations such as Colombia that tap the Mexican distribution system. Although these drug cartels recruit participants of all racial and ethnic backgrounds, increasingly Mexicans anchor the drug trade. Rap videos and media touting enormous riches earned in the drug trade are valid, at least for those in the upper echelon of drug trafficking. Even farmers in Mexico contributing to the drug trade by their cultivation of marijuana and opium reap far greater returns than they could earn from legal crops in the post-NAFTA disruption to Mexican agricultural markets. Drug traffickers are engaged in bloody turf wars in Mexico of monumental scale and face risks ranging from life in prison to torture and execution at the hands of rival drug dealers. No doubt, then, the financial lure must be intense.

Although the financial rewards for the vast majority of Mexican immigrants choosing instead to labor in U.S. fields, yards, kitchens, construction sites, and factories are far less substantial, they are nonetheless sufficient to prompt Mexicans to leave their homelands and, for some undocumented immigrants, to risk their lives in perilous border passages north. Even with the cost of a coyote guide for undocumented entry and the likelihood of exploitation in U.S. labor markets, the lure of daily wages several times greater than those available in Mexico is sufficient to draw immigrants north.

Enabling the enormous potential for profits in the illicit drug industry is the reality that, unlike some other forms of vice trade, such as prostitution and spring break partying in Mexican nightclubs, drug-fueled addictions in the United States often must be fed daily. Therefore, sojourns to Mexico won't relieve U.S. appetites and a delivery service is needed to bring the product to the homes of users. Although chapter 6 discussed pharmaceutical runs for the border by U.S. residents, overall illicit drugs remain more of a delivery than a take-out commodity given the risk of criminal penalties should authorities interrupt the user's border crossing. Therefore, Mexicans become mules for U.S. users, paid to take the fall in the treacherous delivery route originating in Mexico and beyond.

In a similar vein, much of our appetite for cheap labor can't be readily outsourced—U.S. lawns can't be mowed from Mexico, U.S. livestock must be processed here, U.S. crops need to be picked in U.S. fields, and U.S. construction sites need local labor. Cheap labor must therefore come to the United States to quench these demands. Notwithstanding the science fiction film *Sleep Dealer* (2008), the prospect is scant for undertaking these undesirable U.S. jobs using remote control drones manipulated by Mexican laborers from cyber factories south of the border. Instead, our economy will continue to rely as it has for decades on Mexican labor delivered on-site.

Despite the insatiable and ongoing U.S. demand for local delivery of illicit drugs and cheap labor, the overwhelming U.S. government and societal focus concerning the drug trade and undocumented labor is on the Mexican deliverer rather than on the U.S. customer. To the extent that law enforcement targets U.S. drug customers, that enforcement emphasis is on inner-city residents of color, leaving alone the suburban Anglos who fuel the drug demand, especially for cocaine. On the labor side, despite the existence since 1986 of federal penalties for knowingly employing undocumented labor, enforcement against employers has been sporadic. The federal government prefers to throw its considerable weight against the undocumented workers and their vulnerable families.

One aim of this book has been to examine the extent to which differences in laws drive border crossings. In the case of Prohibition-era rum-running, legal differences obviously prompted the illegal trafficking—U.S. companies fled south of the border to produce alcohol in Mexico where production was legal, and then enjoyed profits as traffickers ran the illicit cargo north for underground consumption. Although neither drug production nor trafficking enjoy de jure legal protection in Mexico, widespread corruption has conferred at least de facto legality on the Mexican drug trade, offering parallels to the Prohibition-era alcohol trade. In the case of immigrant labor, differences in laws play only a minor role in the passage of laborers from Mexico to the United States. Although Mexican law requires a minimum wage and U.S. wages are governed by higher minimum wage floors from both federal and, in some cases, state sources, these wage laws fail to directly spur migration. U.S. employers are able to circumvent these wage floors as needed, for example by charging for worker supplies such as gloves and rides to the job-site, and by threatening to call immigration if workers complain about illegal wages or workplace conditions. Despite this manipulation and the conscious lowering of U.S. standards, significant differences in wages actually paid in both countries nonetheless exist that attract Mexican laborers northward.

In contrast to the sustained flow of vice tourism south to Mexico from the United States covered in previous chapters, northbound journeys primarily to exploit differences in laws are more infrequent in border history. For example, previous chapters mentioned incidentally that Mexico's residents have traveled to the United States for legal abortions as well as to engage in legal gambling at tribal gaming facilities. The absence of sustained vice tourism northward may reflect more strict vice regulation in the United States than in Mexico, enhanced U.S. border restrictions on casual passage, and the greater cost of illicit activities on the U.S. side of the border. The materials below therefore focus on financially motivated journeys north to the United States.

In addition to its pivotal role in shaping the negative view of Mexicans and Mexican immigration in the U.S. imagination, drug trafficking potentially impedes southbound border traffic. Drug violence is causing U.S. teens on spring break and other U.S. tourists to shy away from Mexican destinations, particularly border towns and Acapulco. In fall 2010, the Jonas Brothers, a U.S. boy band, canceled their concert in Monterrey, Mexico, over concerns of drug violence gripping that region. College football coaches at Notre Dame and Miami yanked their players' passports during their participation in El Paso's Sun Bowl in December 2010, barring them from entering Mexico. Although its second season (2010) was set in Mexico, the HBO comedy *Eastbound and Down* was actually filmed in Puerto Rico because the cable network feared violence in Mexico. A U.S. government report on the 2009 investment climate in Mexico from the vantage point of U.S. investors seeking opportunities abroad blamed drug violence for Mexico's loss of competitiveness with emerging economies such as China and India.[3] Even immigrants headed north may suffer as comprehensive immigration reform proposals are stymied by their conflation with drug traffickers and as fears of violence creeping northward lead to additional border security measures.

Although the discussion below focuses on smuggling networks of immigrants and drugs headed north, illicit trafficking flows in both directions, as U.S.-produced weapons and drug money are trafficked south to Mexican drug cartels. As explained in chapter 3, over the years numerous consumer goods have also been smuggled south into Mexico with the economic motive of avoiding steep tariffs imposed by the Mexican government on importations.

Apart from drugs, numerous other goods are smuggled north across the Mexican border into the United States. Although not discussed in detail here, for years U.S. residents have smuggled illegal fireworks from Tijuana into the United States. Exotic animals, particularly parrots, are smuggled through Mexico and imported illegally into the United States, as are insects such as Mexican beetles, moths, and butterflies.[4] The demand for cacti in Southwestern U.S. landscaping spurred its smuggling from Mexico. Capturing the broader history of smuggling across the border in both directions is this cogent summary: "Mexicans have always been available to supply whatever Americans want but cannot obtain legally in their own country—just as Americans have always been ready to provide whatever Mexicans want and cannot acquire readily in Mexico."[5]

Similarly, migrations flow in both directions. Although the immigration materials in chapter 9 focus on immigration north into the United States, there is an equally colorful but less sustained history of immigration into Mexico by U.S. residents, and of sometimes restrictive Mexican immigration policies. Entries by U.S. residents into Mexico discussed elsewhere include those by retirees (chapter 2) and Confederates who came at the conclusion of the Civil War (chapter 1). Mexico also received wartime draft dodgers from the United States, such as during World War I when several thousand U.S. "slackers" fled to Mexico to escape service against Germany,[6] and during the Vietnam War when Mexico was the southern version of the better-known Canadian route for draft evaders. Earlier, as mentioned in chapter 1, significant groups of Mormons entered Mexico in the late 1800s, primarily to escape prosecution for polygamy, until their practices alienated their Mexican neighbors.[7] Notably on the restriction front, before the Mexican-American War in the mid-1800s, upon seeing the warning signs of secession that led to that war and the takeover of Mexican terrain in the Southwest, Mexico in 1830 had prohibited immigration into the Southwest from the United States.[8]

Mexico also barred the entry of long-haired U.S. residents—hippies—on occasion in the late 1960s–early 1970s once they started congregating in Mexican locales such as Ensenada in the Baja Peninsula.[9] Mexican border officials patrolled border town bus and train stations, airports, and the U.S.-Mexico border to enforce regulations ensuring that tourists have a visible means of support, as opposed to being beggars and bums who might steal once inside Mexico. Mexican officials were also distressed that hippies were openly smoking marijuana and using LSD. While not excluding everyone with long hair, Mexican immigration officials profiled potential miscreants based on dress and physical appearance as well as entrants' self-identification as "hippies." As one border official stated the border policy in 1970: "If their hair is neat and clean we let them pass. Otherwise, we tell them to go back to their barber shop and get a haircut."[10] In the aggregate, the range of U.S. entries into Mexico has none of the economic urgency of the Mexican immigrant's journey to el Norte for a chance at survival and perhaps prosperity. Indeed, these U.S. crossings are largely forgotten or taken for granted as the prerogative of residents of a rich nation to enter a poor country as they wish. Many U.S. residents regard Mexico as their exotic playground while at the same time demonizing Mexicans who head north for a compellingly virtuous reason—their economic survival.

Rum-Running for the Border

"I'm not talking about dope. I got a racket that's got that licked to death. The wise guys are getting into the liquor business. The market in Los Angeles is wide open, profits are big, and the rap ain't so bad [as drug trafficking] if you get pinched."
—Carroll Graham, *Border Town* (1934), 104–105

Graham's *Border Town* adventure novel outlined the mechanics of Prohibition-era trafficking using specially modified cars to carry a heavy cargo of booze across the border into Los Angeles. The two partners in trafficking each agreed to purchase a couple of cars, paying Los Angeles "punks" $50 a trip to drive each load, and splitting the profits. In a modified car carrying 100 cases of liquor, at a profit of $10–$20 a case, the appeal was obvious: "Johnny [Ramirez] stood on the Mexican side and watched the taillights of the [whiskey-laden] automobiles disappear [into the United States] around a bend in the mountainous road. He rubbed his hands together exultantly. 'Now I'll make some real money,' he said aloud."[1]

Profits of Prohibition-era liquor trafficking from Mexico to the United States indeed were huge. Although prices varied depending on the quality of the liquor, the year of the smuggling, and the destination point, prices in the United States were at least three times and sometimes almost eight times the price paid for the alcohol in Mexico. On the low end, one source compared a cost of $35 per case of liquor in Mexico to a $100 retail price in the United States.[2] Another source contended that smugglers might purchase a case (12 quart bottles) of whiskey in Mexico for $12, yet obtain $90 per case when the booze reached Chicago.[3] With these figures, the actual profits exceeded those anticipated by *Border Town's* fictional bootlegger. The author did his research, however, as some cars equipped with heavy-duty axle springs were able to transport 100 cases (1,200 quarts) of alcohol.[4] Cadillacs in particular were favored. The average car, however, could carry smaller but still profitable amounts:

The booze flowed across the border in those days like marijuana does today. . . . A lot of it came through the [border] ports in automobiles. They had secret compartments in the door panels, tanks under the rear seat and along the drive shaft. A regular passenger car could carry about a hundred and ten gallons [440 quarts]. The trick [for U.S. authorities] was to rock the car and listen for a splashing sound.[5]

Prohibition-era bootleggers used a variety of means to get contraband alcohol north across the border. Boats, cars, and even planes carried cargoes of alcohol. Border travelers often brought back personal use quantities in a flask tucked inside their jacket pockets or in hot water bottles.[6] Maritime routes in the Pacific Ocean and the Gulf of Mexico shipped alcohol cargo on the high seas. The Mexican port of Ensenada on the Pacific Ocean in particular was a smuggling base for the Western United States.[7] In a precursor to present-day drug smuggling, bootleggers in Mexicali even used a tunnel burrowed across the border into Calexico, California.[8] U.S. soldiers stationed at El Paso's Fort Bliss participated in one of the shortest smuggling routes from Juárez to El Paso: "[The soldiers] would line up on the U.S. side of the Rio Grande . . . where the river is the narrowest. Putting a dollar or two in a clean whiskey bottle, they would toss it over the river to waiting Mexicans. They, in turn, would throw back a [quart] bottle filled with reasonably decent liquor."[9] An even shorter route in Texas took advantage of a southern shift in the Rio Grande in one spot in El Paso that left the border a mere line in the sand. A saloon prospered here in the late 1920s, but when it was closed and a wire mesh border fence installed, whiskey smuggling was as simple as passing a quarter southward through the fence for a swig of whiskey in return.

Supplying the speakeasies of the U.S. heartland, however, required a lengthier, riskier, and more substantial cargo shipment. A typical run involved a U.S. bootlegger who arranged in advance with a Mexico-based liquor dealer for a delivery across the border. Rather than travel by car across the international border and risk confronting authorities, traffickers along the Texas border usually ferried the alcohol across the Rio Grande at a prearranged location away from the border authorities. Depending on the river depth, cars or horses might ford the river, or the booze would be brought across in gunnysacks.[10] For this part of the journey, smugglers would use a Mexican worker "who was paid five pesos (U.S. $2.50) for a night's work, was often 'liquored up with fighting whiskey,' loaned a gun, given two gunny sacks full of bottled whiskey which were draped over the back of a horse or mule, and told to deliver the goods at a designated spot on the American side of the river."[11] U.S. authorities often aimed to intercept the smugglers at the border, before the cargo was loaded into cars and trucks that would be hard to detect once on U.S. roads. Violent confrontations were inevitable when authorities intervened in a trade that produced great profits. During Prohibition, some 19 border patrol officers died in the El Paso area alone.[12] Sometimes aiding the cause of smugglers (who suffered numerous casualties themselves) were Mexican border guards, bribed by the smugglers with a reward for each case of liquor passed safely across the river. Even dating to Prohibition, corruption among Mexican authorities facilitated illicit trafficking. These guards would "direct smugglers to points of crossing, spot American officers, and protect the smugglers with rifle fire from the Mexican side of the Rio Grande."[13] Once the cars or trucks were loaded, the race was on to U.S. destinations, whether Dallas, Kansas City, Chicago, St. Louis, or elsewhere. Many times a decoy car sent ahead would telephone back the existence of any roadblocks in a Prohibition-era version of modern-day *Smokey and the Bandit* (1977) bootlegging.[14]

In addition to the risks of gun battles at the border with U.S. enforcement authorities, and of interdiction on the smuggling route, hijackers emerged to seize the cargo in transit, especially on the U.S. side of the border once the Rio Grande had been successfully forded and the booze paid for by the expectant smugglers:

[Hijackers] didn't even need the price of a dollar a bottle for the Mexican whiskey. [They] merely hung around the border getting tips on liquor shipments and then as soon as the merchandise was delivered to the El Paso side of the Rio Grande, [they] moved in on the bootlegger and relieved him of his load—from the business end of a .45 of course.[15]

Along the U.S.-Mexico border, Ciudad Juárez was the alcohol smuggling capital during Prohibition. Several factors contributed to Juárez's stature. Most important was its huge supply of alcohol. With the advent of Prohibition, alcohol manufacturers and retailers had to ship their remaining supply out of the United States. Kentucky distilleries alone had an estimated 39 million gallons of whiskey on hand, and Juárez's location proximate to the railroad line ensured its receipt of a significant portion of this supply.[16] Yet after its arrival by rail into El Paso and then its shipment by truck or wagon south across the border to Juárez, much of that whiskey reversed course through the smugglers' routes.

Adding to the supply delivered from the United States, several U.S. liquor producers relocated to Juárez, such as the Kentucky distillery that made Waterfill and Frazier whiskey.[17] U.S. residents also constructed a brewery in Juárez; it opened in 1922 in a ceremony offering free beer to a crowd of 5,000.[18] These U.S.-controlled interests complemented the many U.S.-owned saloons that relocated across the border from El Paso to Juárez when Prohibition commenced. U.S. alcohol producers moved to other locations along the border; for example, in the 1920s U.S. entrepreneurs established breweries in the Mexican border towns of Nogales and Matamoros.[19]

The illicit liquor supply came not just from U.S. stockpiles stored in Mexico and from Mexico-produced booze. Rather, Mexico served as a smuggling route for international sources of bootleg supply. For example, British liquor exports to Mexico increased eightfold from 1918 to 1922, no doubt eventually finding their way to drinkers in the United States.[20] This Prohibition-era experience is replicated by today's immigration routes using Mexico as the entry point into the United States for immigrants, mostly undocumented, from Central and South America. Further, the international drug trade now funnels through Mexico. In contrast to the rum-running days in which U.S. Anglos controlled the illicit supply chains, today's drug trafficking through Mexico is predominantly a Mexican-run enterprise.

As with Prohibition, the U.S. demand for illicit substances created a black market and swept violence into the borderlands. Once the alcohol smuggling capital during Prohibition, today border town Juárez is the global epicenter for violence inherent in the illicit supply of drugs to insatiable U.S. users. As discussed in the next chapter, that illicit supply chain for drugs dates back to Prohibition and earlier. Once defined by the rollicking Prohibition years and later by maquiladora factories, the Mexican borderlands today are characterized by raging drug violence. The end of Prohibition quelled the smuggler violence and effectively halted the illegal trade north in alcohol; chapters 8 and 12 discuss the need for consideration of legalization for some of the current illicit U.S. drugs of choice in the interest of ending the atrocious violent consequences of this drug war for Mexicans and Mexico.

Acapulco Gold

"There's five hundred dollars in this for you," he said. "All you
got to do is put a package I give you in your bag and deliver it to
a guy in Los Angeles. How does that sound?"
    "And what's in the package?" Johnny asked.
    "What's that to you? You should want to know what's in a
package you get five hundred bucks for carrying?"
                        —Carroll Graham, *Border Town* (1934), 50

Before switching to the equally lucrative practice of Prohibition-
era rum-running, *Border Town's* fictional Johnny Ramirez carried drugs
across the Mexican border to Southern California, earning a substantial payment for each trip given its risks. By the time of the novel's 1920s setting,
the United States prohibited trafficking in the opiate drugs Johnny delivered.
The lengthy history of drug trafficking from Mexico into the United States
might surprise many who regard the drug trade as dating only to the 1960s
era of hippie experimentation. Rather, the U.S.-Mexico drug trade dates to at
least the late nineteenth century and reflects the willingness of Mexican traffickers to supply narcotics as desired by U.S. residents, despite the horrible
cost of violence and the prospect of prison or even a death sentence in the
United States. Although the drugs trafficked have varied somewhat over the
years, and Mexico's stake in the international drug trade has fluctuated based
on external and internal factors, particularly enforcement prerogatives,
unchanged in the last 100 years and more has been the insatiable appetite of
U.S. residents for illicit drugs and the persistence of Mexican traffickers to
meet that demand.

Opium smuggling from Mexico into the United States dates back at least
100 years. Chinese immigrants in the United States brought with them the
custom of opium smoking. Because Chinatowns of the era were populated
with mostly male workers, hysteria spread that Chinese men were seducing
white women with opium, prompting San Francisco to ban opium smoking

in the 1870s.[1] The routine inclusion of opiates in U.S. medicines sold over the counter contributed to widespread addiction. By 1900, an estimated 200,000 U.S. residents were addicted to opium, some of them middle- and upper-class women who used opium instead of even more stigmatized alcohol.[2] Many of El Paso's prostitutes in the late nineteenth century were opium addicts.[3] Eventually, the U.S. government restricted the importation of opium processed for smoking through the 1909 Opium Exclusion Act, and later regulated opium by the 1914 Harrison Narcotics Act that taxed and controlled the distribution of morphine and other opiates through licenses for physicians, dentists, and veterinarians. After these restrictions, U.S. border residents frequented opium dens in Mexico's border towns such as Mexicali and Ciudad Juárez that housed significant Chinese settlements. For those addicts situated farther from the borderlands, an illegal trafficking network developed to supply opium-based narcotics such as morphine. These drugs sold for three times their cost in Mexico, making drug running enormously profitable in relation to lawful trade.

Mexico's production of opium by poppy farmers predated its prohibition in the United States, providing a supply chain for Mexican border town usage and trafficking to the United States. Early on, Mexico served only a minor smuggling role, with the Middle East and Asia constituting the major players. When European chemists in the late 1800s developed the most potent opiate, heroin, Mexican traffickers eventually began processing opium into heroin for sale in the United States. In part to pacify the United States, Mexico prohibited the exportation of heroin (and marijuana) in 1927,[4] but by then Mexican production of heroin and its distribution chain into the United States were firmly established. Serving primarily lower-class users in the United States, the distribution network for Mexican brown heroin remained subordinate in Hollywood fashionable circles and on the East Coast to supply chains from Asia and the Middle East that delivered a purer version of the narcotic.[5] But Mexico stepped into the legal and illegal breach during World War II when Asian and Middle East/European networks broke down, providing both morphine to the U.S. government as a painkiller for injured troops and Mexican brown heroin to U.S. addicts through illegal trafficking markets. Although competing supply routes revived after World War II to displace Mexico, the international drug enforcement imperative to disrupt the so-called French Connection smuggling route through the Mediterranean in the 1970s lifted Mexican production and export markets once again, as did the Vietnam War, which created new addicts among former servicemen who crossed into Tijuana from their borderland residences for their daily fix.[6] Today, almost all of Mexico's opium production is converted into heroin, and most of that product heads north to the United States.[7]

Constituting one of the world's oldest medicines, marijuana first came to Mexico from Spain[8] and became part of the Mexican culture, appearing in the post-Revolution lyrics of the most widely known Mexican corrido, "La Cucaracha": "La cucaracha, la cucaracha. Ya no puede caminar. Porque no tiene, porque le falta, marijuana pa' fumar. (The cockroach, the cockroach. Now he can't go traveling. Because he doesn't have, because he lacks marijuana to smoke)." Mexicans in the Southwest and West Indian sailors brought the practice of marijuana smoking to the U.S. South and the Southwest.[9] In New Orleans, for example, jazz musicians used marijuana imported legally from Mexico, South America, or the Caribbean.[10] The federal Harrison Act covering opiates did not encompass marijuana. Although not outlawed federally at the start of Prohibition, eventually marijuana fell victim to a similar racial dynamic that restricted opium distribution. Akin to the supposed threat of Chinese men seducing white women, inflammatory media warnings of the marijuana menace somehow linked marijuana usage among blacks in the South and Mexican Americans in the Southwest with murder, rape, and mayhem threatening Anglo residents. Fanning these racial flames was the Great Depression, in which Mexican laborers were scapegoated for community economic woes. The resulting hysteria led to state laws outlawing marijuana, particularly in Southern and Southwestern states with significant numbers of black and Mexican American residents. In Texas, for example, it was actually contended on the floor of the Texas Senate that "All Mexicans are crazy, and this stuff [marijuana] is what makes them crazy."[11] By 1931, all but two states west of the Mississippi had outlawed marijuana, and every state in the country did so by 1937.[12] In 1937, Congress held hearings on the marijuana menace. By then, the film *Reefer Madness* (1936) had been released, and Congress heard of murder, rape, and suicide blamed on marijuana usage.[13] In the prevailing climate that associated marijuana usage with Mexicans Americans and blacks, both groups disfavored at the time by society and under the law, Congress responded in a precursor to later stricter laws by regulating marijuana under the Marihuana Tax Act of 1937 that banned unlicensed and nonmedicial uses.[14]

Mexico outlawed the export of marijuana in 1927 by presidential decree,[15] and eventually its cultivation and possession, but the traffickers didn't flinch. In the 1930s and 1940s, marijuana trafficking from Mexico into the United States blossomed amidst the confluence of its universal prohibition in the United States and its growing use. Simple economics dictates that upon prohibition in the face of accelerating demand, prices surge, thus fueling the illegal market.

Unlike opiates and cocaine, marijuana is also grown illegally (aside from lawful medical production in some states) inside the United States in sites ranging from remote fields and forests to greenhouses and amateur attic operations. Although its cultivation remains against the law in Mexico, widespread official corruption (made possible by low government salaries yet huge profits reaped in illegal trafficking) and limited enforcement resources created a de facto allowance in Mexico of marijuana growers and traffickers. As the United States ramped up enforcement efforts on its home turf, more of the marijuana production and distribution market shifted to the Mexican connection. By the 1970s, Mexico supplied an estimated 70 percent of the U.S. demand for marijuana (and 70–80 percent of its heroin).[16] Despite fluctuations over time, the Mexican market share today remains high—in 2006, the President's National Drug Control Strategy blamed Mexican traffickers for 65 percent of all narcotics sold in the United States.[17] In 2010, a U.S. senator heading the Senate subcommittee on homeland security attributed 50 percent of U.S. marijuana and methamphetamine to Mexico, with 90 percent of U.S. cocaine arriving through Mexico.[18]

Cocaine trafficking through Mexico into the United States shares racist origins with other illicit drug trades. As with opiates and marijuana, cocaine came to be viewed in the early 1900s United States as a propellant of undesirable behavior by a disfavored group, in this instance black men: "Allegations spread that black cocaine 'fiends' were raping white women or going on murderous sprees while they were high on the drug. The drug was reputed to give blacks superhuman powers."[19] With this frenzy, regulation came swiftly by means of the 1914 Harrison Act that also encompassed opiates.

As with opiates and marijuana, U.S. legal restrictions spawned the illegal trade in cocaine that eventually swung through Mexico. Although the cocaine trade originated from South American producers in Colombia, Bolivia, and Peru and tended to reach the United States through Florida, concentrated U.S. interdiction efforts in the 1980s targeting traffickers there—the "Miami Vice" model of drug enforcement—rerouted much of the cocaine trade through the established drug trafficking networks of Mexico. While in 1980 only some 30 percent of the U.S. cocaine supply came from Mexico, cocaine trafficking from Mexico increased to more than 50 percent of the U.S. supply by 1990 and eventually to 90 percent as mentioned above.[20]

During roughly the same period, cocaine and marijuana use exploded in the United States as these drugs became more socially acceptable: "The changes that made the drug trade one of the world's biggest businesses grew out of the complex social and political movements that swept across America in the 1960s and 1970s, when marijuana and cocaine became fashionable, then acceptable, and finally indispensable in some segments of middle-class American culture." As evidence, in 1962 only 4 percent of young adults between ages 18 and 25 had tried marijuana—but by 1967, 13 percent had tried the drug.[21] By 2009, marijuana use was well entrenched in the social fabric, with almost half of high school seniors and 100 million current U.S. residents having tried the drug. More than 35 million current U.S. residents at some point used the second-most sampled illegal drug in recent years, cocaine.[22] Pop icon Lady Gaga's confession in a *Vanity Fair* magazine interview in 2010 that she occasionally uses cocaine and Paris Hilton's 2010 arrest for cocaine possession reveal the continued appeal of the drug in the fashionable mainstream.

Today's burgeoning smuggling trade in methamphetamine is a testament to the flexibility of drug traffickers to adapt to newfound demands in the U.S. market as well as to the opportunities that drug enforcement emphasis in another region presents. Once cooked in super labs throughout the United States, U.S. authorities starved lab operations by restricting access to their core ingredient, pseudoephedrine (used in the Sudafed cold remedy). But Mexican cartels took over the trade, importing enormous quantities of pseudoephedrine through both legal and (once the Mexican government banned trade in pseudoephedrine in 2008) illegal channels and in turn sending back meth to the U.S. heartland via established drug trafficking routes. According to one source, within just a few years Mexican trade accounted for at least 80 percent of the meth used in the United States.[23] Surging from 66 tons in 2000 to 224 tons in 2004, imports of pseudoephedrine evidence the growth of meth production in Mexico during the early 2000s.[24] As discussed in chapter 6, Mexican trafficking networks also deliver increasing quantities of pharmaceuticals to supply spiraling U.S. addictions to painkillers and other abused prescription drugs.

Over time, Mexico's role in feeding the U.S. drug habit has accelerated due to factors including proximity and the desperation of poverty that breeds illicit economies. Despite the longstanding U.S. war on drugs, it is abundantly clear that the drug trade is gaining or at least holding ground and that government efforts to combat the drug trade are essentially fruitless. The fatal flaw in the U.S. drug enforcement policy is the same for its strategy to regulate immigration—a focus on the Mexican supply side of the border flow rather than on U.S. demand. U.S. authorities once actively pursued illegal drug users in the United States, but that enforcement emphasis changed when drug use became widespread in Anglo neighborhoods. Apart from continued inner-city enforcement against blacks and Mexican Americans, throughout most of the history of illicit drug enforcement U.S. efforts have favored an interdiction strategy of intercepting drugs in the supply chain, especially at their source, before they reach U.S. users. The Mexican government has cooperated in these efforts over time to varying degrees, but the overriding enforcement dynamic is the U.S. government pressuring Mexico to partner in the interdiction of illegal drugs by using diplomacy or economic policies, or its unilateral actions, to ensure cooperation. This callous approach of allocating blame to Mexico for U.S. drug use has proven devastating to the Mexican people.

Mexico's longstanding reluctance to embrace a full-fledged war on drug running for the border reflects several realities sourced in history, economics, cartel innovation, and culture. First, none of the enforcement approaches employed throughout the last century have succeeded. Mexico outlawed the cultivation and export of narcotics, but the mere existence of laws did nothing to curb the drug trade. U.S. law even imposed the death penalty on traffickers (who commit murder) to no avail. Mexico targeted growers of opium and marijuana in the early 1960s to carry out the U.S. imperative of source-based enforcement, but directing government resources at the most impoverished participants in the drug trafficking network was futile: "[D]espite efforts by Mexico City officials who urged peasants to raise alternative crops, Mexico's drug culture proved resistant to forced change; by the end of the decade [1960s] it easily met a booming North American demand for drugs, especially marijuana."[25]

At the other extreme, militarization of the border by U.S. forces failed to curb trafficking, yet resulted in the tragic border killing by U.S. Marines of an innocent Mexican teenager tending goats on horseback as part of a church project when he was somehow mistaken for a drug trafficker.[26] Militarization of the drug war on the Mexican side of the border simply brought narco corruption among local Mexican police into military circles and sparked the current epidemic of drug violence plaguing Mexico.[27]

Enforcement emphasis on commercial cargo vehicles in the mid-1990s, known as Operation Hard Line, prompted drug traffickers to break up their loads into smaller portions, so that success measured by U.S. authorities in the rising number of drug seizures was misleading.[28] Crackdowns by U.S. authorities on domestic production of methamphetamine created a Mexican production and export market. An emphasis on eliminating the Colombian cocaine supply chain through Florida brought Colombian suppliers into the hands of Mexican traffickers and their alternate supply network. Crop eradication efforts in parts of South America led to development of higher-yield coca plantings and shifting of production to new regions.[29] Development of a borderlands radar net to detect cocaine trafficking by plane shifted smuggling to ground transport that further bolstered Mexican-sourced traffickers, giving them the profits to finance a vast network of corrupt government officials to aid the drug trade.[30]

Neither cooperative nor unilateral efforts have proven successful. The most dramatic unilateral strategy by the United States was Operation Intercept, initiated by U.S. customs agents and military in September 1969 to meticulously inspect every vehicle and pedestrian crossing the border. Primarily meant to get the attention of the Mexican government,[31] the border shutdown idled Mexicans with U.S. work permits, rotted shipments of Mexican produce bound for U.S. markets, kept Mexican shoppers from frequenting U.S. border towns, and stifled the tourist trade headed south that had to face the bottleneck on their return. Less than a month into Operation Intercept, the Mexican government negotiated a compromise enforcement strategy, the equally futile Operation Cooperation, that among other things allowed U.S. agents to conduct surveillance in Mexico of opium and marijuana cultivation.[32] Operation Condor, the campaign initiated in 1975 to eradicate marijuana using airborne herbicide drops and ground troops, had some initial success but ultimately spurred the restructuring rather than the elimination of the Mexican drug trade. As a political scientist recognized, "Thanks to the antidrug [eradication] offensive, the least efficient and competitive smuggling groups were weeded out (jailed or forced out of business), leaving the market open for sophisticated organizations that relied more heavily on violence, corruption, and intimidation."[33]

The economics of an impoverished nation have also frustrated enforcement. Small farmers face no realistic prospects for alternative legal crops: "Both marijuana and heroin . . . [are] windfalls to campesinos, who are unable to survive by planting corn and beans and discover the rewards of cultivation of marijuana and poppies."[34] Taking the cheapest drug as an example, growers can earn as much for one kilo (about two pounds) of marijuana as they can from one ton of corn.[35] Mexican authorities are vulnerable to corruption given the tremendous profits of the drug trade and their otherwise paltry official salaries. Those recruited into the most dangerous roles of the drug trade are the most expendable—given financial desperation and widespread unemployment in Mexico there will always be replacement couriers for delivering drugs across the border, no matter how many of them are arrested or killed while trafficking:

> What else can explain the fact that most drug traffickers die young and the rest get old in jail, and there remains a never-ending supply of men [and women] willing to take the place of the dead or the jailed? . . .
>
> It is quite common in El Paso, Texas, to see young Mexican and Mexican-American men and women being led in handcuffs to jail where they are processed for attempting to smuggle drugs hidden in their vehicles [across the border]. These young men and women—as young as 18 years—are often convinced by drug traffickers to cross a load of drugs on a one-time basis in exchange for hundreds or even thousands of dollars[,] . . . several times what it would take them to make in a single month [of lawful employment].[36]

Further, drug trafficking plays a significant role in the Mexican economy; the drug trade brings more revenue to Mexico than oil sales, tourism, and remittances from immigrants in the United States combined.[37] Although estimates of profits differ widely given the effectiveness of money laundering, they tend to run into the many billions. The U.S. government estimated that the drug trade brings Mexican traffickers more than $13.8 billion annually, with most of that revenue ($8.5 billion) coming from the sale of marijuana.[38] The U.N. Office of Drug Control and Crime Prevention estimated the worldwide annual profit from drug trafficking is perhaps as much as $400 billion; another source estimated the annual profits of Mexican trafficking as $80 billion.[39]

A sizeable chunk of the drug profits traditionally funds Mexican (and U.S.) officials receiving bribes for their complicity or their targeting of competitors. Corruption reaches from low-paid border guards to high officials in the Mexican government. Drug cartels in some instances supplant the Mexican government in delivering needed social services to their home communities, thus protecting against snitching. For example, a Mexican druglord living in the Michoacán mountains is revered "for giving townspeople money for food, clothing, and even medical care."[40]

Despite the huge profits, however, the overall impact of drug trafficking on the Mexican economy is more complex. As discussed in chapter 9, the drug war is prompting wealthy Mexican entrepreneurs to flee to the United States. Tourism has abated some, and U.S. investors are increasingly hesitant to supply capital to borderlands ventures. Thus, the fallout from the drug war clouds the otherwise seductive financial picture offered by the illicit drug trade for Mexico's economy.

Culture plays a role, too, in Mexico's historic reluctance to combat the drug trade. Although Mexico's drug use is rising—in part as the country becomes more Americanized through the infusion of U.S. pop culture and the return of Mexican immigrants working in el Norte—drug use in Mexico overall remains well below the U.S. standard. By 1989, U.S. residents were consuming more than half (60 percent) of the world's illegal narcotics,[41] and that torch has not been passed since. According to United Nations estimates in the 1990s, 60 of every 1,000 U.S. residents, but fewer than five out of 1,000 Mexicans, use illicit drugs.[42] Statistics from 2004 among U.S. residents aged 15 through 64 found marijuana use among 12.5 percent of that population; by contrast, the usage in Mexico in 2002 for the age range of 15 to 65 was a scant 1.3 percent.[43] Because Mexico views drug abuse as a U.S. problem, it is often disinclined to wage full-scale war on its own residents to solve a U.S. dilemma, particularly when U.S. officials condescendingly treat drug trafficking as a Mexican problem needing Mexican solutions:

> In this sense, the Mexican government's reluctance to fight drug trafficking frontally is quite coherent with its traditional perception of the phenomenon as a demand-side problem. If the origins of drug trafficking are in the insatiable appetite of American drug addicts, it makes no sense to combat it where drugs are produced. In other words, if the origins of the program are on the *other* side of the border, it does not seem very reasonable to spend vast economic and human resources, threatening Mexican stability, by fighting the war on *this* [Mexican] side of the border.[44]

Countless scholars have made this point, though perhaps none as powerfully as writer and musician Elijah Wald did in his fascinating journey into the culture of the Mexican narcocorrido genre that blends traditional folk corridos with the defiant lyrics of U.S. gangster rap:

> Mexico is, on the whole, a producing rather than a consuming nation, and the traffickers in marijuana, opiates, cocaine, and, most recently, methamphetamines are generally serving not a local demand but users in the United States, far and away the world's largest consumer. Because of this, even Mexico's moralists and antidrug forces tend to feel a certain resentment toward Washington's approach to international narcotics control. The suggestion that Mexico is somehow responsible for its northern

neighbor's drug crisis—regularly made by US politicians and law enforce-ment officials—is seen as both absurd and insulting. It is a simple fact that if Mexico stopped serving as a supplier, that would not end or even significantly change the drug problem in the United States, whereas if the Yankees stopped buying, most of the Mexican drug trade would disappear virtually overnight. Because of this truth, even conservative Mexicans tend to resent the United States' unilateral policy of "certifying" Latin American countries as compliant with US enforcement efforts.[45]

The United States later dropped this drug certification program that former Mexican President Vicente Fox characterized as "humiliating and useless."[46] Fox also leveled blame on post–September 11 efforts to armor the border against undocumented immigration and the drug trade for contributing to now-rising drug abuse in Mexico, which jumped more than 50 percent between 2002 and 2008:[47]

> Clamping down on the border, of course, did not reduce the demand for drugs in the United States. But it had the unintended effect of increasing drug abuse in Mexico. When the cartels were unable to get their poison into the United States, they "liquidated their inventory" inside our [Mexi-can] borders, spawning a larger consumer market for drugs among our young people. The *narcotraficantes* did what Coca-Cola used to do to expand the market for soft drinks. They gave away free samples at shop-ping malls and soccer games, selling their oversupply on the cheap to a whole new generation of Mexican youth.[48]

Mexico no doubt understands the ingenuity of international drug traffickers who are able to adapt to any enforcement strategy thrown their way. Similar to the reality that undocumented immigration continues no matter the bor-der enforcement methods employed, the lucrative profits of the drug trade offer even greater potential for innovation and technology-based strategies by smugglers. When the U.S. government implemented enhanced border security at urban entry points (a strategy known in San Diego as Operation Gatekeeper), undocumented immigrants simply shifted their crossings to desolate desert terrain. Similarly, when U.S. drug enforcement ramped up efforts to intercept cocaine shipments into Florida from South America, drug cartels merely shifted their loads through the trafficking networks in Mexico. A dramatic drop in the U.S. street prices of cocaine from 1987 to 2003 proves that Mexican supply routes actually enhanced the availability of the drug.[49] The decline in purity and boost in cocaine prices since 2006 likely is temporary as the drug cartels adjust to the drug war that Mexican President Calderón launched upon taking office in late 2006.

A quick review of the history of techniques employed in drug running for the border over the years illustrates the futility of interdiction strategies that are routinely exploited at any weak spot. Overall, despite grandstanding in the media, U.S. and Mexican officials intercept only a small percentage of drugs headed for U.S. consumers.[50] Given the small dose size, only 13 truckloads of cocaine and a single cargo plane of heroin would supply the respective U.S. demands for a year,[51] bringing home the absurdity of hope for effective supply-side enforcement.

Dismal interdiction success reflects the staggering border traffic at the world's busiest border. Without counting the extensive crossings into the United States on foot outside the official ports of entry in border towns or U.S. arrivals by plane or boat, in 2009, despite significant reductions from prior years, the U.S. Bureau of Transportation Statistics counted 4.29 million northbound trucks, 7,475 trains containing 574,299 rail containers, 70 million passenger vehicles with 141 million people aboard, 228,454 buses with 2.4 million passengers, and 41,314,685 people crossing north on foot.[52] Most drug crossings occur at these busy ports of entry, as opposed to the desolate borderlands where many undocumented immigrants cross on foot. Contrary to the wild assertion of Arizona Governor Jan Brewer in 2010 that the majority of undocumented immigrants crossing into Arizona are packing marijuana and other drugs on their backs, the reality is far different. Drug traffickers appreciate the risks and drawbacks of such wilderness crossings: the potential of interception by U.S. immigration officials who regard every remote crosser they encounter as either an undocumented immigrant or a drug smuggler (in contrast to the dynamics of crossings at ports of entry where millions of lawful entrants pass); the potential for hijacking by thieves that target immigrants for their money or cargo; and the carry-on limitations of such a crossing, particularly for bulky marijuana. Rather, Mexican drug traffickers prefer to exploit the world's busiest border using vehicles, especially cargo trucks, that can carry large loads and, courtesy of NAFTA's boost to border trade, are too numerous to search individually.

Illustrating the challenge of detecting illicit substances packaged as legitimate cargo, an eight-ton load of cocaine was discovered in the early 1990s stuffed into jalapeño pepper cans.[53] And in 2010, authorities in southern Arizona found 743 pounds of marijuana packed in bales inside an otherwise full septic tank truck traveling on a highway from Mexico.[54] Border authorities have discovered drugs hidden inside concrete furniture, oxygen tanks, garden hose reels, and even a lawn mower and a big screen television.[55] Although newly developed X-ray technology permits screening of trucks for illicit drugs or human cargo, smugglers have turned their attention to developing compartments impervious to such detection.[56] Smugglers also use passenger vehicles modified by expert craftsmen with secret compartments, often incorporated into the flow of the vehicle such as in part of the gas tank, behind the dashboard, in the seats, or in a spare tire. Although U.S. border officials may deploy sniffing dogs, the smugglers have their own trained dogs with which to pretest the load, wrapped in packaging and soaked in gasoline, oil, or perfume, against detection.[57]

As Operation Intercept demonstrated in the late 1960s, at the world's busiest border it is not feasible to search every crossing cargo truck or passenger vehicle by tearing it down to the frame. Smugglers therefore rely on the odds that their vehicles won't be seen as suspicious and targeted for a more elaborate search. Whether using passenger vehicles or immigrants with temporary visas crossing at border checkpoints on foot, drug cartels improve their chances of navigating drug profiling by hiring teenagers and the elderly as their mules.[58] Smugglers sometimes further enhance those odds by deploying a convoy of vehicles, with one easily detectible (at the expense of the driver who unknowingly takes the fall for the rest of the load), so that the other vehicles might sail through in the commotion of the bust.[59] Surveillance spotters posing as border vendors selling to waiting vehicles search for signs of lax U.S. border officials, information they relay to the cartels by cell phone. Mexican officials on the take allow the load to reach the border—not intercepting planes stuffed with South American cocaine that land on the thousands of remote airstrips in rural Mexico, not targeting the marijuana or poppy fields within Mexico or the labs used to produce heroin or methamphetamine, and not busting the load in transit to the border by car or truck. Smugglers often improve their chances of a safe border passage north by bribing U.S. border officials, who may earn up to half their annual salary just for waving one convoy load through the border.[60] In 2010 the *Washington Post* wrote about one of these corrupt U.S. border guards, whose allegiance to the drug cartels enabled her to own a spacious house and two Hummers and to vacation in Europe.[61] A federal official estimated that between 10 and 25 percent of drugs smuggled across the border crossed with the acquiescence of corrupt U.S. officials.[62] Large Mexican drug cartels have organized networks of corrupt Mexican and U.S. officials that allow them to exploit the chaos at the border ports of entry, thus leaving mostly smaller-scale drug operations to chance smuggler crossings on foot in the desolate borderlands.[63]

Security and detection technology at the border always runs a step behind the cartels, which have their own ample finances to counter those strategies. In fact, a consequence of escalating border security in recent years, rather than deterring overall trafficking, has been to weed out the smaller players in favor of the professional smuggling networks.[64] As explained in chapter 9, border security measures have even drawn drug cartels into the now-lucrative pursuits of migrant smuggling and migrant extortion.

Media portrayals of Mexican drug smuggling often employ techniques ranging from the ingenious to the improbable—including the comedic (the green van in Cheech and Chong's *Up in Smoke* (1978) built entirely of solid and liquefied marijuana), the melodramatic (Catherine Zeta-Jones in *Traffic* (2000), who arranged the smuggling of cocaine mixed into molten plastic shaped as dolls,[65] and the smuggling of heroin packed in the bottom of a parrot cage in 1950's *Borderline*), and the seemingly far-fetched (2012's *The Crossing* with actress Megan Fox as a U.S. tourist forced to smuggle heroin across the Mexican border to gain her kidnapped husband's release). Reality can mirror these portrayals, given imaginative smuggling tactics that extend well beyond car and truckloads at the border and isolated backpackers in the border wilderness. Escalated border security prompted smugglers to use airplanes to cross the border, especially during the 1980s when cocaine-laden planes loaded up in Mexico for low-flying border runs. But enhanced radar detection at the border, including radar surveillance blimps, prompted some innovative traffickers of late to switch to ultralights—essentially motorized hang gliders—to shuttle small loads of drugs above ground. These crafts are less likely to be detected and can be rigged to drop their payload to a waiting car without landing, thereby helping ensure that by the time the ultralight is intercepted, if at all, the illicit cargo is safely on U.S. soil.[66] The proximity of residential and commercial development between the Mexican and U.S. sides of the border enables another pathway for traffickers—underground. In recent years, with the aid of neighbor tips, ground-penetrating radar, and drilling equipment, U.S. authorities have uncovered dozens of drug and immigrant smuggling tunnels, including 16 found from just October 2008 to June 2009. One of the more sophisticated tunnels was framed in two-by-four lumber, with electricity, lighting, and ventilation.[67] Perhaps the longest tunnel stretched 1,200 feet, connecting a farmhouse in Southern California and a home across the border in Tecate, Baja California.[68] One tunnel discovered in 2002 that linked a Tijuana ranch house to a U.S. residence was lined with railroad tracks so that a battery-operated cart could shuttle drugs under the border.[69] In November 2009, the Mexican army, rather than U.S. authorities, discovered a half-built tunnel under a Tijuana building that pointed toward the United States, and confiscated 275 pounds of marijuana in a warehouse where equipment used in building the tunnel was stored. And in November 2010, U.S. authorities discovered a whopping 30 tons of marijuana near a 600-yard-long tunnel that used subterranean rail cars to transport drugs underneath the border into California. Contrasting with subterranean deliveries, the discovery in 2011 of a marijuana-launching catapult used to fling drugs onto the Arizona side of the border suggests an alternate means of breaching a border wall.

The final smuggling frontier, the Pacific Ocean, has seen increased traffic of both drugs and undocumented immigrants in recent years. In the period from October 2007 to October 2008, U.S. authorities seized 6,300 pounds of marijuana on the high seas off the California coast, up from just 906 pounds the prior year. Patrolling the shore with Coast Guard cutters, aircraft, and high-speed watercraft, U.S. coastal officials acknowledge that the vast territory of their patrol often requires "being in the right place at the right time."[70] Colombian cocaine producers using the Mexican trafficking network will bring their product into Mexico either aboard planes, as mentioned above, or aboard container ships docking in Mexican ports such as Veracruz, Acapulco, and Ensenada before they reach U.S.-patrolled waters.[71] In recent years, Colombian authorities have seized some 32 semi-submersible "narco-subs" capable of transporting cocaine to Mexico.[72] At the low-tech end of the coastal smuggling network, dating back at least to the 1960s, some small-time smugglers paddled their cargo into the United States by surfboard; federal agents in June 2009 caught one such smuggler with some 25 pounds of marijuana aboard.[73] Another example of a low-tech strategy is a throwback to Prohibition-era alcohol smuggling used by some drug operatives who swim packages of drugs across the Rio Grande into Texas.[74]

Given the U.S. obsession with border security post–September 11, some Mexican cartels avoid the necessity of border crossing by cultivating marijuana fields on federal or tribal land directly in the Western United States, thus explaining the percentage decline in recent years of marijuana supplied from Mexico. In the summer of 2009, for example, Oregon officials seized some $400 million worth of plants from these remote marijuana plantations, arresting several Mexican nationals.[75] Overall, the war on drugs targeting Mexican suppliers remains "a fight between technology and the ingenuity of smugglers."[76]

The strongest argument that justifies a refusal by Mexico to wage a supply-side campaign against drug trafficking is the epidemic level of drug warfare in recent years that has fundamentally damaged Mexico, particularly its borderlands region. In the four years from December 2006 when Mexican President Felipe Calderón took office to January 2011, more than 30,000 Mexicans were killed in the drug war. Most were traffickers, but the body count includes several authorities as well as hundreds of innocent bystanders. Border cities are at the epicenter of the violence, particularly Ciudad Juárez, where 1,650 murders occurred in 2008, more than 2,500 were committed in 2009, and more than 3,100 drug violence casualties occurred in 2010.[77] Former President Fox launched the current crackdown on Mexican drug lords, calling it "The Mother of All Battles," and his successor, Calderón, turned up the heat by using the Mexican military and federal police to quash drug traffickers and to replace corrupt municipal police,[78] while extraditing alleged Mexican traffickers for prosecution in the United States. Violence erupted from two angles—ramped-up enforcement created a power vacuum among the cartels, sparking a turf battle that had traffickers killing traffickers in their quest to fill the resulting supply voids.[79] Fox described this warfare over the spoils: "Who would take over for the leaders we had arrested? Drug traffickers sought to outdo each other in shadowy violence against their rivals, dismembering the corpses of their competitors."[80]

Violence also took a second route. As a Mexican journalist put it, when Calderón "took a stick and whacked a beehive,"[81] he drew the Mexican military into a bloody firefight with cartels. The traffickers responded with execution-style murders and torture to deter the military campaign, their drug assassins "chopping off heads, dissolving bodies in acid and posting notes on mutilated corpses taunting the authorities."[82] For example, in 2009 drug traffickers in the Mexican state of Michoacán left 12 dead federal police officers, who showed signs of having been tortured, at a remote roadside location. Drug warfare routinely claims innocent victims who include bystanders as well as families of authorities or of entrepreneurs who resist enlistment in the drug trade.[83] Especially in the border town of Juárez, gun battles in public places such as restaurants and nightclubs have slaughtered scores of innocent bystanders and scarred the soul of the Mexican people. In January 2010, gunmen in a drug-related massacre killed 16 people celebrating a birthday at a Juárez residence, most of them teenagers, an attack mirrored by the killing of 17 young people at a birthday party in Torreón, Mexico in July 2010. Sometimes, innocent victims are intentionally targeted for execution. As national columnist Ruben Navarrette Jr. recognized, "The cartels are essentially terrorizing the Mexican people in the hopes of convincing them to put pressure on the [Mexican] government to relent in its efforts to put the bad guys out of business."[84] The Mexican government did replace its military presence in the drug war epicenter of Juárez with federal police officers in April 2010, but the body count hasn't slowed.[85] During just a 72-hour stretch in early 2011, 53 people died in the Juárez violence, including four police officers.

The U.S. response to this Mexican drug violence includes frighteningly ill-conceived urgings to treat the drug war in Mexico as a cross-border military conflict that demands U.S. engagement. Toward this end, in March 2009, a U.S. military leader implored President Obama to approach the Mexican cartel challenge the same way as our struggle with insurgents in Iraq and Afghanistan, suggesting that the U.S. military was ready to offer "intelligence support, capabilities and tactics that have evolved for us in our fight against networks in the terrorist world."[86] Through the Mérida Initiative, the United States already helps finance the Mexican military campaign against its drug cartels, funneling hundreds of millions of dollars since 2008 to outfit the Mexican military with helicopters, surveillance airplanes, and other equipment, money that could be better spent on Mexico's crumbling educational and other infrastructure than on a perpetual military campaign against the drug cartels that now results in more casualties than the ongoing U.S. war in Afghanistan.

Although most U.S. media paint a one-sided picture of blame on Mexico for the escalating drug violence, the United States must acknowledge its responsibility for sparking the bloodshed. Secretary of State Hillary Clinton, at least, has admitted candidly that the United States shares blame for the crisis: "Our insatiable demand for illegal drugs fuels the drug trade. Our inability to prevent weapons from being illegally smuggled across the border to arm these criminals causes the deaths of police officers, soldiers and civilians. So, yes, I feel very strongly we have a co-responsibility."[87] Such admissions of joint responsibility are an important step toward overcoming the longstanding tendency to blame Mexico and Mexicans for drug trafficking, which blinds us to mutually cooperative solutions that address U.S. demand.

No doubt guns (and drug money) flowing south from the United States to Mexico are contributing to the horrific upheaval in Mexico. As drugs head north, similar trafficking networks shuttle blood money and assault weapons south into Mexico. The U.S. Bureau of Alcohol, Tobacco, and Firearms estimates that 90 percent of the firearms seized in Mexico originated in the United States, most of those from the bordering Southwestern states housing some 6,500 gun dealers.[88] The Houston, Texas, area alone is home to about 1,500 licensed gun dealers.[89] In contrast to the strict laws in Mexico for purchase of weapons, rabid resistance to gun control in the United States contributes to a substantial market in trafficked weapons. Drug cartels run some of the market, with the rest controlled by Mexican gun dealers that sell their illegal weapons to the cartels and other criminals at considerable mark-ups over the U.S. cost—the converse of the drug trade flowing north. Licensed gun dealers in the Southwestern states of Arizona, New Mexico, and Texas can sell unlimited rifles to buyers with a clean criminal record and a driver's license without reporting their sales to the government. Gun show sales are even less regulated, not even requiring a record of the buyer's name and therefore accomplished without any background checks. The *New York Times* documented the smuggling of weapons into Mexico as employing the following pattern:

> [T]he [Mexican] drug cartels hire [U.S. residents] in need of cash with no criminal records to buy guns from legal sources [in the United States], often just one or two at a time. . . .
>
> Sending straw buyers into American stores, cartels have stocked up on semiautomatic AK-47 and AR-15 rifles, converting some to machine guns, investigators in both countries say. They have also bought .50 caliber rifles capable of stopping a car and Belgian pistols able to fire rounds that will penetrate body armor. . . .
>
> Once the smugglers have amassed a cache of weapons, they drive them across the border in small batches, stuffed inside spare tires, fastened to undercarriages with zip ties or bubble-wrapped and tucked into vehicle panels.[90]

Given the fervent gun lobby, reform addressing the ready sale of assault weapons in the United States is unlikely. Therefore, as it does for drugs flowing north, the United States employs an interdiction strategy for weapons headed for Mexico. Homeland Security Secretary Janet Napolitano explained in summer 2009 that the United States has:

> ramped up southbound inspections to search for illegal weapons and cash, adding mobile X-ray machines, license plate readers, more Border Patrol agents, and K-9 detection teams to that effort. For the first time we have begun inspecting all southbound rail shipments into Mexico. . . . We've seized just in the past few months $69 million in cash . . . more than 95,000 rounds of ammunition, more than 500 assault rifles and handguns[,] . . . materially more than we did at this point last year.[91]

In the same way that the U.S. government points the finger at Mexican drug cartels, without acknowledging U.S. demand except in rare instances, the Mexican government has accused the United States of supplying guns to arm the Mexican cartels without sharing some of the blame. For example, in 2007 the Mexican Attorney General blasted the United States, arguing: "It's truly absurd that a person can get together 50 to 100 high-powered arms, grenade launchers, fragmentation grenades, and can transport this cargo to our country. It's a task that needs a much more decided and determined effort from the U.S. government."[92]

Drug money follows a similar path southward to Mexico. As Cheech reminded Chong in their cinematic drug comedy *Nice Dreams* (1981), the first rule of drug dealing is "don't take a check!" Enormous proceeds of cash, in the many billions of dollars annually, then, must find their way back to Mexican drug cartel leaders who in turn disburse significant sums to corrupt officials to grease the distribution chain. The passage of money into Mexico uses some of the same techniques for drugs flowing north and weapons south. Commonly, the money is collated and packaged in a U.S. border town house,[93] then hidden in vehicle compartments and smuggled across the border by car or truck. Corrupt border officials are paid to look the other way. Once in Mexico, the profits not needed in the cartel operations may be laundered in the Mexican banking system, the Mexican stock market, or offshore.[94] Mexico's burgeoning tourism industry is a favorite laundering vehicle for drug cartels. Some of the profits may even be laundered within the United States, avoiding the risk of transport and of taxation in Mexico.[95] Both Mexican and U.S. authorities of late have targeted drug money shipments for interdiction. Related to these efforts, in March 2007, U.S. and Mexican agents working cooperatively uncovered the largest money stash ever found, earned from the U.S. methamphetamine trade: $205.6 million in U.S. dollars and $1.5 million in pesos, hidden in the walls and closets of a home in a wealthy Mexico City neighborhood.[96]

Overall, the drug war that the last two Mexican presidents have waged with U.S. blessing and financial aid is a colossal misstep that plunged Mexico into the depths of violence and despair. As urged in chapter 12, the United States must replace its interdiction strategy with demand-side measures that reduce the unceasing U.S. demand for illegal substances. Failing that, Mexico should abandon its complicity in an enforcement strategy that fails to appreciate the economics, complexities, and history of the drug trade through Mexico to satisfy the voracious habit of its neighbor. A return to the prior protocol in

Mexico that allowed the drug trade to operate within tight limits of civility (in exchange for sizeable bribes) will restore a semblance of order to Mexico. Despite the obvious shortcomings of regulating drug trafficking through a system of organized corruption, at least this former practice spared innocent lives and demonstrated that the drug cartels might ultimately operate within the realm of legitimate business like the alcohol industry. Mexico's former President Vicente Fox, who initiated the current drug war, admitted as much in August 2010, stating that Mexico should "consider legalizing the production, distribution and sale of drugs."[97]

The United States must accept responsibility for its demand and refrain from escalating the struggle to a U.S. military conflict. The Mexican people have suffered enough for our illicit habits, and we cannot take the fight to their already-bloodied streets. If the United States unilaterally ramps up the drug war on its own turf with military engagement, that firefight would at least take place in the terrain of demand for illicit substances. Rather than remaining invisible to U.S. policymakers, the shift in violence from south of the border to U.S. streets might supply the interest convergence for bold U.S. strategies of legalization coupled with efforts to reduce U.S. demand that for decades has failed to wane. Alternatively, U.S. policymakers might have the foresight and courage to implement Fox's suggestion of legalization on our side of the border without the motivation of a full-scale drug war on U.S. streets. Chapter 12 explores the viability and framework of such legalization.

Coming to America

The U.S.-Mexican border es una herida abierta [is an open wound] where the Third World grates against the first and bleeds.

—Gloria Anzaldúa,
Borderlands/La Frontera: The New Mestiza (1999), 25

As long as everything remains this way, we will keep crossing. If they throw out two by Nogales, ten will enter by Mexicali. And if they deport five by Juárez, seven will come through Laredo. If today they throw me out, tomorrow I'll come back.
—Remarks of undocumented immigrant in Rudy Adler, Victoria Criado, and Brett Huneycutt, *Border Film Project: Photos by Migrants & Minutemen on the U.S.-Mexico Border* (2007), n.p.

Reviewing the history of border crossings into the United States by immigrants—documented and undocumented—confirms two fundamental points. First, immigrants are lured by compelling economic forces sourced in el Norte, namely employment opportunities and wages in the United States that far surpass those available in Mexico. Second, no means of border enforcement ever undertaken will deter immigrants driven to improve their life and especially their families' futures.

As with the U.S. drug interdiction campaign, undocumented immigration enforcement tends to concentrate on intercepting the undocumented crosser at the border, as well as within U.S. territory.[1] Quelling the demand side of the immigration equation—here employers that throughout U.S. history have sought out desperate immigrant laborers willing to work for substandard wages in miserable conditions—is a lesser focus of immigration policy, ensuring the continued cycle of border crossings and deportations back to Mexico that marked the last 100 years of border history.

U.S. residents often regard Mexican immigrants as greedy hordes chasing an undeserved American dream. For the vast majority of Mexican immigrants, however, there is no gold rush of riches awaiting their journey. Rather, they will toil for cut-rate wages in the shadows of the American dream, lured by U.S. labor demand and the desperation, not greed, it invokes. Despite what the history detailed below suggests, many xenophobes contend further that criminal motives draw Mexican immigrants northward. Jim Gilchrist, founder of the Minuteman Project vigilante group, offers this unsympathetic characterization of Mexican immigrants:

> Supporters have tried to portray illegal aliens as hard-working men and women who just want to earn a living, even if their jobs involve picking strawberries or cleaning our offices and homes. The truth is that hard-working immigrants are not the only people snaking their way across the border under cover of night. Criminals and terrorists cross the border right along with them. Drug runners smuggle drugs, sowing the seeds of violence, despair, and broken lives associated with drug abuse. . . . Illegal immigrant gangs ravage the streets and terrorize our citizens.[2]

Some politicians further conflate Mexican undocumented immigrants and criminals, such as Tom Tancredo who wrote during his campaign for the 2008 U.S. presidency that even "some of the illegals who are not directly con-nected to drug trafficking have been very . . . aggressive . . . to the ranchers in the area," by threatening and physically assaulting Southwestern ranchers and their families.[3]

Others accuse immigrants, particularly undocumented immigrants, of streaming north to claim government benefits in the United States, especially welfare, health care, and public education—the latter constitutionally man-dated for children of undocumented immigrants.[4] Supporters of the anti-immigrant Proposition 187 in California (adopted in 1994 by voters but even-tually gutted by a federal court) painted immigrants in unflattering terms in their campaign materials: "Welfare, medical and educational benefits are the magnets that draw these ILLEGAL ALIENS across our borders. . . . Vote YES ON PROPOSITION 187. ENOUGH IS ENOUGH!"[5] These sentiments, of undeserving Mexican immigrants crossing the border to collect govern-ment benefits, prompted Congress in 1996 to exclude undocumented immi-grants from receiving most federal public benefits, including Medicaid, food stamps, and unemployment compensation.[6]

Although family reunification is a goal of some U.S. immigrants, immi-gration laws deny admission to family members without an affidavit of finan-cial support from sponsoring relatives. In other words, an immigrant seeking reunification who is likely to depend on the U.S. government for subsistence is excluded from entry. Thus, arriving relatives, assuming they navigate the lengthy backlog for most family reunification admissions, tend to join their U.S.-based sponsor who no doubt is engaged in productive employment in order to deliver that support affidavit. Likely these new immigrants, too, will join the U.S. workforce.[7]

Many hostile voices urging anti-immigrant laws decry what they call anchor babies—the perception that Mexican immigrant women strategically launch themselves across the border in time to give birth to a child of privilege in the United States who will be entitled (along with the mother) to lifetime receipt of generous government benefits. Pursuant to the U.S. Constitution and also federal immigration law, children born in the United States to undocumented parents generally are U.S. citizens.[8] As Patrick Buchanan describes "anchor baby" abuse: "Pregnant women who sneak in or overstay their visas automatically entitle their babies to a lifetime of benefits at the expense of U.S. taxpayers, including twelve years of free schooling. The parents stay to collect the benefits. When the child reaches eighteen, he or she can sponsor relatives coming in."[9] In fact, Buchanan badly misstates the law. The U.S. government routinely deports undocumented parents of U.S.-born children, likely on the assumption the parents will take their child with them. Moreover, the U.S. citizen child must be 21 years old to sponsor his or her parents for eventual citizenship. Outside of immediate family (the child's parents), the U.S. citizen child must seek reunification of other family members in accordance with annual and per country numerical limits that have created substantial backlogs.[10] Contrary to the belief that undocumented immigrants get a free ride for themselves and their children, immigrant families help finance local schools through their payment of property tax (and other taxes) whether as renters or as homeowners in the community. With the facts corrected, the lure of giving birth in the United States is far less compelling. Accordingly, although 8 percent of the children born in the United States in 2008 had at least one undocumented parent, rarely had the expectant mother made a run for the border. A demographer for the Pew Hispanic Center determined that of the 340,000 babies born to undocumented mothers in 2008, some 85 percent of the parents had been in the United States for more than a year, and more than half for at least five years. In almost all cases, economic opportunity brought the prospective parents across the border, not the possibility of citizenship for their U.S.-born child.[11]

Buchanan and other manic critics of immigration also warn of La Reconquista—a nonmilitary retaking of cultural and perhaps even physical control of the southwestern United States by Mexican immigrants. This threat coincides with the image of the fertile Latina that underlies the "anchor baby" outcry. These multiple images of the threatening Mexican immigrant animated the Internet game "Border Patrol," the aim of which was to shoot at three menacing crossers of the desert landscape—an armed "Mexican Nationalist" presumably with designs on a hostile Reconquista, a "Drug Smuggler" carrying a sack of marijuana, and a female "Breeder" presumably intending to drop her "anchor" in the United States.[12] These stereotypes accompany media stories when one of the some 11 million undocumented immigrants living in the United States is accused of a crime, and they are hurled whenever comprehensive immigration reform is up for debate, as when one commentator attacked the 2009 federal immigration reform bill introduced by Illinois Democrat Luis Gutierrez, claiming: "[T]housands of American citizens of all ages, from infants to senior citizens have been terrorized, raped, robbed and murdered by this invading army of foreign nationals illegally in this country."[13]

Countering these fear mongers are numerous scholars who recognize that the overarching motivation that draws immigrants, documented or not, to the United States from Mexico and other countries is economic opportunity, particularly for immigrants desperate to provide for their families. As one scholar put it: "Mexicans travel to the United States because they find work there. If they did not, they would stay home—that is obvious."[14] Another elaborated: "There is no evidence whatsoever that the availability of health care or any other kind of public service in the United States is an important incentive for Mexicans contemplating a move to the U.S. Their motives are overwhelmingly income, job, and family-related. They come to the U.S. to work and get ahead, not to consume public services."[15] Moreover, undocumented immigrants in particular are ineligible for many government benefits and choose instead to disdain any government contact while working and living in the shadows. Their contributions to the U.S. social security system through wage withholdings under fake numbers not eligible for collecting benefits are a windfall to our retirement funds. Many of these immigrant workers are young and in their prime years of labor productivity. Mexico (and other countries) bore the cost of their education. These realities of border-crossing motivations and impacts are common knowledge to any reasoned and compassionate observer of history, with one such commentator reminding: "In our heart of hearts, we all know the answer [to why undocumented immigrants risk their lives to come here]. Immigrants come in pursuit of the American Dream. They come for jobs. They come to join family members. Indeed, even for the undocumented, the United States is a land of great opportunity."[16]

The review of history below makes clear the economic motivation behind Mexican immigration to the United States, which ebbs and flows based on prosperity and decline in the U.S. and Mexican economies. Also evident in this historical review is the variety of methods of entry utilized by undocumented immigrants in their journey to the land of opportunity, and the futility of legal impediments to entry. Clearly apparent is that, regardless of the allowances for legal entry at the time, when U.S. employers beckon, Mexican immigrants will come as they have for decades.

Shortly after the present U.S.-Mexico border was established in the mid-nineteenth century under the Treaty of Guadalupe Hidalgo and the Gadsden Purchase, immigration from Mexico was insubstantial. Moreover, traffic initially flowed south as Mexicans living in what became the United States sometimes left their new country and migrated south to Mexico. In order to protect its newly drawn boundary with the United States, Mexico's government offered land and even compensation to those Mexicans willing to relocate south of the border.[17] But racial prejudice in the United States laid the foundation in the late nineteenth century for the dynamic that has prevailed to the present day—one in which Mexican laborers are relied on as a fluid supply for U.S. labor needs, but regarded as disposable when those needs ebb. Ironically, despite the low regard among many in the United States for Mexican laborers, it was even greater racial prejudice against Chinese workers that launched migratory runs for the border that still follow similar paths.

With few exceptions, the federal Chinese Exclusion Act of 1882 denied entry of Chinese into the United States.[18] Japanese immigrants were similarly cut off pursuant to the 1907 Gentlemen's Agreement with Japan, and broader anti-Asian sentiments culminated in 1917 U.S. legislation to exclude all Asians, including immigrants from India. After the Chinese Exclusion Act, Mexico served as an entry point for illicit Chinese immigration to the United States. One common method of Chinese border crossing was a roundabout trek that brought thousands of Chinese by ship from Asia to San Francisco, where they boarded a ship bound for Mexican ports of call, such as Ensenada, Cabo San Lucas, and La Paz in Baja California. Although significant numbers of Chinese settled in Mexico, whose government encouraged Chinese immigration to help populate the borderlands, many headed through Baja or Sonora, Mexico into the United States using overland smuggling routes. Nogales, Arizona, became the principal entry point into the United States by means of stagecoaches, rail boxcars, and even burros, from which smugglers escorted Chinese immigrants to Los Angeles or San Francisco.[19] Once in the United States, the smuggled Chinese relied on forged certificates of residency and blended with pre-exclusion immigrants. Only a handful of U.S. border inspectors were responsible for the U.S.-Mexico border, and they bore duties of customs inspections and opium interdiction as well as enforcing the exclusion law, thereby ensuring easy passage for smuggling networks. In 1914, the U.S. government bolstered the border forces to address the smuggling of immigrants—hiring more border guards and supplying them with horses, cars, and boats to patrol the U.S.-Mexico border.[20]

Particularly during World War I, labor needs in the United States, combined with anti-Asian immigration laws, ushered in a special legal treatment of Mexican immigration that survived until the 1960s. Under this approach, while immigration from most other countries was carefully regulated and limited by federal statute, Mexicans enjoyed a system of apparent permissiveness that disguised harsh impediments that could be flexed as needed to curtail or encourage Mexican immigration as U.S. labor markets dictated. This was accomplished primarily by shielding Mexico and other Western Hemisphere countries from the immigration law limits imposed on other countries under the Immigration Act of 1924. Despite its phrasing as a quota, the 1924 Act aimed to restrict immigration from southern and eastern Europe—primarily of Jews, Italians, Slavs, and Greeks—by imposing a discriminatory national "quota" system. That Act exempted Mexico and other Western Hemisphere countries, thereby imposing no numerical limits on immigration of Mexicans to the United States. Though some urged restricting Mexican immigration, the Southwestern agriculture and transportation industries, and other industrialists, lobbied to keep Mexicans shielded from quotas.[21] But a raft of discretionary restrictions enforced at the administrative level allowed control of Mexican immigration like a faucet that was opened as needed. These restrictions included a head tax on each immigrant, first levied in 1882 at 50 cents, but increased by 1917 to eight dollars a head and supplemented in 1924 by a ten-dollar visa fee on entry.[22] The 1917 Immigration Act imposed a literacy test on all immigrants over age 16, requiring them to be able to read English or some other language in order to be admitted to the United States. Moreover, federal immigration laws forbade admission to those likely to become a public charge. The latter exclusion was particularly susceptible to discretionary application based on the prevailing labor needs and economy. Using these and other administrative impediments to entry, U.S. immigration officials could serve labor needs while excluding Mexicans in times of economic distress. For example, the prerogatives favoring entry of Mexican laborers were so strong in 1917 that the U.S. Secretary of Labor waived some of these restrictions—the head tax and the literacy requirement—for Mexican immigrant workers.[23] At other times, immigration officials closed the door by strictly enforcing these conditions to formal entry. Given the lax border enforcement at the beginning of the twentieth century, oftentimes Mexican immigrants responded to insistence on these conditions by simply crossing the border without documentation, in a precursor to today's more sustained push by the undocumented into the United States: "The decision to utilize a smuggler could save the Mexican worker not only about half the cost of the head tax and visa fee but also the trouble of passing the literacy test and the time and expense of a seemingly endless wait in some border town before being processed for admission[] by American officials."[24]

During the 1910s, the combination of anti-Asian immigration restrictions, growth in U.S. industry such as agriculture, railroads, meat packing, steel mills, and mining, World War I labor shortages, and the upheaval of the Mexican Revolution all began to push and pull Mexicans into the United States in significant numbers. From 1910 to 1920, about 200,000 Mexican immigrants entered the United States.[25] Almost half a million did so during the Roaring 1920s,[26] most legally.[27] Instead of using burros and stagecoaches, by 1920 Mexican immigrants crossed the border by train or automobile. My grandfather Fernando Troncoso, for example, left Chiapas, Mexico, in 1918 at age 18, traveling by train to Los Angeles, where he found work as a car painter, a musician, and later as an electrical switchboard mechanic. My grandmother Ramona Montes de Oca emigrated from Guadalajara, Mexico, in her uncle's car in 1921 to California's Coachella Valley, where she worked the fields at age 12.

Undocumented entrants could cross easily on trains headed for U.S. cities such as Los Angeles, as immigration enforcement didn't stretch beyond the borderlands. A U.S. immigration official in El Paso remarked around 1920 that "practically any [undocumented] alien desirous of entering the United States and possessed of ordinary intelligence and persistence could readily find the means to do so without fear of detection."[28] Despite the infusion of border enforcement resources in 1914 mentioned earlier, by 1919 U.S. authorities had amassed only 151 immigration inspectors to cover the 2,000-mile southern border. When a downturn in the U.S. economy and double-digit unemployment prompted a temporary immigration quota in 1921 targeting southern and eastern European immigration—a precursor to even more restrictive rules under the 1924 Immigration Act—unauthorized European immigrants began entering the United States, as the Chinese had for decades, through the Mexican border. With the passage of that 1924 Immigration Act came appropriations to establish a U.S. Border Patrol that grew in resources over the years as it was tasked with, among other things, policing the smuggling of alcohol from Mexico during Prohibition.[29]

The economic downturn in 1921–1922 provided an early glimpse of how the United States would treat Mexican immigrants in lean times. Employers fired them, mobs ran them out of town, and police and government officials helped terrorize and displace Mexican workers and their families in the United States.[30] By the late 1920s, as the economy reeled toward the Great Depression, immigration officials were able to staunch Mexican immigration using the illiteracy standard (from which Mexican immigrant laborers were no longer exempt), the likelihood of becoming a public charge, and a long-standing immigration restriction against contract labor that barred entry of laborers with a work contract or its equivalent.[31] Implementing these discretionary standards slowed Mexican immigration as needed. More importantly, Mexican immigrants tended to follow the ups and downs of the labor market and were unlikely to leave Mexico in times of waning U.S. labor need. Illustrating the connection among the U.S. economy, Mexican immigration, and U.S. immigration enforcement are statistics that while 87,648 documented Mexican immigrants came to the United States in 1924, and 66,766 in 1927, by 1930 at the outset of the Depression that number fell to only 11,915, and in 1931 to just 2,627.[32] Scholar Bill Ong Hing exposes the strategic immigration policy of this era as applied to Mexicans that survived calls to include Mexicans within the prevailing inflexible quota limits:

> The State Department opposed quotas as violative of the policy of Pan-American goodwill. . . . Rather than risk economic retaliation if restrictionist efforts to impose quotas on the Western Hemisphere were realized, the State Department devised a clever palliative to decrease Mexican immigration [in lean times]. It simply required strict enforcement of existing immigration law, including old provisions like the head tax, the literacy test, the Contract Labor Law and the prohibitions against immigrants likely to become public charges. The short-run result was sharply curtailed immigration; the long-run advantage was the continued retention of virtually unlimited federal flexibility for the future admission of temporary labor.[33]

As in 1921, during the Depression era Mexican laborers were routinely deported to Mexico—an option that didn't exist for European immigrants given the distance those immigrants had traveled and their dispersal throughout the United States. For Mexicans who tended to settle primarily in the Southwest, however, removing them to Mexico was a convenient option. During 1929 and the early 1930s, rather than a run to the border to immigrate to the United States, most migrant border traffic flowed southward as Mexican immigrants, many of them involuntarily, were removed from the United States. Removal was accomplished through public and private means, using vigilante and government tactics encompassing violence and coercion. For example, Oklahomans chased off Mexican residents by threatening to burn them out of their homes; in Texas, signs warned Mexicans to leave town.[34] Government denied welfare benefits to many unemployed Mexicans, prompting some to return voluntarily to Mexico. Federal immigration officials launched raids in U.S. cities, seeking Mexicans who had entered the United States outside of official immigration channels.[35] Local governments sometimes aided departing Mexicans by providing transportation to Mexico—Los Angeles County organized special trains to transport Mexicans across the border. Scholarly estimates of those returning to Mexico during the Depression range from 350,000 to 600,000.[36] Overall, some 20 percent of the U.S. Mexican population left during those years.[37] In the frenzy of the uprooting and removals, many of those deported were U.S. citizen children born to undocumented or noncitizen entrants. Moreover, even U.S. citizen adults of Mexican descent were removed in the deportation campaign that relied on racial profiling rather than on careful examination of citizenship or legal status. Only when the economy rallied and labor shortages occurred in the United States during the start of World War II did immigration from Mexico recover.

These wartime labor needs arose in the 1940s, particularly in Southwestern agricultural regions as Japanese farmers and workers were interned and Mexican Americans and other U.S. laborers were deployed in the military. Agribusiness manipulated some of the labor "shortage" in agriculture. Bolstering unions in industrial arenas by protecting the organizational rights of employees, the 1935 National Labor Relations Act succumbed to the strong lobby of growers and excluded agricultural employees. Industrial unionization took hold in the 1930s and 1940s and reached a peak in the mid-1950s when 30 percent of U.S. workers were protected by union contracts,[38] but agriculture proved more formidable for labor organizing and advances. Already depleted by the war effort, the Anglo labor force moved to more lucrative employment in union-organized workplaces, prompting agribusiness to turn to Mexican labor:

The defeat of the labor movement in the fields in the late thirties encouraged growers to continue to use immigrant labor as a retaining wall against further union incursion. As white, native-born workers fled the low wages, grueling conditions, and totalitarian structure of work in the fields in favor of urban union jobs, a shortage of "exploitable" labor did truly arise, from the vantage point of the growers.[39]

To address the labor shortage, whether real or contrived by growers, the U.S. and Mexican governments negotiated an importation structure for Mexican labor in 1942—the Bracero Program—that survived in various forms until Congress let it lapse in December 1964. During its operation, the Bracero Program brought 4.8 million Mexican laborers across the border,[40] the majority of them to work in the Southwestern agricultural industry. Although only about 2 percent of U.S. farm operators used bracero workers, these workers were the staple of the largest agribusiness farms.[41] Other bracero laborers were employed outside the agriculture industry, particularly for railroad maintenance. Breaking from past U.S. imperatives against contract labor that dated to 1885 and that equated contract labor with involuntary servitude, the Bracero Program specified the terms of employment and immigration for the Mexican workers, thereby minimizing the potential for collective bargaining in the fields. Wages were predetermined, as were the other terms of employment such as housing and transportation. The bracero protocol side-stepped administrative hoops otherwise applicable to immigrants, but the United States did not want these favored workers to overstay their welcome. Mexican bracero workers were thus bound to return to Mexico upon completing their employment—usually the end of the harvest.[42] Ensuring their departure was the structure in which the spouses and children of bracero workers were left behind in Mexico, and deductions were taken from paychecks and retained by the U.S. government as a pension fund available only after the workers returned to Mexico.[43]

Despite the negotiated protections, many bracero workers were short-changed and abused. For example, employers evaded wage requirements with payroll deductions for meals and by paying with the piece-rate system of crops picked rather than by hourly wage.[44] Braceros sometimes worked overtime without pay, and their working conditions were often dangerous and oppressive.[45] Living quarters were substandard and unsanitary, and bracero workers endured segregation and discrimination during their stay in the United States.[46]

The Bracero Program, at least for agribusiness, was a tremendous success in ensuring the development of a low-wage labor system that survives to this day with an agricultural labor force of mostly undocumented workers boasting even fewer rights. Particularly in the mid-1940s, bracero workers offered an endless source of strikebreakers to quell labor unrest in the U.S. fields.[47] Due to the ready supply of bracero labor, agriculture wages stagnated or declined during the 1950s to the point where farm wages constituted only 36.1 percent of U.S. manufacturing wages.[48]

Failing to protect the rights of bracero workers and future generations of farm laborers, the Bracero Program was also a missed opportunity at bilateral cooperation between the United States and Mexico. While on the surface the Bracero Program appeared to be a monument to the negotiations and cooperation of the two countries to supply critical labor needs in the United States, initially in aid of the U.S. war effort, the reality is that growers and the U.S. government betrayed that potential. Throughout the tenure of the Bracero Program, growers undercut its protections by luring undocumented workers across the border to work for lesser wages and without the official safeguards. For example, between 1947 and 1949, more undocumented workers came to the United States from Mexico than did bracero workers.[49] A 1951 study found a majority (about 60 percent) of tomato pickers that year were undocumented.[50] As with the bracero workers, these undocumented immigrants reached other sectors of the economy: "New York's and Los Angeles' garment factories, and restaurants, laundries, hotels, and hospitals nearly everywhere willingly employed persons without proper papers."[51] Although the Mexican government initially refused to allow bracero workers to enter Texas, given widespread discrimination practiced there against Mexicans, Texas growers circumvented this prohibition by using undocumented labor. When the Bracero Program briefly expired in December 1947 and negotiations stalled over Mexico's insistence on enhanced wages, federal immigration authorities cooperated with U.S. growers to allow undocumented Mexicans to cross the border on foot into the waiting trucks of farmers departing for U.S. fields.[52] The U.S. government repeated this negotiating tactic in 1954, drawing criticism: "Opening the border . . . served notice to Mexico that it had better negotiate [on more favorable terms] because the United States had the power to get all the workers from Mexico it wanted—agreement or no agreement. It was evident that the United States would act unilaterally and that it completely controlled the *bracero* program."[53] Most blatantly, during a period of hiatus from the Bracero Program, the U.S. government allowed and encouraged bracero workers to return a few feet into Mexico at border checkpoints and then reenter the United States as undocumented laborers, free from the protections provided under the program.[54] Eventually, ongoing abuses of workers in the Bracero Program prompted Congress to heed the calls of César Chávez and other labor leaders, as well as religious and Mexican American organizations, and allow the labor importation accord to lapse in late 1964.

Into the 1970s, Chávez complained of an illicit arrangement between federal immigration authorities and U.S. growers to impede efforts to organize fieldworkers by ensuring a ready supply of undocumented workers from Mexico. In 1974, he issued a press statement contending "there is a conspiracy between the Nixon Administration and agribusiness to make sure that this flood of desperately poor workers continues unchecked."[55] More broadly, Chávez decried the grower-friendly posture of U.S. immigration policy during the Bracero Program and beyond:

> The immigration service and the border patrol always worked on the assumption that it was not really illegal for these [undocumented] people to be here provided they are working, are being useful to the growers. The moment they stop being useful—either because they strike or because they don't work any more since the crops are finished—then of course it becomes very illegal and they are thrown out. It's a very corrupt system.[56]

Perhaps to cover up the cozy relationship, or to silence critics of unchecked Mexican immigration who clamored most in times of economic downturn, U.S. immigration authorities in the 1950s through the 1970s occasionally flexed their muscle with enforcement campaigns against the undocumented. Most notably, in June 1954 the U.S. attorney general launched a military-like effort along the border and in interior locations using planes and ground teams in jeeps—Operation Wetback—that resulted in massive-scale deportations of undocumented workers. Between 1954 and 1959, some 3.7 million Latinos/as, mostly Mexicans, were deported. As during the Great Depression sweeps, families were separated and many U.S. citizens were wrongly deported. Also akin to the Great Depression removals, an economic recession from 1953 to 1955 scapegoated Mexican immigrants and prompted this derogatorily titled Operation Wetback.[57] Similarly, civil liberties were cast aside and racial profiling was undertaken to identify those subject to deportation. Operation Wetback did prove to be perhaps the most effective strategy to successfully close the border to unwanted immigration. Still, it inflicted horrendous costs in ripping apart families and ignoring the human and civil rights of deportees, many of whom were denied the opportunity to present evidence to contest their deportation.[58] Moreover, in contrast to today's restrictive immigration policy, the border was theoretically open during that deportation campaign, as the Bracero Program remained in effect to supply any U.S. labor demand and an unlimited number of Mexican immigrants were allowed to seek legal entry into the United States. Therefore, documented entrants could serve U.S. labor needs without risking their lives in crossing.

By the 1960s, however, fears mounted of looming immigration threats from south of the border.[59] Those concerns were manifested in legislation enacted in 1965, the Immigration and Nationality Act, meant to finally remove the widely varying and discriminatory national quotas in place since 1924 and replace them with an immigration system (carrying a uniform per-country annual maximum of 20,000 persons) for the Eastern Hemisphere grounded in preferences for family reunification. For the first time, Western Hemisphere immigration was also limited, initially to 120,000 persons a year, without individual country limits given the dominance of past hemispheric immigration from Mexico and Canada. As one scholar summarized the outcome of the legislation, "In effect, Congress coupled more generous treatment of those outside the Western Hemisphere with less generous treatment of Latin Americans."[60] In 1976, Congress imposed a per-country annual limit on permanent visas within the Western Hemisphere of just 20,000 immigrants. Because the Bracero Program of contract workers had terminated in December 1964, the new limit on Mexican legal immigration to just 20,000 entrants, together with reunification of immediate relatives and the limited possibility of temporary entrance under commuter and other visa programs, were now the only legal avenues left for Mexican immigrants to work and prosper in the United States. As one commentator summarized the remarkable shift in permissible legal entry, "Mexico went from enjoying access to 450,000 annual guest worker visas [under the Bracero Program] and an unlimited number of residence visas to having no guest worker visas at all and just 20,000 visas for permanent residence."[61] At the same time, U.S. employers kept calling, creating today's undocumented immigration dilemma.

Deportation statistics of the Immigration and Naturalization Service (INS) confirm the shift in Mexican immigration patterns from a combination of temporary bracero laborers, other legal immigrants, and undocumented immigrants to a primarily undocumented workforce. In 1961, during the pendency of the Bracero Program and before the 1965 Act, the INS deported 30,000 Mexicans. In 1967, the INS deported 108,000 Mexicans, and the annual number grew to almost half a million by 1970.[62] Once the 1976 per-country restrictions were enacted, the number of undocumented entrants skyrocketed further, as reflected by INS deportations nearing the one million mark in 1977.[63] Mexicans seeking legal admission under the new limits faced huge backlogs. For example, in June 2009, the U.S. State Department was still processing immigrant visas for unmarried adult Mexicans who were the sons and daughters of U.S. citizens who filed in October 1992—a 17-year backlog for family reunification.[64] Any student of statistics could foretell the dilemma for Mexican immigrants under these unrealistic constraints. During the early 1960s, annual legal Mexican immigration consisted of some 200,000 braceros and another 35,000 admitted for permanent residency,[65] in addition to already active undocumented traffic. Once these open-ended programs were removed and replaced with the 20,000 annual cap, no doubt undocumented immigration would balloon. Under the current immigration system, few legal avenues exist for unskilled workers seeking entry who lack relatives who are U.S. citizens.[66] Only 5,000 immigrant visas each year aim to accommodate the entire demand for low-skilled workers in U.S. jobs such as construction, assembly lines, housekeeping, and landscaping.[67] These workers must enter without papers to meet the insatiable, near-narcotic demand of U.S. employers for cheap labor.

Despite increased border enforcement in recent decades, significant numbers of undocumented border crossings annually reflect the failure and futility of those efforts. By the early 1980s, estimates of the undocumented population in the United States, many of them Mexican, ranged between two and eight million.[68] Concerns mounted over the millions of border crossings routinely occurring as undocumented Mexican workers traveled back to Mexico for holidays and special occasions such as weddings and funerals, and then returned to their employment in the United States. President Reagan warned of the dangers of a porous border, announcing, "we've lost control of our borders and no nation can do that and survive."[69] The mid-1980s federal immigration reform package, then, included a significant boost in funding of border enforcement on the assumption the U.S.-Mexico border could be effectively shut down with adequate resources. At the same time, undocumented workers had found employment in numerous sectors beyond agriculture such as manufacturing, hospitality, and construction, and many middle-class families relied on them for domestic help. Lawmakers were reluctant to undo long-term relationships between undocumented workers and their U.S. employers. Therefore, the reform package adopted as the Immigration Reform and Control Act of 1986, signed by Reagan, contained a pathway to citizenship for undocumented workers who had lived in the

United States since January 1, 1982. Reflecting the continued clout of agribusiness, undocumented workers who had spent just 90 days of a qualifying period engaged in U.S. agricultural labor were also eligible for legalization. Ultimately, the 1986 Act was the gateway for between 2.7 and 3.1 million undocumented workers to secure legalization.[70] About 90 percent of these workers were from Mexico, and many of them (about 750,000) were farm workers.[71] For the first time, the 1986 Act attempted to confront the pull side of immigration from Mexico by mandating U.S. employer sanctions. Congress previously had resisted this approach, even expressly excluding employment of the undocumented from its prohibition in 1952 of harboring, transporting, or concealing undocumented entrants.[72] Latino/a organizations opposed such employer sanctions, arguing employers would use the specter of sanctions to discriminate against Latino/a hires generally.[73] But lawmakers felt that employer sanctions in the 1986 Act of civil fines and criminal penalties for knowingly hiring an undocumented laborer, coupled with enhanced border security, would suppress undocumented entry into the United States.

Of course, those assumptions were flawed, as neither augmented security nor employer sanctions decreased undocumented immigration. As discussed later, enhanced border security merely increased the costs of passage as Mexican undocumented immigrants engaged professional escorts ("coyotes") and embraced new, more dangerous tactics to ensure their entry. Testifying before Congress, an INS official acknowledged: "[A]lien smugglers have developed a sophisticated infrastructure to successfully counteract U.S. Border Patrol operations."[74] Employer sanctions in turn were frustrated by a cottage industry of false documents for migrants that enabled employers to satisfy the documentation requirements of the 1986 Act, as well as by inconsistent enforcement of the employer sanctions. The Act assumed that legalizing the status of millions of undocumented workers would quell the future labor needs of U.S. employers; this was profoundly naïve. Employers kept beckoning Mexican labor to feed their unceasing addiction to abundant cheap labor pools, and Mexican immigrants, saddled since 1976 with unrealistically low legal immigration limits, found ways to enter the United States to serve this labor demand. By the 2000s, the U.S. undocumented population was estimated at 11–12 million. Ironically, rather than deterring employer hiring or immigrant journeys to the United States, employer sanctions in practice contributed to the race to the bottom for labor organizing and worker rights. Particularly under the Obama administration's emphasis on workplace enforcement, employers under investigation gained immunity from prosecution by firing employees, immigrant or not, with ostensibly invalid social security numbers. Moreover, employers used the enhanced enforcement campaign to stave off union organizing and to replace suspected undocumented workers receiving fringe benefits with part timers not entitled to benefits under existing union contracts.[75]

Methods of undocumented entry have varied over the years in response to changes in U.S. enforcement strategy. In the 1980s, entry was less risky than crossings today. At the time of the 1986 Act, about half (48 percent) of undocumented entrants came through Tijuana as the most direct Mexican gateway to the primary destination of undocumented entrants—California.[76] Most crossed the border at Tijuana's Zapata Canyon, sometimes using the banzai run technique that Cheech Marin portrayed comedically in *Born in East L.A.* (1987), in which Cheech followed hundreds of migrants down a Tijuana hillside past a single overwhelmed border patrol truck to the soundtrack of Neil Diamond's uplifting ode to immigration, "America." Sometimes these immigrant groups would rush the San Ysidro border-crossing station, running onto the southbound lanes of Interstate 5 and prompting a conservative California talk-show radio host to suggest motorists receive sombrero-shaped bumper stickers for each undocumented migrant they hit on the freeway.[77] These crossings in prominent urban settings gave the impression of an uncontrolled border, and formed the backdrop for Pete Wilson's notorious California reelection commercial in 1994 that warned: "They keep coming."

Following the terrorist bombing of the World Trade Center in 1993, securing the U.S.-Mexico border took on a new urgency. Unchecked migration, particularly flagrant entries in visible urban terrain, came to be seen as fostering terrorism. This specter of terrorist entry has influenced border policy for the last 20 years. During the Clinton administration in the mid-1990s, the imperative of border security led to beefed-up border enforcement in urban centers, notably the San Diego/Tijuana border (where the policy was known as Operation Gatekeeper) and the El Paso/Ciudad Juárez boundary (Operation Hold the Line). Congress enacted the Illegal Immigration Reform and Immigration Responsibility Act of 1996 to arm the border with significant additions of Border Patrol agents, construction of more fencing and walls, and implementation of advanced detection systems such as night-vision goggles and underground sensors. From 1994 to 1998 alone, the Border Patrol's annual budget more than doubled, from $354 million to $877 million.[78]

Tragically, this border build-up strategy was fatally flawed. At best, the U.S. government may have assumed that undocumented immigration would halt once easier routes proximate to urban areas were impeded. At worst, the government foresaw the likelihood that immigrants would find alternate but highly treacherous routes, causing many to die, but discounted the likely deaths of migrants "as collateral damage in the 'war' on illegal immigration."[79] Whatever the intent, the outcome revealed the foolishness and inhumanity of any strategy to prevent undocumented entry by arming the border. The build-up had no appreciable effect on the number of undocumented cross- ings, aside from sending the death rate soaring. As one report concluded, "[t]here is no evidence that the border enforcement build-up . . . has substan- tially reduced unauthorized border crossings"; and moreover, that "[d]espite large increases in spending and Border Patrol resources . . . the number of unauthorized immigrants increased to levels higher than those [before the build-up]."[80] The border build-up symbolized our scant regard for laborer lives, particularly in relation to wealthy capitalists:

> The ten-foot iron wall separating Tijuana from San Ysidro spreads east along the border—a potent symbol of the U.S. government's attitude toward poor Mexicans, denying hungry people the same free passage NAFTA extended to money and goods. While a river of trucks also trav- els north, bearing the products of the border factories, Mexican workers who are caught in the United States, trying to find a better standard of liv- ing than the maquiladoras are willing to support, are deported back to the south, in a reverse flow.[81]

Contrasting the U.S. public's scant regard for the welfare of Mexican immi- grants with our impassioned reaction to the Gulf Oil Spill in 2010, one journalist lamented: "The arrest and/or deportation of hard-working immi- grants never spawned the broad moral outrage that accompanied the *New York Times* photo of an oil-soaked pelican."[82] Similarly, neither deaths in the desert of crossing migrant laborers nor the scores of innocent deaths in the Mexican drug war seem to register on the U.S. scale of sympathy and thus transform our policies. Until we accept responsibility for these deaths and regard reform of our immigration (and drug) laws as moral imperatives of a compassionate country, we will continue to move in the wrong direction that relies primarily on draconian enforcement strategies.

Following the mid-1990s border fortifications, crossings into the United States by undocumented migrants shifted from urban banzai runs for the border to isolated groups trekking through remote, perilous terrain in the deserts and mountains of California, Arizona, New Mexico, and Texas. The build-up succeeded only in rendering most crossings less visible and more deadly. A 2009 ACLU report revealed that an estimated 5,600 undocumented immigrants died during their Mexico border crossing since the border build-up strategy was implemented in 1994.[83] These deaths reflect the desperation of immigrants and the futility of efforts that place the appearance of security ahead of actual human life. The nature of the thousands of deaths reveals the treacherous passages migrants face and the many tactics of border crossing undertaken despite the border-armoring. Many deaths occurred on foot in the cruel, isolated terrain. For example, in 2001 a group of 14 Latino men and teenagers died near the Cabeza Prieta National Wildlife Refuge in the remote Arizona desert when their guide lost his way—their bodies were found burned and mummified from the scorching heat.[84] At the opposite extreme, a freak snowstorm in April 1999 that brought a foot of snow and freezing temperatures to California 20 miles north of the Mexican border took the lives of eight migrants. Incidents such as these even prompted the Border Patrol to erect signal towers in the Arizona desert to allow desperate migrants who stumble across them to summon authorities for help. Torrents launched by desert downpours on unyielding soil washed away scores of immigrants—eight Mexican migrants drowned just inside the Arizona border in 1997 when a 15-foot-high wall of water swept them away. Some died crossing rivers and streams into the United States—in 2000 alone, 26 migrants drowned in the swift-moving All-American Canal that runs along the California border.[85] Others died when wildfires tore through the outskirts of San Diego in 2007. Mexican migrants take advantage of NAFTA cargo traffic across the border and often are smuggled en masse through border and interior checkpoints stuffed into the cargo holds of semi-trucks or even trains. In October 2002, the skeletal remains of 11 migrants were discovered in Iowa within a sealed railcar arriving from Mexico.

The entry on foot, afloat, or by truck across the border does not complete the migrant's hazardous journey. Once the immigrants reach U.S. roads, smugglers arrange for them to be picked up and delivered to safe houses near the border, such as in Phoenix and Tucson. From there, smugglers transport the migrants to their desired location in the United States, often in converted vans with the back seats removed, in which the immigrants huddle on the floor to avoid suspicion. Probably the most wrenching example of the hazards of transport of the undocumented within the United States occurred in May 2003, when 19 immigrants, including a five-year-old, died by suffocation in a stifling 18-wheeler while being transported from a Texas safe house to Houston by a trucker who was paid $7,500 for the trip.[86] Similarly, in 1999, a van carrying undocumented migrants toward the U.S. South collided with a tractor-trailer on an icy New Mexico highway, killing 13 migrants traveling without seatbelts, most of them from the Mexican state of Chiapas. In another awful incident, the Border Patrol pursued a pick-up truck in California with 25 migrants stuffed into a camper shell—eight died when the truck failed to negotiate a curve in the high-speed chase.[87] Other journeys with tragic conclusions include an SUV carrying 19 undocumented immigrants that flipped in Arizona, killing nine in 2008, and a similar accident in 2009 that killed nine when an SUV crashed with more than 20 men crammed aboard.[88]

One irony of the borderlands gauntlet created by fortifying the border is that some smugglers previously trafficking drugs found even greater fortunes (with lesser potential jail sentences if caught) in human smuggling as "coyotes" or "polleros" with fees for passage running between $2,000 and $6,000 per "pollo" (migrant).[89] Passage through the desert may involve several operatives of the coyote smuggling operation—including a trail guide and U.S. drivers to whom that guide delivers the migrants. Armoring the border pushed migrants toward experienced coyotes with networks of guides, safe houses, and drivers, and prices rose considerably for the border passage, prompting the additional irony for U.S. xenophobes that migrants could no longer afford to return to Mexico at the end of a growing season, or for holidays and special occasions. Instead, they settled more permanently in the United States, sometimes bringing their families to join them.[90]

Our border-arming prerogatives eventually drew the Mexican drug cartels into the smuggling process. Already versed in smuggling techniques, some drug cartels have undertaken to smuggle migrants, even using border tunnels constructed for drug transport. Alternatively, the cartels may charge the pollo smugglers a head tax for the privilege of transporting migrants through the cartel's Mexican territory. Most ominously, some cartels have begun to intercept and extort undocumented immigrants on their journey north, particularly those impoverished migrants from Central or South America who must navigate their way through the entirety of Mexico to the border. Cartel operatives have employed several heinous extortionate techniques, including holding the immigrants for ransom to be paid by relatives, in the United States or countries of origin, whose names the migrants are forced to reveal. Alternatively, the drug cartels might enlist the migrants as hit men to carry out the violent cartel campaign to terrorize the Mexican government and people, or as mules to smuggle drugs across the border. The 2010 massacre in Mexico of 72 mostly Central and South American migrants headed for the

U.S. border is thought to have been prompted by those migrants' refusal to assist a cartel in smuggling drugs.[91] Killing the migrants sends the unmistakable message to subsequent captured groups that they had better cooperate or face death.

The forced enlistment of migrant laborers into drug cartel operations mirrors the increasingly common practice of involuntary servitude of migrant workers once in the United States. Arming of the border and increased enforcement within the United States to intercept undocumented immigrants contribute to a climate in which near-insolvent migrants are beholden to those who stealthily transport them into and within the United States and procure employment for them. A 2004 University of California, Berkeley study found that in addition to the sex trade, forced labor is prevalent in other U.S. labor sectors, notably domestic service (27 percent), agriculture (10 percent), sweatshops (5 percent), and restaurants/hotels (4 percent).[92] In the agriculture industry, use of labor contractors as intermediaries who hire and pay laborers helps keep the exploitation under the radar. In one Florida case, migrant workers transported from the Arizona desert to Florida orange groves were threatened with beatings if they left before repaying their transportation debt. Each week, these workers were paid only a tiny sum after the labor contractor deducted for their housing, work tools, and their cross-country transport.[93] Undocumented immigrants are uniquely susceptible to these extortionate tactics, resulting in modern-day slavery within the United States.

The current method of border passage into the United States may turn on the resources of the migrant—significant money might earn the migrant a chance at a safer crossing through an urban border checkpoint, either hidden in a car or truck (with greater risk of capture for the driver), or brazenly crossing through the checkpoint with false documents after lessons in Americanization from a coyote[94] akin to the sessions Cheech Marin held for aspiring border crossers in *Born In East L.A.* on barrio slang, clothing, swagger, greetings ("Waas Sappening!"), and sports lexicon ("Go Raiders!"). Those migrants with fewer resources can look forward to a guided journey by foot through the molten Southwestern desert[95] as well as the prospect of extortionate encounters with the drug cartels or involuntary servitude once they reach U.S. fields of dreams to repay their debt to the smugglers.

As with drug smuggling, coyote networks also deploy bribes among their tactics. A corrupt border or internal checkpoint guard is as helpful to wave through a car or truckload of undocumented immigrants as a shipment of illegal drugs. A 2003 Mexican government report suggested that one-third of the coyote's smuggling fees end up in the hands of corrupt border officials.[96]

The smuggler strategies of supplying false documentation and dispensing bribes expose flaws in the latest border proposal to address the shift away from urban crossings to those undertaken in isolated areas—construction of a seemingly impenetrable border wall the length of the U.S.-Mexico border. Patrick Buchanan led the charge for a wall along the entire border that he claimed would "halt the mass illegal immigration across our southern border cold."[97] Congress embraced this exorbitant strategy in adopting the 2006 Secure Fence Act that authorized the construction of 700 miles of fencing along the 2,000-mile border. These barricades are easily overcome with homemade ladders, rope, blow torches, and other means of incursion.[98] Of course, even a fence constructed high and strong enough and with sufficient detection equipment that it cannot be breached or surmounted is vulnerable to underground tunneling, as drug traffickers have shown. And NAFTA truck traffic, along with tourists and other travelers with appropriate documentation, will still be able to cross at border checkpoints. Given the tremendous amount of traffic through those checkpoints—in 2002 the two Tijuana entry stations of San Ysidro and Otay Mesa alone had more than 7.5 million crossings[99]—as well as the enhanced potential for bribes as crossing options narrow, no doubt even more undocumented crossings would occur at legal entry points.

A gaping hole in the border wall strategy is that the Pew Hispanic Center, in a 2006 report, found that only somewhat more than half of undocumented immigrants in the United States crossed the border using smuggling techniques. Rather, almost half (45 percent) of unauthorized migrants entered the United States legally by plane, car, or on foot, using visas that allowed them to visit or reside temporarily in the United States, and then overstayed those visas. Employing a similar tactic were some holders of border-crossing cards that allow the holders short stays in the United States, including those issued for daily commuters to work in the United States within specified borderlands terrain. In 2004 alone, there were 179 million authorized entries into the United States by foreigners for temporary stays, the vast majority of them (148 million) by Mexicans or Canadians with border-crossing cards (visitor visas).[100] Mexican citizens have used border-crossing cards for decades to work in the borderlands, particularly in the two major U.S. urban centers within the permissible work zone—San Diego and El Paso, both proximate to large Mexican border town cities. Mexican daily commuters, for example, provide the cheap labor force for San Diego's formidable convention hospitality industry.[101] Adding to the utility of border-crossing cards, some are stolen (or found) and end up in the hands of smuggling networks that sell them to prospective migrants who roughly fit the photo identification in the smuggler's library of cards.[102] Once the migrant is safely across the border station, the smugglers retrieve the card for further use.

The impetus for the border-spanning wall came from the September 11 terrorist attacks and the consequent war on terror that views the porous border as a national security threat. Despite the fact that all of the September 11 terrorists came to the United States legally through airports, mostly using six-month tourist visas (only a couple of them had overstayed their visa entry), advocates of increased border security have warned that terrorists will tap the established undocumented immigrant trafficking network in Mexico. For example, in 2005, a Homeland Security official testified to Congress that al Qaeda planned to use Mexico's coyote network to smuggle terrorists across the Mexican border into the United States.[103] Jim Gilchrist, founder of the vigilante Minuteman Project, bangs the same drum in pointing to a suspected terrorist convicted in 2005 of raising money for the terrorist-classified organization Hezbollah who allegedly arrived from Mexico in the trunk of a car, as well as to the statistic that U.S. border authorities annually capture many "Other Than Mexicans," some of them from Middle Eastern countries.[104] However, these interceptions overwhelmingly (perhaps 99 percent)[105] consist of undocumented immigrants from other Latin American countries who employ the smuggling networks of Mexico much as Colombian cocaine traffickers do. Many of these Other Than Mexican detainees are Guatemalans or, of late, Brazilians.[106] As former Mexico President Vicente Fox observed in 2007, "few realize that Mexico receives somewhere between 300,000 and 400,000 immigrants a year from Guatemala, El Salvador, Nicaragua, and the rest of Central America—nearly as many as the half million or so Mexicans [until that number dropped in the 2007 recession] who go north [into the United States] to work every year."[107] Thus far, the Hezbollah fundraiser is the sole suspected terrorist known to have used the Mexican network. Still, the specter of terrorist entry through the Mexican smuggling networks contributed to the militarization of the border, both by state governments when the governors of Arizona and New Mexico declared immigration emergencies and sent National Guard units to their respective borders, and by armed civilian Minutemen who gathered in the Arizona desert beginning in 2005 to patrol the border.

Neither the Minutemen nor other state and federal border initiatives in the wake of September 11 markedly interrupted migratory flows of undocumented workers from and through Mexico into the United States. As scholar Kevin Johnson reminds us:

Few events could generate the political support and incentive for aggressive border enforcement created by the terrorist acts of September 11. Given that the aggressive border enforcement that followed has failed, it is difficult to envision any event that could prompt the sustained efforts to close the borders or provide the resources necessary to achieve that goal. Today [2007] undocumented migration continues at the same levels as prior to September 11.[108]

Although responses to September 11 did not stem the border traffic, beginning in 2007, the worst U.S. economic crisis since the Great Depression has proven effective to considerably slow northbound migration. A Pew Hispanic Center report in 2010 revealed that while between 2000 and 2005 the annual inflows of undocumented immigrants from (and through) Mexico averaged 500,000, and from 2005 to 2007, 325,000 annually, that number fell to just 150,000 undocumented immigrants annually from March 2007 to March 2009.[109] On a smaller scale, a Homeland Security agent in El Paso confirmed that before the recession, "We had 75 to 80 [undocumented] crossers a night." By 2009, the situation had changed: "[W]e are lucky if we get 75 a week. Or a month. The biggest threat to the Border Patrol now is boredom."[110] Mexico's economy, intertwined with the United States', plunged too. The drop in number of crossings suggests that Mexican immigrants are not lured by any prospect of government benefits—otherwise there would be a mass exodus to the United States in the throes of the Mexican economic crisis, not for jobs, but to obtain benefits. The migration slowdown during the recession confirms also that the only effective border strategy is not walls or armed vigilantes, or employer sanctions and workplace raids, but economic strategies. Because the United States of course does not want to artificially induce an internal economic crisis to stave off migration, immigration reform will need to look south of the border at the equally compelling push factors of immigration—primarily the economies of Mexico and other feeder countries in Latin America. Mexican immigration into the United States traditionally has increased when the Mexican economy deteriorates or the country suffers upheaval, as during the Mexican Revolution.

In the regrettable spirit of the Mexican removals during the Great Depression and Operation Wetback during a 1950s recession, deportations have marked the current recession during the Obama administration. Far eclipsing the Bush administration in numbers of deportees, U.S. officials established a frenetic pace of raids and deportations. In 2009, the federal government deported 387,000 immigrants, most of them Mexican and almost every one of them Latino/a. That removal pace by 2010 was 60 percent higher than during the last year of the Bush administration.[111] At the same time that northbound border crossings by Mexican working-class undocumented immigrants have slowed, these deportations have ramped up.

Ironically, as the shrinking of U.S. employment opportunities curtails undocumented immigration of low-wage laborers, the ongoing drug war in Mexico propels legal immigrants at the opposite end of the income spectrum to leave for the United States, with deleterious consequences for Mexico. Wealthy Mexican families increasingly are coming to the United States, fleeing the drug violence that claims innocent bystanders and which targets the wealthy for extortionate kidnappings. These kidnappings help finance the illegal cartel operations or serve as a complementary side business of their well-armed and feared activities. Investor and inter-company transfer visas are available to wealthy immigrants who invest considerable funds in U.S. enterprises, offering a special entry line when other administrative routes are clogged. In one reported example, a Mexico City entrepreneur and kidnapping victim invested $200,000 in a San Antonio restaurant business, which enabled him to leave Mexico with his family.[112] Instead of investing their wealth to create jobs in Mexico, these immigrants fleeing Mexican violence wrought by U.S. drug demand are creating jobs in the United States. The Mexican border towns of Ciudad Juárez and Tijuana are particular victims of this emerging capital flight to the relative safety of the United States. U.S. cities such as El Paso, Houston, San Antonio, and San Diego are luring these wealthy expatriates in an exodus being likened to the Mexican and Cuban Revolutions. In moves reminiscent of the Prohibition era, when U.S. tavern owners simply relocated south of the border, many of these wealthy migrants are moving restaurants, nightclubs, and other businesses from Mexico to the United States, in part to service the other expatriates fleeing drug violence. Some of these business owners saw their customer base shrink in Mexico as patrons avoided restaurants and nightlife for fear of violence. Once in the United States, they are jumpstarting U.S. borderland economies and are part of the reason Texas has fared better than much of the United States during the current recession. In El Paso alone, immigrants from Juárez started more than 200 companies within a year.[113] These transplants leaving for the more expensive terrain of the United States may share sizeable financial resources with the U.S. residents retiring or purchasing second homes in Mexico, but otherwise their motivations differ considerably. While U.S. residents migrating to Mexico aim to take advantage of cheaper living or the allure of the Mexican beach, well-to-do Mexican families are seeking the security and safety of a home and business away from the front lines of the Mexican drug war. As with migrating Mexican laborers seeking to feed their families, these wealthy Mexican migrants have the welfare of their families foremost in mind in their border crossing. They belong in contention for the most virtuous of border crossers.

As the U.S. economy recovers, employers once again will call for additional low-wage immigrant workers from Mexico, as they have for decades. As before, the vast wage differential will continue to serve as a tremendous lure of Mexicans and other Latino/a immigrants on the lower end of the economic spectrum. At the same time that Mexicans can earn only $5 a day or less in their home country, they might earn between $7 and $10 an hour in the United States,[114] thereby justifying over time the cost of the expensive coyote-led journey to the United States. Chapter 11 addresses border and immigration reform in light of this economic reality by offering fresh ideas instead of the failed U.S. policies of border arming, granting of one-time amnesty, and raiding U.S. workplaces and homes in search of the undocumented.

PART V

A Framework for
Comprehensive Border Reform

Comprehensive border reform requires a framework that goes beyond the border-security-centric proposals of late that assume higher walls, more border officers, and advanced technology implemented through unilateral action by the United States will snuff undocumented immigration and drug trafficking. Rather, the framework below abandons the failed U.S. obsession with interdiction strategies and instead relies on legalization in areas where the underlying justifications for impeding border flows are misinformed by stereotypes and even, in the case of marijuana criminalization, racially rooted. Still, legalization as a strategy has its limits when applied to border crossings, as some potential crossings, such as those connected to the sexual trafficking of minors and the entry of fugitives fleeing authorities, are not amenable to a legalization protocol.[1] For these areas, U.S. policies must reach beyond the borderlands as well as embrace dialogue and accord with Mexico toward mutual solutions to regional threats. As detailed below, proposed border strategies should encompass an economic stimulus in all reaches of Mexico that is grounded in fairness as well as interest convergence. For the gravest threats to human rights posed by terrorists, sexual trafficking, and trafficking of methamphetamine, cross-border cooperative efforts of U.S.-Mexico law and intelligence authorities can operate more effectively once the nettlesome issues of immigration and marijuana trafficking are cleared. This would allow redirection of the considerable government resources dissipated on the current futile battles to keep marijuana and cheap labor from their U.S. users.

In some of these policy areas, Mexico is ahead of the curve, having recently taken the bold step of decriminalizing user quantities of drugs and having a record of advocating for the safe passage of its citizens who venture across the border as undocumented immigrants.[2] In other areas, notably its lack of environmental enforcement, its strict anti-abortion stance, and its tacit encouragement of sex tourism through low ages of sexual consent and lack of enforcement, Mexico lags behind the United States in human rights standards.

While preserving the sovereignty of the two nations, the discussion below nonetheless contemplates the vision of a shared destiny between the United States and Mexico in which border crossings by migrant workers, rather than maintaining their current shroud of menace, are acknowledged and celebrated for their contribution to an economic and cultural partnership between nations that extends far beyond a line in the desert or a river bottom. Once the two countries reach a shared understanding of truly deleterious crossings, their eradication can be confronted and prioritized. Although the Mexican government currently views drug trafficking as a threat to Mexico, its decriminalization of drug use suggests to the United States that it is the trafficking itself rather than the use of drugs that causes the most societal harm, a position that Mexico's staggering murder toll certainly corroborates.

Lessons from 150 Years of Border Crossings

Comprehensive immigration reform proposals are too often dictated by biases and prerogatives of the moment that are blind to history. The history of border crossings, detailed above, supplies perspective on the shape of reform that reaches beyond just migration northward, and which situates those northbound migrants arriving to labor in the United States as deserving our appreciation rather than our resentment. Whether sourced in socioeconomic factors or in vices and addictions, border crossings in both directions must be considered first as a whole, as this chapter undertakes, before passing judgment on virtuous crossings that should be encouraged and those that should be deterred through mutual cooperation.

Over the last 150 years, the border has evolved in perception of the U.S. public to its present state, where undocumented immigration and drug trafficking dominate that construction. As illustrated above, border traffic moves in staggering numbers in both directions, with most crossings for lawful purposes such as legal immigration, NAFTA freight, and tourism. But, over time, the stereotypes of the drug-dealing Mexican and the lazy, criminally inclined Mexican immigrant have come to define the unilateral view in the United States of border crossings as northbound and nefarious. Throughout the last century, however, U.S. residents routinely crossed the border into Mexico for purposes that included engaging in some act otherwise illegal in the United States or taking advantage of the vast economic disparity between the two countries. Mexican residents tolerate annual invading hordes of drunken youth—Los Spring Breakers—and are known for their friendliness toward retirees and second-home owners that live in Americanized resort enclaves. U.S. companies are solicited by Mexican officials, and once in Mexico they exploit cheaper labor without the same rigorous enforcement of fair labor and environmental standards. U.S. gun dealers supply the weapons that arm the murderous Mexican drug cartels. Yet the U.S. media and public tend to focus only on northbound crossings of the stereotypical Mexican menace. To the extent southbound crossings are relevant in policy debates, they are connected to these deleterious stereotypes and centered on Mexicans or their blood money headed south—either as fugitive bandidos running for the border for sanctuary after committing some heinous crime in the United States, or in the form of remittances seen by some as earned in labor appropriated from U.S. citizens and destined for ill-deserving family members in Mexico.

Every time Congress debates immigration reform, or states consider localized immigration regulation, the debate turns ugly and border crossings transform into the image of a sombrero-wearing Mexican immigrant crafty enough to traffic illicit drugs but otherwise a lazy charge on the public benefits system. The more industrious Mexican immigrant laborers are seen as stealing U.S. jobs and plotting la Reconquista to return the southwestern U.S. language, culture, and terrain to Mexican hands. These images are familiar to anyone with a television, radio, Internet access, or a newspaper. The purveyors of these images wildly essentialize the Mexican immigrant experience and with seeming impunity hurl hateful, hurtful accusations into the core of mainstream media. Latino/a organizations and organizers are targets of the barrage of these sometimes menacing messages. For example, in early 2002, dozens of Latino/a lawyers across the United States, along with community groups and activists, received a hate letter laced with a white powdery substance mimicking anthrax, with the following description of the threat posed by border-crossing Mexicans and Latino/a immigrants from other countries:

> [S]ince you grease balls still can't run your own countries effectively, like rats escaping a sinking ship, we get more and more of your wet back asses to care for. If that isn't bad enough, your whore-women can't keep from getting knocked up and producing more mongrel-spics that the rest of us have to provide welfare for.
>
> I never had anything given to me for nothing, and I am college educated and own my own house that is big enough to hold an entire barrio of you useless drug pushers.[1]

Conveying the entrenched images of lazy but fertile Latinos/as, dirty Mexicans ("rats" and "grease balls"), undocumented immigrants, and Latino/a drug dealers in the same communiqué, each letter depicted the subhuman image of Mexican immigrants in the U.S. imagination. Against this backdrop of incessant negative images, meaningful reform is challenging. Worse, anti-Mexican forces have succeeded in tapping every prevailing frightening image to construct Mexicans and other border-crossing Latinos/as as a threat to the United States. In the wake of the September 11 attacks, for example, Mexican immigrants were portrayed either as terrorists or as potentially aligned with terrorist forces. Given the longstanding social construction of Mexicans and other Latinos/as as violent, foreign, criminal-minded, and disloyal to the United States, numerous grounds exist to construct Latino/a immigrants as a direct terrorist threat.

Even if not viewed directly as terrorists, Latino/a immigrants stand accused of readiness to aid terrorists in anti-American plots. For example, the head of a Utah anti-undocumented immigrant group applauded a pre–2002 Winter Olympics sweep of undocumented airport workers in Salt Lake City, suggesting they were poised to aid terrorists, then run for the Mexican border with their payoff:

> [T]his may be stereotyping, but, if you go to an illegal Mexican working at the airport, and he has access to airplanes, or he's manning a baggage check or whatever, and an Arab terrorist walks up to him and says, "I'll give you $10,000 if you plant a 9-millimeter on the airplane for me," well, here's an individual who's never stood up, held his hand over his heart and said, "I pledge allegiance to the flag and to the country for which it stands." You think that Mexican is going to head south with the 10 grand? You betcha.[2]

Yet another avenue exists for constructing the Latino/a border crosser as aligned with terrorists—the conflation of drug dealers with terrorists. The U.S. government has already laid this foundation. In 1986, President Reagan issued a security directive that classified drugs as a national security threat. Following the September 11 attacks, the U.S. Office of National Drug Control Policy emphasized the connection between illicit drugs and international terrorism,[3] and in 2010 a Manhattan U.S. attorney created a Terrorism and International Narcotics unit to address extremist groups turning to the drug trade to finance their operations.[4]

The most recent negative construction relied on the flu pandemic to attack Mexican immigration. When swine flu alarmed U.S. residents in 2009, anti-immigrant pundits wasted no time in blaming Mexican immigrants for carrying the swine flu across the border. After decades of xenophobes accusing Mexican immigrants of bringing disease to the United States, the swine flu presented an opportune target. The inflammatory commentator Michael Savage put it bluntly: "Make no mistake about it: Illegal aliens are the carriers of the new strain of human-swine avian flu from Mexico." Savage even found a way to blend terrorism, swine flu, and Mexican immigrants into an irresistibly menacing threat: "[C]ould this be a terrorist attack through Mexico? Could our dear friends in the radical Islamic countries have concocted this virus and planted it in Mexico knowing that . . . [Homeland Security] would do nothing to stop the flow of human traffic from Mexico?"[5] Ironically, some more prescient observers pointed to a U.S.-owned mega hog farm in Mexico as ground zero for the emergence of the 2009 swine flu pandemic. The irony is that the agri-giant allegedly left the United States post-NAFTA for Mexico to escape strict U.S. regulation of treating and disposing of its hog waste, prompting this witty article (t-shirt) caption, "Smithfield Foods Fled US Environmental Laws to Open a Gigantic Pig Farm in Mexico, and All We Got Was this Lousy Swine Flu."[6]

The portrayal of Mexican border crossers as a security threat and as potential terrorist operatives has led to abysmal border policy—the militarization of the border and the imperatives for border walls and technology that have marked the last twenty years of U.S.-Mexico border relations. Most important, the conflation of all border crossings, most of them legitimate, into the image of the terrorist/criminal/drug-dealer/Mexican undocumented immigrant has reinforced and entrenched the supply-side policies of confronting and suppressing border traffic. Supply-side enforcement favors patrolling the border zone for drug smugglers and undocumented immigrants while prioritizing internal U.S. raids on undocumented workers and drug dealers over sanctioning exploitative employers and Anglo drug users. As detailed extensively in the discussions of drug trafficking and immigration in chapters 8 and 9, these interdiction strategies historically have failed to staunch border traffic of drugs and undocumented laborers and stand virtually no chance of success because the desperation of the undocumented, and the vast financial resources of the drug traffickers, will find any crack in the armor.

Although certain border issues such as immigration and drug trafficking require strategies unique to the separate challenges they pose, overall the United States and Mexico lack any comprehensive, cooperative border strategy despite the interconnectedness of many crossings. Formulating a comprehensive border policy first requires the United States to acknowledge its significant role in creating the problems many U.S. policymakers decry. Recognizing mutual fault is also critical to the following reform agenda that articulates the need for meaningful bilateral decision making on issues of border concern. The United States has too often regarded Mexico as the laggard on border policy and responded by attempting to enforce its will on Mexico. This unilateral approach to policymaking is consistent with the widespread belief that Mexicans are somehow to blame for all negative consequences whatsoever associated with their entry to the United States, however active or complicit a role U.S. actors play. Rather than fault the U.S. drug addict, we blame the drug dealer. Rather than place blame on U.S. employers exploiting cheap labor, we vilify the Mexican immigrant laborer. Instead of acknowledging the "ugly American" john who frequents prostitutes south of the border, we regard the prostitute as the whorish Latina whose insatiable appetite for sex, particularly with Anglos, renders her deserving of mistreatment. And so on.

Media invite this supply-side allocation of blame. U.S. media, for example, focus obsessively on the drug dealer of color, reserving any sympathetic treatment for users. Casual imbibers usually are depicted as fun-loving, ordinary folk; addicts are portrayed as tragic victims; dealers are vile at their core. Most vivid was the film *Traffic*'s (2000) dichotomy of the black dealer and the Anglo upper-class suburban user. In a pivotal scene, a naked addicted white girl lay barely conscious under her dealer, a black man, who interrupted his sexual pleasure to inject her foot with heroin. His role was brief and menacing, in contrast to the suburban addict whose likeable character, the young daughter of the film's star, Michael Douglas, and her descent into the cauldron of drug abuse, were fully charted. As I questioned elsewhere, this imagery "had the effect of vilifying dealers, by portraying them as savaging White girls, and of garnering sympathy for the tragic illness of addiction that would cause a White girl to sell her body to a Black man for poison." [7] These media images reinforce our supply-centric enforcement focus on drug trafficking and undocumented labor, which falls disproportionately on poor persons of color. This enforcement emphasis is a throwback to the impact of Prohibition-era temperance laws disproportionately used against poor southern and eastern European immigrants, who were racialized at the time, as well as against African Americans. [8]

Should it wish to do so, it would be surprisingly easy for Mexico to construct an image of the United States, and of U.S. residents, in reverse-stereotypical terms in the same mold as many in the United States negatively view Mexican immigrants. The blueprint for that construction in fact has been detailed throughout this book. Mexicans might understandably view U.S. residents as committing crimes and then running south for the Mexican border to elude U.S. authorities, in the footsteps of such high-profile fugitives as Andrew Luster and Christian Longo. Los Spring Breakers might be seen as representative of U.S. youth—flashing loose morals, fighting in the streets, and drinking to excess. Mexicans have seen the hedonistic party side of U.S. residents for years, dating to Prohibition-era incursions, followed by U.S. servicemen and now U.S. youth crossing the border on weekends to go swimming in alcohol in Mexican border towns. U.S. residents might be constructed as sex fiends, crossing the border to sow their virgin oats with prostitutes and returning for sordid sex shows and encores with Mexican prostitutes and even entering Mexico for the despicable aim of sex with children, then running for the U.S. border. U.S. residents could be regarded as unwilling to assimilate. They vacation at Mexican resort hotels owned by U.S. hoteliers and purchase residences in Mexican resort enclaves built by U.S. developers, in both venues expecting service in English. I once witnessed two U.S. residents complaining that Mexican employees of a U.S.-owned time-share resort on a Mexican beach didn't sufficiently understand their slurred and boozy demands delivered in English. Rather than offering economic opportunity to Mexicans, U.S.-owned maquiladora factories might properly be seen as circumventing fair labor and environmental standards, while disdaining any commitment to local quality of life for their workers. Rejecting their construction by some U.S. observers as subhuman threats to U.S. values, these factory workers might recognize the subhumanity inherent in this corporate business model that views them as mere commodities rather than as workers with families and health needs and dreams of security the maquiladoras will never deliver. Looking at the U.S. lure of Mexican immigrants, Mexican residents might understandably regard U.S. residents as the lazy ones. What else, one could imagine, would explain that jobs of considerable drudgery in sweltering fields, or on hot construction roofs or in U.S. yards, or in filthy hotel rooms or disgusting slaughterhouses, go routinely unfilled by U.S. citizen labor, calling for immigrant workers to save the day? Even Mexican drug dealers might marvel at the voracious appetites of U.S. residents for marijuana, cocaine, heroin, methamphetamine, and other illicit drugs that feed billions annually into the Mexican drug cartels. Mexican President Felipe Calderón lamented appropriately in 2010 that: "It's as if our neighbor were the biggest drug addict in the world."[9]

Yet, the Mexican people don't hold these negative views. In general, they regard U.S. residents favorably and welcome them as tourists, retirees, or vacation-home owners with visas unlimited in number. In 2011, Calderón beckoned U.S. retirees and tourists, telling tourists they "shouldn't worry" about drug violence and assuring retirees that Mexico is "a great place to live and enjoy."[10] Mexico also continues to support U.S. corporate investment despite the dismal labor and environmental record of the maquiladoras. At the same time, although not always having viewed these emigrants favorably,[11] Mexicans now accept that laborers headed north to the United States are trying boldly to carve out a better economic future for their families. They are admired for their initiative rather than vilified.

This background should temper the outcry of U.S. residents over Mexican entries. The considerable majority of U.S. border crossings by Mexicans are by those entering as documented tourists or as documented workers, particularly as daily commuters working in the borderlands. For those arriving as undocumented workers, or as smugglers of drugs or other illicit cargo, the United States must acknowledge its substantial and definitive role in luring them through its addictions to drugs and cheap labor. Or by its flooding the Mexican markets with cheap corn under NAFTA, decimating the agricultural industry and launching many Mexican farm laborers north to the maquiladoras and then across the border while prompting other farmers who stay behind to turn to illicit crops. We must also acknowledge the hypocrisy of our prevailing attitudes against Mexican immigration. At the same time that U.S. residents flock unfettered to Mexico for retirement and second homes, in the interest of living more cheaply south of the border, and as U.S. corporations cross the border to exploit undervalued Mexican labor, we limit entry to Mexican laborers headed north aiming to improve their economic prospects and the health and welfare of their families.

Taking the last 150 years of border crossings as a group, some motivations are manifestly despicable, such as child sex tourists headed south, or the trafficking of children and even adults north for sexual slavery in the United States. Other entries are cowardly, particularly the entry into Mexico of fugitives from justice (even if they might now avoid capital punishment, most fugitives are unaware of the protections under the extradition treaty). In the category of meritorious or at least benign crossings are tourists who aid the economy and strengthen cross-border relationships between the two countries. Crossings for profit are sometimes meritorious, unless the profit is illicit in the form of the drug trade or weapons trafficking that supports the drug trade. U.S. retirees and second-home owners aim to maximize wealth, or live better on the wealth they already have. U.S. companies head south of the border to fulfill what I mentioned previously as their raison d'être—to earn the most possible wealth for their shareholders, although some exploit cross-border differences in labor and environmental laws and their enforcement. Viewed against all these crossings, a strong case can be made for Mexican immigrants, both documented and undocumented, as possessing the most justifiable and honorable motivation of all border crossers north or south. The sacred American dream is to build a financial haven for one's family through hard work. Immigrants from Mexico, as well as those from other Latin American countries entering through Mexico, often have left needy families behind, dependent on the money the immigrant earns in the United States. Once across the border, these immigrants tackle labor in the most grueling and dangerous conditions. They deserve a crossing badge of honor for their belief in and labor toward that American dream. Rather, what they get is rhetoric typical of the Southern California radio host mentioned earlier who suggested that those motorists hitting undocumented immigrants crossing the borderlands freeway deserved the medal—a sombrero sticker for their bumper as good Americans. We vilify immigrants and classify them with the drug traffickers, desperados running for the border, and even terrorists. Instead, I urge we examine the motives of border crossing and better reward and separate the virtuous from the despicable.

Toward this end, I articulate a harm reduction agenda that reconfigures U.S. border policy on several fronts. Its first attribute is to sweep aside the current protocol in which undocumented immigration, drug trafficking, and the amorphous terrorist threat define our border agenda and push us toward militarizing the border, thus subjecting Mexican immigrants in pursuit of the American dream to treatment as dangerous criminals or even as terrorists. In its place is a proposal described in chapter 11 in which the U.S.-Mexico border is open to Mexican (and other Western Hemisphere) immigrants, yet protected from entry by those who intend to do grievous harm. Obviously, there is no place in any border admissions allowance for terrorists who enter with aims to kill U.S. residents. Fortunately, these crossings are exceedingly small in number. An immigration policy that allows entry to unlimited numbers of those seeking to enter the United States to work in alignment with prevailing labor demand would enable the U.S. government to better focus on the evil few who come to inflict harm.

Child sex traffickers, and equally those who frequent Mexico for sexual crimes with youth and then run for the sanctuary of the U.S. border, ought to be prioritized by U.S. authorities for prosecution, as should traffickers of adults for sex. By contrast to prostitution, sexual trafficking "is a form of slavery where individuals are forced into sexual service either knowingly or through trickery."[12] Should prostitution be coerced on either side of the border, it should be prohibited and prioritized for enforcement, as should coerced labor of any variety by migrants or other workers.[13] Similarly, fugitives crossing the border in either direction are a threat to both countries, as is the menace of child pornography produced in impoverished countries and crossing virtual borders into U.S. computers. And, as discussed in chapter 12 below, drug traffickers in methamphetamine carry poison that dissolves dignity and decency in the United States. The border policy discussed in chapter 11, while ostensibly open to Mexican laborers (and their families) seeking to improve their lives, as well as to those retirees from Mexico wishing to spend greater time with family already in the United States, should be resolutely closed to terrorists, fugitives, meth cartels, and sex traffickers and their customers.

In contrast, other border crossings, and lures of border crossings, generally should draw lesser enforcement emphasis, particularly on the supply side. A harm reduction agenda would focus on mitigating damage to individuals and communities, which is often aggravated by supply-side measures. For example, immigration restrictions have proven deadly to migrant border crossers entering the United States. But allowing unlimited immigration can harm vulnerable U.S. workers and the communities they reside in through a race to the bottom for wages and working conditions that a surplus of labor might create. Thus, the proposal in chapter 11 for relaxing border restrictions on immigration from Mexico and other Western Hemisphere countries must be accompanied by vigilance on the labor front for employers that take undue advantage of fluctuations in the labor market. The drug reform proposal articulated in chapter 12 couples decriminalization of certain drugs with increased regulatory emphasis on the demand side in the form of funding addiction treatment programs. For prostitution, harm reduction on the demand side would protect prostitutes from abusive customers and pimps, as well as protect all parties from the spread of disease.

Licensing plays an important regulatory role in reducing harm in many of the areas confronted in this book. For example, licensing the sale of some previously illicit drugs, particularly marijuana, can raise revenues as well as ensure the safety of the product to the extent possible. Licensing of prostitutes can encourage safer sexual behaviors through public health education and required medical exams, although the Mexican experience demonstrates that some prostitutes will operate outside the law to avoid the expense of licensing.

As discussed in more detail in chapter 14, border crossings motivated by differences in laws are often problematic for both countries. In light of the special history of the United States and Mexico, chapter 14 articulates a framework for confronting the differences between laws across borders and their effect on border crossings. Specifically, I address the extent to which laws prompting border crossings ought to be synchronized to dampen the motivation for law-shopping.

Bilateral cooperation is the touchstone of any comprehensive border policy. As mentioned, the United States and Mexico are more inclined to finger-point than to cooperate on the two defining issues of border crossing—immigration and drugs, The drug trade aptly illustrates this dynamic, as U.S. officials blame corruption and historically lax enforcement in Mexico for fueling the drug trade without fully acknowledging the feverish demand-side pull of drugs north. At the same time, as discussed in chapter 8, Mexican officials decry the lax U.S. enforcement of gun laws that allows weapons trafficking south, without accounting for the equally compelling demand for weaponry among the Mexican drug cartels. As part of sharing blame for harmful effects in both countries of certain border crossings, the United States and Mexico must better cooperate on the underlying issues of immigration and drug trafficking to confront the current climate in which immigrants perish in their desert crossings toward U.S. employers, and Mexican police, kidnapped migrants, and innocent bystanders in Mexico die in the pursuit of satisfying U.S. drug demand.

In these areas where bilateral cooperation is key, the United States and Mexico have tended to act unilaterally in the past to the detriment of building a cooperative alliance. Examples in drug policy include the Operation Intercept closure of the border by U.S. customs and military in 1969 and, on the other side of the border, Mexico's unilateral decision to decriminalize small possessory amounts of all drugs in 2009. In the immigration arena, the U.S. border-arming policy launched in the 1990s, the subsequent efforts at enhanced border security that led to the Secure Fence Act of 2006, and the cataclysmic workplace and community immigration raids of the Bush and Obama administrations are examples of the history of mostly unilateral policymaking by the United States on immigration. At the local level, Arizona's Senate Bill 1070 is the most prominent example of states acting unilaterally and even contrary to the U.S. government in designing their own restrictive immigration policy. In his first state of the union address in September 2007, Mexico's President Felipe Calderón scolded this longstanding U.S. approach: "We strongly protest the unilateral measures taken by the U.S. Congress and government that have only persecuted and exacerbated the mistreatment of Mexican undocumented workers."[14]

Most policy areas exhibiting the appearance of cross-border cooperation nonetheless beneath the surface are flawed or coerced by U.S. pressure. On the drug front, the pollyanna-ish- titled Operation Cooperation, an ultimately futile policy in the early 1970s described in chapter 8, was the result of U.S. pressure applied through the border closure strategy of Operation Intercept. Although the Bracero Program of the mid-twentieth century appeared to constitute a cooperative cross-border immigrant labor policy, the U.S. government consistently undercut its protections by such tactics as inviting entry of undocumented labor to sabotage efforts of Mexican negotiators to secure higher guaranteed wages for Mexican workers. Moreover, the massive deportation strategy of Operation Wetback undertaken during that labor program delivered the message to Mexico that its workers were only welcome when the United States beckoned. Similarly, the United States has routinely circumvented its criminal extradition treaty with Mexico by tactics including kidnapping suspects in Mexico and failing to inform suspects of their rights under the treaty when the death penalty looms. Although the maquiladora structure and the NAFTA accord were cross-border initiatives to boost mutual trade, they were flawed by their failure to fully consider monumental human migration and labor consequences within their scope. By ignoring the impacts on potential immigration in negotiating NAFTA, the United States and Mexico "missed a historic opportunity to squarely address labor migration."[15]

Both countries ought to acknowledge that the underlying motives for border crossings are increasingly interrelated and demand mutual attention to address those posing a threat to each country (primarily terrorism and sex trafficking) as well as crossings threatening the safety of crossers themselves (undocumented immigration) or borderlands residents (drug trafficking). Many of these areas would be best engaged by mutual accord, as NAFTA did with trade. Although the United States and Mexico were able to reach an accord for the free movement of goods, the United States continues to legislate unilaterally on human migration. As under NAFTA, the countries sending and receiving migrant labor—primarily Mexico and the United States but also those Latin American countries channeling immigrants through Mexico into the United States—ought to work toward a migration accord or treaty that specifies compromise policies with the safety and human rights of migrants and protection of labor rights among its foremost objectives. A 2006 resolution adopted by the Mexican government titled "Mexico and the Migration Phenomenon" recognized this need for cross-border cooperation by embracing "the principle of shared responsibility, which acknowledges that both countries must do their share in order to obtain the best results from the bilateral management of the migration phenomenon."[16]

Arguably the United States and Mexico are already treaty-bound to pursue mutually cooperative solutions to the so-called immigration crisis. For example, the Treaty of Guadalupe Hidalgo, as reaffirmed in the Gadsden

Purchase Treaty of 1853, contemplates that disagreements between the two countries with respect to "political or commercial relations" shall be resolved by "mutual representations and pacific negotiations."[17] Failing establishment of definitive cross-border migration policy by the mutual accord of a treaty agreement, the United States and Mexico might at least engage the ongoing issues of migration by means of a border commission. Congressman Luis Gutierrez (D-IL) introduced a comprehensive immigration reform bill in late 2009 that would create a United States-Mexico Border Enforcement Commission but, given the limitation of unilateral U.S. legislation, its membership would consist only of appointed officials from U.S. border states. To be effective, a border commission must include representatives from at least the United States and Mexico.

Cross-border cooperation is vital in areas of fugitive crossings, terrorism, and trafficking, the latter encompassing sexual trafficking of both children and adults, the involuntary trafficking of human labor, and varieties of the drug trade that survive the reform proposals laid out in chapter 12, particularly meth cartels. For these areas, technology networks and cross-border enforcement initiatives should share resources to address these damaging crossings. Today, the intergovernmental emphasis on border crossings is between the U.S. federal and state/local governments cooperating on detecting and deporting virtuous undocumented immigrant workers through 287(g) agreements and the Secure Communities program,[18] while the truly dangerous border crossers continue their profitable operations. The U.S. government and Mexico don't see eye-to-eye on the supposed threat of undocumented immigration, making cooperative efforts on migration unlikely. Spurred particularly by the policymaking debacle in Arizona surrounding its adoption of Senate Bill 1070, Mexico has defended its emigrants and exposed the chasm between the two countries in attitudes toward northbound immigration. Both countries can agree, however, on the threats posed by certain damaging crossings, and real progress is possible in those areas where both countries are genuinely aligned in interest.

Both countries must also recognize the connectedness of migrations north and south. Flows of goods and capital south to Mexico have disrupted and destabilized Mexican families. Heavily subsidized agricultural staples have decimated rural Mexican agricultural economies, with borderland factories reaping the benefits of the resulting desperation and displacement. Obviously, flows of capital and trade between the United States and Mexico are matters of mutual concern that demand bilateral engagement and cooperation toward solutions that recognize the humanity of the Mexican workforce.

Perhaps the most important avenue for mutual cooperation between the United States and Mexico would be to recognize the interconnectedness of the two economies and to work toward stimulating the Mexican economy. Boosting Mexico's economy holds promise for decreasing Mexican immigration as well as undermining the lures of joining the Mexican drug cartels fed largely by economic despair in Mexico. As one commentator characterized the economic underpinnings of the Mexican drug trade:

> [M]uch of the drug trade along the border cannot be attributed to the morality or immorality of the border, or the good or ill intentions of those who participate in the production and trafficking of illicit drugs, but to the sheer economic incentives that the business itself offers and the structural forces influencing border asymmetries such as differences in income levels, unemployment, and the low-skill levels of many Mexican workers.[19]

Despite my argument of the bona fides of the vast majority of undocumented immigrants entering the United States, there are still reasons to reduce their number. Foremost among them is that many immigrants leave their homes and families behind for extended periods in search of economic survival. Economic strategies to enable these immigrants to prosper in Mexico (or their country of origin), should they choose, would be meritorious. As then-Mexican President Vicente Fox asked:

> How can we narrow the gap on income on both sides of the border? How can we in the long run equal the levels of development between our countries so that we can become real friends, real partners and real neighbors? How can we build up the opportunities in Mexico so that our kids 12-, 14-year-olds, don't have to leave home, don't have to move to the United States looking for opportunities?[20]

One worthwhile strategy would stimulate the Mexican economy to create jobs in Mexico, an imperative that extends to other Latin American countries. From 1970 to 2000, the number of Latin American residents living in poverty almost doubled from 120 million to more than 220 million.[21] Earlier missed opportunities sealed the economic fate of the region. In the 15 years after World War II, the United States provided Europe with $30 billion in aid but gave only $2.5 billion to the Americas.[22] We intervened previously with billions more spent outside the Americas in fighting World War II, but fail to regard the threat of the Mexican drug war to the Mexican people in similar terms that require deployment of financial resources in aid of protecting humanity from devastation. Helping ensure job and wage growth in Mexico will contribute toward easing the two border flows that define Mexicans in such negative terms in the United States—undocumented immigration and the drug trade.[23] Among other things, ensuring economic growth in rural regions will be critical to replacing the income farmers earn from illicit crops. Economic growth in Mexico may even treat the roots of that country's susceptibility to child sex tourism and to sex trafficking, as well as to child pornographers who rely on financial despair to locate abandoned children or parents willing to offer up their children.

Arguments for U.S. economic assistance to Mexico are grounded in fairness as well as interest convergence. Mexican bracero laborers played a significant role in developing the U.S. economy during boom years in the twentieth century, while preserving our agricultural industry during wartime. Mexican labor on farms and in factories, much of it undocumented, contributed to economic growth of the United States after that guest labor program ended. In contrast, NAFTA benefited some U.S. farmers but devastated the livelihoods of many smaller Mexican farmers when subsidized U.S. corn flooded the market of Mexico's staple commodity. As immigration scholar Bill Ong Hing explains:

> Mexico has lost far more jobs than it has gained under NAFTA. Incredibly, because of the lifting of tariffs under NAFTA and continued U.S. farm subsidies, for example, Mexico is now importing most of its corn from the United States. Mexican corn farmers have gone out of business, undercut by U.S. prices. So farm workers who once harvested corn in Mexico lost their jobs, and where did they look for work? Across the border.[24]

Overall, jobs in the Mexican agricultural industry shrank from 8.1 million before NAFTA to only six million in 2006.[25] Hing argues that just as the wealthy European Union countries supplied subsidies for and investments in economically weaker countries entering the Union, such as Portugal, Spain, Poland, and Greece, the United States (and Canada) should boost the Mexican economy to ease pressures of mass migration. He urges investment in critical sectors such as Mexico's inadequate road system, its underachieving educational system, and its reeling subsistence farms.[26] As Hing concludes, "There is a good argument that the United States has a historical debt to pay for what it has done to the agricultural sector in Mexico."[27] Of course, the current political climate for supplying Mexico with aid, particularly in its educational sector, is likely quite hostile given outcry over educating Mexican immigrant students in U.S. schools, requiring resort to more self-interested arguments.

Lately, the escalating drug war supplies another argument for economic aid that straddles fairness and interest convergence. The threat of violence is cutting off investment capital flowing into Mexico, staunching tourism, and even sending those Mexican families with financial means fleeing across the border for their safety. At the bottom of the drug war is the insatiable U.S. appetite for drugs that cares little about how many innocent people are dying in pursuit of the drug trade, or its financial costs to Mexico. Yet the voluntary role of the Mexican drug cartels in the violence dampens this fairness argument, requiring resort to the convergences presented by the drug war and immigration.

On the interest convergence side, economic despair in Mexico drives immigration and drug trafficking north. Growing the Mexican economy through means of economic stimuli, such as micro-loans for start-up businesses,[28] that create jobs in rural and urban terrain would reduce the pressures for these border crossings. Grounds for interest convergence on immigration range from the laudable views of those concerned with the strain on Mexican families of expensive and treacherous passages north that separate families into two countries, to the unjustifiable but nonetheless active sentiments among many that Mexican immigration is somehow undermining the cultural legacy of the United States. Justifications for an economic stimulus extend to other Latin American countries, particularly those Central American countries whose economies and infrastructures were scarred in unrest manipulated by the U.S. government and its interventionist policies, particularly during the Reagan years, prompting residents to flee for opportunities in the United States through the Mexican human smuggling networks.

Admittedly, providing economic stimulus to Mexico is a supply-side measure. Nevertheless, there are important distinctions from the current and historical U.S. supply side, interdiction-based strategies for curbing drug smuggling and immigration. For example, interdiction tends to be border-centric, as when the U.S. drug czar (played by Michael Douglas) in *Traffic* (2000) headed to what he called the "front lines" of the drug war—the Mexican border. Economic aid to Mexico would move emphasis away from the "front lines" of the borderlands and concentrate on developing opportunity deep within Mexico. Unlike U.S. interdiction strategies, which have tended to be unilateral and have included the condescending process of certifying Mexico as adequately waging the drug war, infiltrating its drug cartels, and even kidnapping drug suspects in Mexico, economic aid better preserves Mexico's sovereignty. Although some might argue that economic intervention undercuts Mexican sovereignty, that consequence would depend on the nature of any strings attached to the stimulus. Today, remittances from Mexican immigrants working in the United States, and monies laundered into Mexico from U.S. drug dealing, constitute at least a de facto form of economic stimulus to Mexico that, given the transaction costs and risks of interruption, surely provides lesser economic security to the country than the prospect of long-term economic growth through U.S. aid. Further, interdiction regards Mexicans as criminals, while economic aid connotes the more favorable message that Mexico and Mexicans are worthy of foreign investment that will return dividends in economic partnership among the Americas.

Engrained corruption in the Mexican political system[29] poses a challenge to these economic-based strategies. Simply delivering an economic stimulus in bulk to the Mexican government would likely prompt the same outcome as the Wall Street stimulus in which the U.S. recipients feathered their own nests with huge bonuses and little trickled down to laborers. Should the United States find the political will to deliver meaningful economic aid to Mexico, that aid must be supplied through grants to trusted international foundations that can ensure accountability for stimulating local jobs and economies within Mexico.

Finding that political will to engage Mexico as an economic partner no doubt is challenging. Many U.S. residents refuse to acknowledge the debt we owe to Mexican labor both within the United States and in the borderlands maquiladoras. They may be willing to fund military intervention and law and order strategies against the Mexican drug cartels, while unwilling to support aid to develop alternate economies to the drug trade. Yet boosting our interconnected economies is the only realistic path to long-term stability in the Americas.

Discussed next in chapter 11, the justification for a return to the good neighbor immigration policy that prevailed until the 1960s, with no fixed limits on Western Hemisphere immigration to the United States, is grounded in our legacy of reliance on Mexican labor. More than any country, Mexico's history is interwoven with the United States', and its people have shaped the current economic, cultural, and social state of the union. It may seem contradictory to reopen the border to Mexican immigration at the same time we supply economic aid to develop jobs within Mexico, but the two strategies are coherently linked. Today, economic desperation drives Mexican residents north to the border, where our emphasis on controlling immigration makes their crossing perilous. Removing immigration limits for Mexican laborers, while helping ensure their safety in crossing the border, would not address the painful conditions that lead Mexicans to leave their homeland in economic desperation. At the same time, supplying an economic stimulus within Mexico while continuing to armor the border would stymie reunification of Mexican families with the millions of existing undocumented (and other) Mexican workers who may wish to remain living in the United States. The cohesion, then, of working toward an economically viable Mexico and a compassionate immigration policy that recognizes the contributions of Mexican immigrants is that these dual approaches allow meritorious laborers and their families the freedom to choose where to pursue their livelihoods and futures.

Good Neighbor Immigration Policy

U.S.-Mexico border history suggests that laborers will follow economic opportunity across borders if necessary, and that no barriers or other enforcement strategies will impede migrant flows driven by such economic necessity. In the compelling words of a Tucson artist: "How far would you walk to feed your children?"[1] As NAFTA did for goods, the best approach for immigration reform would place migrants at least on equal footing with trade and allow their free passage across borders toward sources of labor demand. Below is one possible framework for a labor model of immigration that relies on freedom of markets as well as on regulatory safeguards to create a system in which Mexican laborers need not die in the desert to reach their American dream.

For most of the twentieth century, a labor model, albeit one-sided, dictated our immigration policy toward Mexico. As described in chapter 9, the U.S. economy regulated entry of Mexican immigrant labor as needed in the fields, railroads, and beyond. Whether coming as immigrants desiring citizenship, as temporary bracero laborers, or as undocumented workers in times when border officials would look the other way, Mexican immigrants entered in sufficient numbers to supply U.S. labor need. The 1965 Immigration and Nationality Act upset this call and response by imposing the first numerical limits on Western Hemisphere immigration. Meaningful immigration reform must include a return to the pre-1965 good neighbor exemption from immigration limits accorded to Western Hemisphere countries.[2] So treated, Mexican laborers would be free to come to the United States to work and to bring their families as they desired.

This immigration proposal differs from those of open border advocates who suggest a labor market-driven immigration system open to entrants from all countries. Yet it is broader than a NAFTA North American-centric immigration policy allowing free passage among Canada, the United States, and Mexico.[3] Although the case can be made for Mexican exceptionalism in our immigration laws, especially in contrast to the prevailing anti-Mexican sentiment singling out Mexican immigrants for enforcement and vilification, there are good reasons to restore a hemispheric allowance. U.S. military intervention and meddling in Central America, prompting unrest and migration, as well as the imbalance of U.S. global aid disbursed primarily outside the Americas,[4] suggest an immigration framework of regionalism more akin to the European Union model. Under the model of European Union citizenship, citizens of member states enjoy freedom of movement similar to U.S. residents moving within the United States. They may freely relocate for work opportunities, bringing their dependents. Those without jobs, such as retirees, may stay beyond three months if they have sufficient resources for themselves and their families to avoid becoming a burden on the host country's social assistance program.[5] Perhaps because of this labor emphasis, fears of mass migration from poor to rich countries in the European Union proved unfounded.[6] Applying this framework of labor mobility to the United States might ease concern of an influx seeking social assistance, a concern already debunked above in the historical record of immigration patterns from Mexico.

In addition to establishing a migratory and labor partnership among the Americas, the United States must break from the one-sidedness of its twentieth-century immigration model that welcomed Mexican immigrants in times of labor shortages, yet ushered them out of the United States when downturn hit. Given our cyclical economic history of boom and bust, Mexican immigrants deserve better than to be treated as a commodity that is thrown out when it has served its initial usefulness. The U.S. labor markets must accept that the quid pro quo for a ready supply of Mexican immigrant labor in the good times is to offer Mexican laborers their rightful place to receive the safety net of government assistance during downturns. For this reason, temporary "guest" labor programs with their history of exploitation and exile of workers are no part of meaningful and compassionate immigration reform. Rather, labor markets must be allowed to beckon the workers they need on terms those workers are willing to accept, but at the same time those laborers must receive the protection of opportunities to obtain permanent residency and citizenship if they choose and to receive government benefits during downturns.[7] Employers must be accountable for these costs by paying more of their share of the expense to government and communities of sustaining immigrants in times of economic distress. U.S. employers today pay paltry wages to most Mexican immigrants and expect local government and community groups to provide any necessary services during downturns. The worst of these employers will resort to contacting deportation authorities in times of economic distress or of union organizing of their undocumented workforce. We must also ensure against the manipulation of noncitizen laborers to the detriment of other workers. Employers should contribute through a tax for each noncitizen laborer used, with the money helping to fund the necessary government safety net. Under this approach, in theory it would be cheaper for employers to find U.S. citizen workers, and employers presumably would seek to employ them first. Therefore, those noncitizen workers employed would likely not be taking U.S. citizen jobs.[8]

Realistically, the prospects are scant for a federal immigration policy that protects U.S. workers and Mexican immigrant laborers. U.S. employers over time have become accustomed to manipulating labor flows as they do goods—simply moving jobs to the cheapest global labor markets. In the current globalized production economy, there is little likelihood for private initiative to protect labor during economic downturns. Nor is there opportunity for significant government initiative to sustain laborers through realistic minimum wages, adequate health care and benefits, and other protections given the ready mobility of jobs and capital overseas as companies race to the global bottom, away from jurisdictions with the vision and courage to implement labor protections.

Despite research findings that legalizing the undocumented workforce and allowing future immigration in line with U.S. labor needs would help grow the U.S. economy,[9] immigration reform has been stymied through boom and bust in the twenty-first century U.S. economy. In the current climate of scapegoating Mexican immigrants, comprehensive immigration reform likely will continue to look narrowly within the U.S. borders to tighten border security while at best authorizing a legalizing of status and perhaps a route to citizenship for longstanding undocumented immigrant workers in the United States. The immigration bill introduced in late 2009 by Congressman Gutierrez, for example, followed the recent progressive approaches by coupling enhanced border security against future entries with the possibility of legalization of status for the present undocumented (known as "earned legalization") who have contributed within the United States by way of their employment, education, military service, or community volunteerism. Notwithstanding any enhanced border security that these proposals may supply by means of compromise to restrictionists, once the U.S. economy recovers and undocumented immigration jumps in future years, pressure will mount again for another amnesty, while immigrants suffer awaiting that reform as they are today. Eventually, however, U.S. residents might realize the futility of border impediments and consider other options to regulate immigration.

As argued in chapter 10, more than any border wall or workplace raid, stimulating economic development in Mexico will best stabilize immigration flows. Instead of the current dynamic in which U.S. employers rely on the glut of Mexican immigrants to find the most desperate willing to work for the least wages and benefits, U.S. employers would be forced to lure immigrant workers with sufficient wages to support the immigrant's family in reasonable comfort. In contrast, today's Mexican immigrant laborers might sleep crowded into apartments or houses ten or more deep, if they are fortunate, or in shacks made from scraps, in cars, or even on the hard ground. Their wages are insufficient to support their basic needs and those of their families left behind, prompting local outcry that scapegoats immigrant workers for their overcrowded housing and other consequences of poverty rather than the real culprits paying cut-rate wages that ignore community values.

Sources of funding an economic stimulus for Mexico are obvious when comparing the costs of ongoing and proposed border security measures. For example, the border fence contemplated under the Secure Fence Act will cost at least $9 million a mile,[10] resulting in billions of dollars in construction costs, and once completed will require ongoing maintenance. Reflecting the mounting costs of border enforcement, in the summer of 2010 alone, Congress added $600 million in emergency funding for border security to the fiscal year's budget. Additional billions spent on internal immigration enforcement away from the border can be avoided by allowing labor markets to dictate immigration flows without artificial legal ceilings on immigration.[11]

The economic stimulus model nonetheless has some drawbacks. Foremost, enhanced wages in Mexico might prompt even more borderlands maquiladora companies to flee Mexico for cheaper international labor markets. There are some minor drawbacks too. Stimulating the Mexican economy by creating jobs and enhancing wages no doubt will increase costs for hundreds of thousands of U.S. transplants in Mexico who take advantage of cheap Mexican labor as retirees and second-home owners.

Realistically, immigration and labor reforms are works in progress that must be constantly revisited and reworked in light of a framework of overarching goals and principles. Today, border security imperatives, protection of U.S. industry, and even dubious concerns over cultural preservation shape our immigration policies. We should add a recognition of worker rights and the human rights of immigrants and push aside concerns of Anglo-cultural preservation as we embrace our neighboring countries in a new vision of enhancing life and work in the Americas that recognizes the virtue of Mexican immigrants. Mexican and other Latino/a immigrants point to the future with many of the traits U.S. residents hold dear—love of family, dedication to hard work, and loyalty to the United States that offers them economic opportunities. Stripped of hurtful derogatory stereotypes, this vision of the meritorious Latino/a immigrant laborer can help ensure we meet the best of our aspirations for a productive nation of immigrants.

Reefer Madness

> If there is a war on drugs, then many of our family members are
> the enemy. And I don't know how you wage war on your own
> family.
> —Michael Douglas as the U.S. drug czar in *Traffic* (2000)

The last 100 years of U.S.-Mexico border history reveal the futility of the war on drugs. The Prohibition-era experience of the 1920s demonstrated convincingly that legal restrictions fail to curb U.S. demand for an illicit product. Instead of quelling demand, Prohibition launched organized crime deep into the U.S. heartland and proved to be "the supreme error of our political history."[1] As with alcohol, the U.S. habit for mind-altering substances stretches across the socioeconomic spectrum and is relatively unswayed by legal restrictions. Replicating the experience of liquor trafficking during Prohibition, the drug smuggling networks through Mexico are undeterred by enforcement strategies, all of which failed to have any significant impact on the entry and reach of illicit drugs into the United States. For each shipment of drugs intercepted, a replacement load makes it through, just as for each undocumented immigrant laborer deported, another reaches the United States.

Prohibition, the current war on drugs, and the undocumented immigration crisis all confirm that supply-side enforcement is doomed to fail, particularly when a rich country and a relatively poor country share a physical border and the economics of supply are compelling. As discussed in chapter 8, no matter the consequences, a ready supply of replacement traffickers will continue to serve the U.S. drug habit as long as Mexico fails to offer sufficient upward economic mobility for its residents through legal means of employment. But even the approach of building Mexico's economy has its shortcomings as long as the U.S. habit for illegal drugs survives. Although strategies to boost economic opportunity in Mexico may eventually lessen the attractiveness of illicit enterprise, any such economic growth would nonetheless take considerable time to alter the decision making of generations of poor in Mexico, as some no doubt see illegal enterprise as the only chance for prosperity. Moreover, despite the so-called American dream in the United States that hard work will reap economic reward, the reality in one of the world's richest countries is that economic opportunity exists for some U.S. groups and less or not at all for others. Even significant economic advances in Mexico would leave some behind, and for them the luster of drug trafficking profits would still shine. Drug prices might also rise to meet countervailing pressures on supply, thus more lucratively rewarding participants and luring some operatives regardless of their ability to attain a modest living through legitimate means. Most important, without addressing the demand side of illicit drugs, trafficking networks would re-form and emerge through the residents of other less fortunate countries. As illustrated by the inroads of enforcement efforts to staunch the "French Connection" heroin network and the "Miami Vice" cocaine connection, drug trafficking adjusts to find alternative routes and alternate carriers willing to brave whatever new risks emerge.

Still, the challenges of shifting to a demand-side strategy are daunting. Among other things, the longstanding stereotypes of the criminal and treacherous Mexican prove irresistible to law and order politicians and voters in scapegoating the Mexican people for the drug trade and other U.S. ills. These negative views of Mexicans contributed in the first instance to the criminal classification of marijuana with heroin and cocaine, themselves tied to racist origins of regulation as detailed in chapter 8. Yet only through demand-side reform can we effectively dismantle trafficking networks. As with Prohibition, demand-side reform holds the best potential for ending trafficking and the violence that surrounds it. Arguing for decriminalization of personal-use quantities of drugs, legal scholar Paul Butler predicted: "Just as Al Capone and his ilk disappeared when Prohibition was repealed, so too will the violent warfare between the profiteers, once the high profits of an unregulated market leave the drug trade. Budweiser and Heineken battle with cute commercials during the Super Bowl, not drive-by shootings."[2] With drug cartels mooted, government could concentrate on terrorists, sex traffickers, and fugitives from justice—border crossers that can harm both countries.

Addressing illegal drugs from the demand side invites at least two regulatory approaches—more rigorous enforcement against users or decriminalization.[3] On the enforcement side, arrest numbers suggest an already draconian anti-use campaign. Today, more than 750,000 people are arrested annually in the United States for marijuana possession,[4] among them musician Willie Nelson in late 2010. Behind those numbers is the reality that enforcement against U.S. users is decidedly racially skewed. Despite studies confirming that young Anglos use marijuana at higher rates than blacks and Latinos/as, youths of color are disproportionately arrested for drug possession. In 2008, for example, although constituting only about half of its urban population, blacks and Latinos/as comprised 87 percent of the 40,000 arrests in New York City for marijuana possession.[5] As I argued elsewhere, racial profiling and concentrations of police resources in communities of color lead to more vehicle stops, confrontations, stop-and-frisk searches, searches incident to arrest, and consequently more drug violations.[6] The enhanced criminal status of crack cocaine over powder cocaine is just one of the manifestations of discriminatory enforcement policies that target dealers and users of color while mostly ignoring Anglo users.[7] Ramping up enforcement among Anglo users across the socioeconomic spectrum might deter use in the most lucrative markets for dealers. Rather than concentrating on interdiction of traffickers at and beyond the border, police might more aggressively seek out users in Anglo communities and settings, such as high school football games, concerts, and the like, by use of sobriety checkpoints, drug-sniffing dogs, and undercover operatives. Should we be concerned about the decline of civil liberties in such a campaign? Perhaps not when authorities in the liberty-free zone of the border permissibly search Mexican border crossers and their vehicles without any need for reasonable suspicion.[8] Police might focus on one of the bastions of drug dealing and illicit use—college campuses where the "dorm room dealers" and users tend to be Anglos who carry on their transactions with relative impunity while interdiction concentrates on Latino/a and black communities.[9] In addition to targeting different groups of users, police might employ the same twisted logic that Maricopa County Sheriff Joe Arpaio uses to charge undocumented immigrants with conspiring to smuggle themselves into Arizona. Why not charge drug users with conspiracy or complicity in the drug trafficking that delivers drugs to their hands, thereby elevating mere possessory misdemeanors to serious felonies with lengthy jail sentences?[10]

Obviously, such aggressive enforcement among users has considerable drawbacks. Prisons are overflowing primarily as a result of the war on drugs, and local government cannot afford additional officers and prison beds. Imagine how Anglo parents with substantial financial resources might clog the criminal justice system with lawyers waging full-scale defenses against possession charges, given the stigmatizing consequences of conviction and the potential for prison that would be needed to deter causal use. Most Anglo parents understand that Barack Obama, an admitted casual user of drugs in his youth, would never have overcome the stigma of conviction had he fallen into the enforcement net. No doubt, then, they would throw whatever resources they could into keeping their children's pathway to greatness clear. Enhanced enforcement, in sum, would be prohibitively expensive and invite further erosion of civil liberties.

As an alternative demand-side strategy, to many observers decriminalization would launch a jubilee among current occasional users and those inclined to try drugs, as well as grease the gateway skids to more dangerous drugs. But the experience of other countries is that decriminalization does not necessarily open these floodgates. Notably, a 2009 study of Portugal's decriminalization of drugs in 2001 found deaths from drug overdoses down, while drug use failed to increase.[11] As is the case with alcohol, government regulation and taxation of sales of currently illicit drugs would derail trafficking networks overnight. Although, as with alcohol, youths must be restricted from legal access, after legalization they would likely gain their illicit supply from less cutthroat connections than today, primarily by using false identification and purchasing from older friends who buy from regulated sellers. Mexican traffickers aren't hauling kegs across the border to supply high school parties in the United States, and neither would there be a lucrative international drug trafficking network to minors under a decriminalization system for adults.[12] Using a harm reduction approach, law enforcement could focus its enforcement on the harmful externalities of drug use as it does for drinking, primarily driving while intoxicated and domestic violence. Government officials could channel revenue from taxation toward addiction treatment programs that are far less expensive and dramatically more cost effective at reducing demand than interdiction efforts that cost the federal government alone $14.8 billion in 2009.[13] Given the estimate that taxing just marijuana on a level with alcohol and tobacco would produce about $10 billion in revenues annually, not counting savings of perhaps equal amounts currently spent on interdiction of marijuana, considerable revenues would be available for treatment.[14] As with alcohol and tobacco, private standards of conduct, primarily those established by employers, might set stricter norms for those within their purview, but otherwise marijuana (and perhaps other narcotic) possession and use would be legalized.

Reacting to the rampant drug violence gripping the country, Mexico decriminalized user quantities of drugs in 2009, eliminating jail for small amounts of marijuana (the equivalent of no more than four joints), cocaine (four lines), heroin (50 milligrams), methamphetamine (40 milligrams), and even LSD (0.015 milligrams).[15] Mexico's reform reflects a similar trend of decriminalization sweeping Latin American.[16] Some U.S. officials responded by expressing alarm that U.S. youth and adults might run for the border for their high; for example, an Arizona sheriff's official worried that Mexico's allowance lures not only juveniles but also adults to Mexico: "Anyone who wants to go across the border and experiment."[17] Intended to quell alarming drug violence, as well as to confront rising Mexican drug use, decriminalization on the Mexican side of the border will do little, if anything, to suppress cross-border drug trafficking and the violence it creates. The major population serviced by Mexican traffickers remains in the United States, and there is little chance that addicts or casual users in the United States will abandon their ready local sources and run for the border into Mexico en masse every time they want to partake in illegal substances. Therefore, the Mexican drug cartels will remain in business if the United States fails to take the drastic but logical action of decriminalization/legalization.

Unlike the Mexican reform decriminalizing possession of user amounts across the board, the United States should more selectively decriminalize narcotics. Colombia, for example, decriminalized marijuana and cocaine for personal use, but retained criminal penalties for other drugs.[18] Argentina's highest court struck down a law severely penalizing marijuana possession for personal use, effectively decriminalizing that drug.[19] In the United States, drugs should be classified on a spectrum of external societal harm, as well as damage caused to the user. Alcohol, too, should be placed on the spectrum, with drugs not materially more harmful than alcohol decriminalized and regulated on similar terms. Under any educated assessment of harm, marijuana should fall well below the harm index for alcohol, both externally and internally,[20] despite its longstanding categorization under federal law, along with LSD, as a Schedule I controlled substance punishable by up to one year in jail. On the internal side alone, while numerous youth and adults die annually of alcohol intoxication, there has never been a recorded overdose death in the history of marijuana smoking.[21] At the other end of the spectrum is methamphetamine, a horrible chemical poison that destroys health and family life. Still, a case can be made for legalizing meth, if only to better regulate and test the nasty chemical composition of the drug. Falling closer to alcohol are cocaine and heroin (and other opiates such as Oxy-Contin pills), each with addictive properties and potentially serious health effects (particularly in the case of heroin, where unregulated purity may be deadly),[22] although externalities are less apparent. Accusations of murderous rampages and seductions of white women by minority users of cocaine and opiates have since been exposed as the regrettable legacy of racial paranoia in the early twentieth century. Characterizing drugs on a spectrum of harm to public health, French scientists in 1998 reinforced these observations of harm by grouping alcohol, cocaine, and heroin in the most dangerous category, while placing marijuana into the least dangerous category.[23] A 2010 British study ranked alcohol the most harmful drug studied when accounting for harm both to the user and to others, with alcohol posing the most external harm and the drugs of heroin, crack cocaine, and methamphetamine causing the most harm to the user.[24]

A reasonable middle ground is to start by decriminalizing and taxing marijuana production, distribution, and possession, and to gauge the impact on the viability of the Mexican cartels as well as the impact on marijuana use and user health in the United States. According to some estimates, marijuana constitutes more than 60 percent of the profits earned by Mexican drug cartels, with only 28 percent derived from the cocaine trade.[25] If so, decriminalization of marijuana should have a cataclysmic effect on the Mexican drug trade. With the illicit marijuana trade scuttled, cooperative cross-border enforcement imperatives could more easily tackle remaining drugs such as heroin, whose base ingredient of opium can only be cultivated in specific regions of Mexico.[26] Moreover, enforcement might find a foothold once the profits of the drug cartels take a large enough blow to prevent traffickers from using their riches to finance local infrastructure, such as schools and hospitals, that help immunize the cartels from snitching. Until the Mexican cartels are disbanded, the entire U.S. demand for marijuana could be supplied through U.S. cultivation, either home-grown by users or purchased through regulated U.S. suppliers, allowing later expansion to legal Mexican markets and brands that might emerge akin to the popularity of Mexican beers such as Corona. As with immigration policy, U.S. drug law should be considered a fluid work in progress that undergoes constant scrutiny to mitigate external harm while taking advantage of the best science and addiction treatment and abuse prevention techniques that come along to ease demand, using the example of tobacco. A public health focus means that government can concentrate on funding studies and technology to curb addiction rather than striving to entrap smugglers, dealers, and users.

As to whether decriminalization stands a realistic chance of approval from lawmakers, hopeful as well as discouraging signs abound. In 2009, a California poll in the throes of that state's fiscal crisis found that a majority (56 percent) of voters favored legalizing and taxing marijuana.[27] Although an initiative to legalize and tax marijuana failed among California voters in 2010, the cause attracted considerable national attention and donations. A Gallup poll in October 2010 found that 46 percent of U.S. residents support marijuana legalization, the highest poll number ever and ironically the same percentage of approval that the California initiative garnered the next month.[28] Marijuana use has decisively entered the mainstream of pop culture with its comedic use in television shows such as the Showtime series *Weeds* and countless films such as *Pineapple Express* (2008), *Harold & Kumar Go to White Castle* (2004), and *Something About Mary* (1998). At least the last three U.S. presidents have smoked (although one may not have inhaled) marijuana. A 2009 study found that use of most illicit drugs by U.S. teens declined over the past decade, notably of methamphetamine, cocaine, and hallucinogens. In contrast, marijuana use rose slightly in the last couple of years, perhaps reflective of the study finding that fewer teens considered occasional marijuana smoking to be harmful.[29]

Still, the prospects are slight for federal domestic and international (the United States is party to a host of drug treaty obligations) reform to fully legalize even the single drug of marijuana. Preoccupied with fighting terrorism and growing the economy, congressional leaders likely will defer any talk of drug reform despite the potential to appropriate some drug profits for the treasury.

The ice is thawing some in progressive states such as California, where then-Governor Arnold Schwarzenegger, while still opposing legalization of marijuana, admitted in 2009 that it was time for a debate on drug legalization, adding, "I think that we ought to study very carefully what other countries are doing that have legalized marijuana and other drugs, what effect it had on those countries, and are they happy with that decision."[30] Taking a step in this direction, Schwarzenegger signed state legislation in 2010 reducing possession of small amounts of marijuana to an infraction equivalent to a traffic ticket. But few federal and state leaders are willing to risk their political capital on meaningful drug reform through legalization, despite the likelihood that many of them used drugs themselves. Most remember how Dr. Joyce Elders, briefly the U.S. Surgeon General under President Clinton, was literally run out of Washington, DC for her stance on controversial issues, including suggesting we explore whether legalization of drugs might reduce crime. As long as enforcement campaigns target interdiction of Mexican drug cartels and black and Latino/a users, none of whom holds much political clout, U.S. politicians will be slow to move. Deborah Small, executive director of Break the Chains, a drug reform organization working within communities of color, suggests change will take a U.S. society that cares about the futures of black and Latino/a youth instead of criminalizing them.[31] Given prevailing negative stereotypes of these groups, either a sea change in attitude must occur or some significant interest convergence must emerge. Possible catalysts include desperation for sources of government revenue or fear of the spread of Mexican drug cartel violence into the United States. Thus far, cartel violence has plagued only Mexico, while across the border in cities such as El Paso the streets are relatively quiet. Should drug violence on par with bloodshed in Mexico reach U.S. streets, particularly those beyond neighborhoods of color, it is likely that U.S. reaction will center more on enforcing the border than in curbing illicit demand. Generating interest convergence toward legalization, then, may prove daunting.

Across the border, Mexico has demonstrated its own willingness to boldly legislate in the face of wrenching drug warfare by decriminalizing user amounts of drugs. Additionally, Mexico must reverse its militarization of the drug war that has pushed cartels into murderous rage. That federal intervention has not markedly impeded the journey of illicit drugs into the United States, while spawning violence that irreparably harms Mexico. Even a return to the days of Mexican government corruption that for decades tolerated the drug trade (for a healthy cut, of course) as long as the traffickers acted more like businessmen than thugs is a better choice for Mexico than the continued chaos and bloodshed.[32] The tension here is that the United States orchestrates much of the Mexican drug enforcement policy through cajoling, money, and other means as it has done throughout the last century, and a rejection of the interdiction campaign by Mexico might inflame relations between the countries.[33]

A better outcome that preserves mutuality of cross-border policymaking would be shrinking the illicit trafficking networks through reduced demand. As the world's most voracious drug consumer, the United States can abruptly staunch demand for illicit drugs through selective legalization as outlined above. But the United States should not legislate in a vacuum. As with immigration, both countries must realize their connectedness and work toward a mutual drug policy that reflects the historical realities and honors foremost the safety of communities on both sides of the border. Because the drug trade resonates throughout other countries in Latin America, particularly Colombia, Peru, and Bolivia, an inter-American dialogue on the drug trafficking crisis must occur to formulate and implement policy alternatives to prohibition.[34] Moreover, because of the possibility that Mexico (or Latin

American) trafficking routes will continue or begin to supply drug demands in other countries such as Canada, a hemispheric and even global dialogue must engage the international trend toward selective legalization.

Failing legalization imperatives, we must rely on moral abstinence as a strategy to curb our role in the Mexican drug wars. Given the directness of the connection between U.S. demand and the deaths of innocent Mexican officials and bystanders in the drug war, users of illicit drugs in the United States must accept a personal responsibility to refrain from fostering that violence. Of course, there are daunting challenges here, too. Drug supply chains are not always readily identifiable by users, and U.S. residents seem to care little anyway about the fate of Mexicans dying at the hands of drug cartels. This is particularly true for those addicted to illicit drugs, whose moral compass might be impaired. For example, no U.S. cocaine user seemed to care about the devastating violence in Colombia's civil war between the cartel-financed rebel group Revolutionary Armed Forces of Colombia (in Spanish, FARC) and right-wing paramilitaries. Even U.S. government efforts after the September 11 attacks to connect the international drug trade to terrorist organizations killing innocent U.S. residents fizzled. The legalization of medical marijuana use in some states also clouds the moral issue with the perceived health benefits for illegal users in states without such authorization. Given these difficulties of rallying meaningful public participation in moral abstinence, federal and state government legislation decriminalizing select drugs may be the only hope for ending the borderlands bloodshed. Indeed, once marijuana is decriminalized and home or government production authorized, users could readily control the source of the drug and avoid the murderous cartels.

Similarly, on the labor immigration front there is no realistic chance that any moral imperative against cheap labor will take hold in the United States to protect the undocumented from perilous border crossings and from exploitative and sometimes involuntary labor once here. In much the same way that many in the United States are addicted to narcotics, as a country we are addicted to cheap labor that supplies our food and consumer goods at Wal-Mart pricing. Even if U.S. jurisdictions embraced living wage protections, it is unclear whether demand would cease for undocumented immigrants, given the ready circumvention of such protections by unscrupulous employers that can undercut the meager existing wage guarantees by charging immigrant employees outrageous prices for transportation, housing, and work supplies. Here, too, legalization of entry is the most effective strategy to reduce the vulnerability of our virtuous immigrant labor force.

A Framework for
Southbound Crossings

Focusing nearly obsessively on northbound crossings they find threatening, whether by undocumented immigrants or drug couriers, most every U.S. politician contends that these crossings must be halted. In response they offer simplistic and narrow solutions of enhanced border enforcement that, as shown above, will fail to deter these entries. These policymakers give little thought to reverse traffic from the United States into Mexico, as border policy from a U.S. perspective emphasizes northbound entries, and lately their suppression. Yet north- and southbound crossings are historically and inexorably connected, as the northbound migratory response to NAFTA's decimation of Mexican agriculture revealed.

Assuming the United States had a comprehensive border policy for southbound crossings, what might it entail? Might Mexico's vision of a comprehensive policy for such crossings differ in key respects? I examine these questions below, along with my own suggestions for regulating U.S. crossings into Mexico.

Of the varieties of southbound crossings considered in this book, U.S. policy has focused most on the expansion of trade and corporate presence south of the border, especially through NAFTA. To the extent that the United States has regulated vice tourism, it has been the externalities of vice that draw regulatory attention. For example, U.S. authorities are concerned about underage drinking in Mexico that leads to drunk driving in the United States on the return trip. Child sex tourists are a hazard even within the United States, as they may not confine their illicit activities to south-of-the-border sojourns. Similarly, on the subject of fugitive crossings, U.S. authorities aim to restrict the southbound flight from justice that can impede criminal prosecution in the United States. In the interest of troop safety, the United States has regulated entry of military personnel to Mexico over the years, as illustrated by the restrictions discussed in chapters 4 and 5 on entries for illicit sex and for carousing in border towns. Similarly, the U.S. government has issued warnings of late to U.S. tourists about drug violence in Mexico. Apart from these situations and for the entry of guns and drug money flowing south to Mexican drug cartels as discussed in chapter 8, there is no call within the United States to comprehensively shut the border to U.S. resident and corporate entry into Mexico, or to that of U.S. goods. While campaigning for the 2008 election, Barack Obama did urge the renegotiation of NAFTA to strengthen its dictates on environmental and fair labor standards. Yet the economic crisis that followed squelched any such plans to constrain the prerogatives of corporate capital.

Many U.S. residents are threatened by the changing demographics of the United States and argue for sealing the northbound border to better preserve the Anglo culture. They fail to realize that a similar shift is occurring in Mexico, where Americanization is under way. Despite similar cultural criticism south of the border from some as the Spanish language morphs to Spanglish and U.S. business gains a foothold, this cultural shift is inevitable given the rich history of border crossings and border relocations in our relationship with Mexico. As I have written elsewhere, the cross-pollination of Mexicans and Anglos is a recipe for cultural exchange that transcends borders and border closures.[1] Sealing the border in either direction runs against this strong current.

From a Mexican perspective, there is no call for comprehensively closing the border to southbound crossings. Of course, the Mexican government currently decries the shipment of guns into Mexico and at times has been hostile to U.S.-owned industry, particularly after the Mexican Revolution when the government expropriated the mostly extractive and land-dominant U.S.-resident and -corporate holdings of the time. Foreign investment has also been tightly controlled in the coastal and borderlands restrictive zone, as chapter 2 explains, although these restrictions are readily circumvented. In contrast, Mexico generally welcomes tourists and retirees to its vacation spots and spends considerable resources to attract U.S. retirees and vacation-home owners as well as U.S. tourists to resort regions such as Cancún and Loreto Bay. Mexico's relationship to vice crossings by U.S. residents is considerably more complex. These crossings have at times threatened moral standards in Mexico, particularly in the early twentieth century when moral values clashed with the revenue stream that accompanied the vice trade and financed local government. As described previously, the late 1960s/early 1970s entry of U.S. hippie youth led Mexican authorities briefly to bar their admission for fear they might corrupt Mexican youth with their drug use and rebellious lifestyle. The assumption that these vagabond migrants had no financial means of consequence avoided the more familiar tension in Mexican history between vice revenues and Mexican values that often gave way to the revenue stream.

Of late, Mexican upset with southbound crossings has focused more on trade imbalances and the smuggling of weapons than on crossings by U.S. residents. Mexicans have taken to the streets to demand renegotiation of NAFTA's agricultural provisions, specifically to remove the Mexican food-stuffs of corn and beans from the agreement.[2] In the interest of food sovereignty, some have called more generally for removal from NAFTA of all agricultural products, while others have urged the reconsideration of U.S. farm subsidies that unfairly advantage U.S. agri-giants over smaller-scale Mexican ejido farmers. Although President Obama's campaign promise to renegotiate NAFTA presumably would supply a venue for discussion of how NAFTA harmed Mexican farmers, the global economic crisis delayed that opportunity.[3]

Mexico's policy emphasis of late on southbound crossings has been on the smuggling of weapons destined for the drug cartels. As with the U.S. obsession in defining border policy based on trafficking of drugs and the passage of undocumented immigrants, the Mexican emphasis is misplaced. Utilizing the world's busiest border, weapons smugglers have the same advantage of chaos as drug smugglers headed north. Even if the Mexican government were to somehow stem the weapons trade from the United States, no doubt new sources of entry would emerge, or, as with marijuana in the United States, weapons production would shift to local sites as enforcement impeded trafficking routes. The solution to weapons trafficking fueling bloodshed in Mexico, of course, is to attack the root of the drug trade through legalization, as argued in chapter 12.

A meaningful comprehensive border policy for southbound crossings must take note of the history of border crossings. In particular, it should be mindful of the interrelationship of north- and southbound crossings. For example, the weapons and drug money headed south are the product of the U.S. demand that draws drug traffickers north. Similarly, immigration to the north funds remittances south that buoy communities throughout Mexico. An additional interrelationship that should inform any comprehensive border policy is one of the themes of this study: whatever is needed or desired in one country historically will be supplied by the other. On the southbound side, the thirst for alcohol and illicit sex has drawn U.S. residents south, as the desire for cheaper wages and production costs, along with reduced regulation and enforcement, has lured U.S. corporations and investors south of the border. Border flows therefore may change over time in relation to differences in laws (and economies), a topic explored in greater detail in chapter 14.

The tension identified above between revenues generated from U.S. presence in Mexico and damage to Mexican values and communities complicates any such comprehensive policy. For example, while maquiladoras create jobs and fuel economic growth in Mexico, they fail to pay living wages in the more expensive borderlands region and exploit their expendable workers. U.S. tourists and retirees create jobs in tourist enclaves, yet their presence drives up costs of living for Mexican workers who deliver needed services. As another example, borderland and tourist zone prostitution supplies jobs but exposes women to alarming threats to their health and to dead-end careers.

In fundamental ways, then, much of the U.S. economic presence and influence in Mexico is deeply flawed. As demonstrated above, free trade disrupts rural regions, sending residents fleeing to the borderlands in search of survival in the often-exploitative maquiladoras or the sex industry. Those who find work serving tourists and retirees in Mexican resorts earn paltry wages, with the profits often going to U.S. companies. Revenues from U.S. tourists rarely contribute to financing of local infrastructure, with tourism instead straining municipal services such as police and street maintenance.[4] The combination of the sex industry, maquiladoras that exploit and commodify their workers, and the violent drug trade ignites volatility in the borderlands region. Those workers who venture across the border to el Norte seeking better wages are underpaid by U.S. employers and stigmatized as "illegals" undeserving of protection. Although returning vast profits to Mexico, the U.S. illicit drug trade has devastated Mexico's soul with wrenching violence that threatens more legitimate sources of economic growth through tourism, retirement, and foreign entrepreneurship.

Comprehensive border policies must confront this dismal economic picture by facilitating and encouraging U.S. investment that delivers meaningful economic security without the exploitation inherent in past and present models of U.S. involvement. The blueprint for this beneficial U.S. presence may be drawn from the borderlands and coastal zone regulation discussed in chapter 2 that purported to constrain direct U.S. investment in these restricted zones. Surmounting those restrictions, most U.S. presence nonetheless is concentrated in these borderlands and the beach resorts. Vice tourists head to these border cities and beach resorts. Tourist families flock to Mexican beaches. Retirees and vacation-home owners seek out coastal enclaves. U.S. corporate interests brought maquiladoras to the borderlands and opened hotels and restaurants in the tourist regions.

As signaled by the restricted zone policy, Mexico should better encourage U.S. presence and investments away from the borderlands and tourist havens and into the territory left devastated by NAFTA and other economic factors. Wal-Mart, despite its substantial presence throughout Mexico, displaces small business and thus doesn't meaningfully stimulate the Mexican economy, particularly in the rural regions. Ironically, the United States does supply a semblance of economic stimulus to these interior regions in the form of the drug economy that offers rural farmers an alternate but problematic subsistence. Indeed, the U.S. contribution that best bolsters the Mexican economic core in these regions away from the borderlands and coastal zones is the most controversial—Mexican immigrants, both documented and not, working in U.S. jobs and sending remittances back to all reaches of Mexico. In 2008, Mexicans working in the United States sent $23.5 billion to their families in Mexico.[5] Studies have shown that Mexican households with U.S. immigrants invest more in small business, with one study crediting remittances with underwriting 21 percent of new Mexican businesses.[6]

At least two approaches would help deliver economic stimulus to these desperate Mexican regions. One is the U.S.-supplied economic aid discussed in chapter 10 that should aim to create jobs and economic opportunity. The other approach is comprehensive immigration reform for northbound crossings, as outlined in chapter 11, that offers the possibility of greater earnings through stability and lesser exploitation, and decreased costs of border passage to Mexican immigrants, presumably increasing remittance revenues as an indirect form of economic aid to Mexico. Given the history of U.S. corporations racing to the bottom of protective labor and environmental laws, remittances may be a better approach than encouraging U.S. companies to invest directly in rural Mexican regions. Still, the long-range security and health of Mexico depends on its workers having opportunities in their homeland regions, rather than relying on a remittance economy of emigrants. This will require better supervision of U.S. investments in Mexico, public and private, to ensure the absence of exploitation that plagued the maquiladora model. Moreover, the Mexican government's problematic history of institutionalized corruption demands watchdog organizations comprised of representatives of both countries to oversee disbursal of economic aid, with human lives and prosperity for the region hanging in the balance.

Laws the Border Leaves Behind

Addressed previously are a variety of cross-border differences in law that have affected border crossings. Some are very subtle, such as the lower property tax rate structures in Mexico, in relation to most U.S. jurisdictions, that add to the appeal of a Mexican retirement or second home. Others are more substantial, such as Mexico's lower drinking age and its abolition of the death penalty, the latter in contrast to its resilience in most U.S. jurisdictions. Almost across the board Mexico offers less strict regulation on the issues engaged in this text. Examples include capital punishment, drug possession, the minimum drinking age, the age of sexual consent, and prostitution. In contrast, Mexican law is more resolute than U.S. law with regard to abortion and gun control. The two countries may also articulate similar laws on many subjects in terms of strictness, yet they may differ substantially in their rigor of enforcement in large measure due to corruption engrained in Mexican government. Drug trafficking (historically, at least) and environmental regulation of borderlands factories are the two areas that stand out here.

As demonstrated above, many varieties of border crossings are spurred by prohibitions in the country of departure where the destination country permits the activity or at least offers a semblance of tolerance. Ironically, immigration north for economic advantage breaks this mold—labor of course is legal in Mexico, and Mexico supports its emigrants to the United States who migrate to pursue an American dream. In contrast, the United States criminalizes their unauthorized entry, regardless of the immigrant's virtuous purpose. For undocumented immigrants, then, legality flows in the opposite direction from many of the crossings considered in this book. The discussion in this chapter thus assumes the dynamic in which the border crosser aims to escape, rather than invoke, some more stringent law.

Any consideration of U.S.-Mexico cross-border law differences must take account of the potentially equal import of interstate differences within the United States. For example, consider the many legal subjects addressed above. Regarding marijuana possession, apart from federal regulation, with

Arizona's Proposition 203 in 2010 and Delaware's legislation in 2011, 16 states now authorize medicinal marijuana possession of some form, while others have significantly decriminalized possession for any purpose. Sixteen states have abolished the death penalty. Prostitution is legal in much of Nevada. Gambling is lawful in Nevada and at tribal casinos throughout the United States. Revelers in Las Vegas can order drinks around the clock with no last call. The age of sexual consent varies across the United States—in most states that age is 16, while in others it is as old as 18.[1] Certain states regulate gun purchases more rigorously than others. Before *Roe v. Wade*, states varied more widely than today in abortion allowances, and before the advent of no-fault divorce some states such as New York offered extremely limited grounds for divorce. These interstate differences in law sometimes prompt interstate travel. For example, before federal law coerced states into raising the minimum drinking age, familiar party routes emerged from strict to more lenient states. In particular, I remember summer weekend trips to Idaho, once a haven for Washington and Oregon youth with its lower drinking age of 19. Some legal differences are less likely to trigger interstate travel for purposes of eluding a stricter state. For example, it is unlikely that a serial killer would gravitate toward a state without capital punishment in order to carry out his or her grisly agenda (which says something about the minimal deterrence effect of capital punishment). In sum, given the permissibility in many states of vice tourism in the areas mentioned above, often there is no need for U.S. residents to head for Mexico to satisfy their urges.

Similarly, an illicit market exists in the United States for much of what prompts vice tourism into Mexico. During Prohibition, U.S. drinkers situated far from the borderlands frequented local speakeasies for their hard alcohol. Today's youth, unable to drink legally, either purchase fake identification, obtain alcohol from older friends or family, or purchase an alternate substance, particularly marijuana that in many locations is easier than alcohol for youngsters to procure and secret away. No doubt a baggie of marijuana is easier to conceal from one's parents and authorities than a case of beer. Before legalization, abortions were available in clandestine venues throughout the United States. The outlawing of gambling (aside from state-sponsored lotteries) in most U.S. jurisdictions has no impact on informal gambling through weekend card games and sports betting pools. Johns seeking prostitutes need not cross the border, or even venture across state lines to a Nevada brothel. By means of Internet sites or by frequenting a local massage parlor or escort service, customers can readily engage prostitutes in most U.S. cities. Although less apparent, child sex can be found, too, in U.S.

locations. While perhaps produced more often in Mexican locations, child pornography might be viewed over the Internet from any U.S. computer.

With these practical circumstances in mind, consider the options for cross-border lawmaking. As now, Mexico and the United States could legislate independently of one another, marching to their own regulatory drums. Conversely, the two countries could aim to synchronize all their laws, particularly in areas that affect border crossings. A middle ground would be to revisit each set of laws in light of cross-border traffic and the growing alliances and cultural connections between the two countries and evaluate each law individually in terms of the advantages and drawbacks of synchronizing the two legal regimes. The same approach could apply to new sectors of regulation that may impact future cross-border traffic. A cross-border organization comprised of both Mexican and U.S. policymakers would best undertake this policy analysis and recommend synchronization as appropriate.

I favor this middle ground approach and suggest a workable framework for its application. Among the factors to be considered in evaluating the benefits of synchronizing a cross-border area of the law are the extent to which the law generates border crossings, the externalities in both countries of those crossings, and the geographical regions affected. For example, in the case of the legal drinking age, border crossings on weekends produce harmful externalities in both countries, with drunken fights and sexual abuse south of the border and likely drunken driving on the road home north. Query, however, whether a change in Mexican law to raise the drinking age, or to prohibit younger entrants from crossing into Mexico on weekend nights, might simply cause U.S. youngsters to reach for locally available intoxicants with similar adverse impacts in the United States, and even effects in Mexico if alcohol is replaced with marijuana supplied to the United States by the Mexican cartels. Similarly, weapons supplied by U.S. dealers that reach Mexican druglords contribute to the wrenching violence in Mexico border towns. But addressing the problem by restricting access to guns in the United States, aside from its political infeasibility in the guns and guts terrain of the Second Amendment, would not quell the drug gunfire. Rather, should the U.S. supply line be terminated, Mexican cartels would no doubt obtain their weapons from other sources as long as the illegal drug trade persists, likely through the international underground market in military weapons.[2] In the same vein, should efforts to interdict marijuana arriving from Mexico ever succeed through some unlikely combination of government resources and cooperative enforcement, that choking of the supply chain would only result in the increased production of the crop within the United States or its arrival from external sources through other trafficking routes, such as through Canada.

Probably the most important factor is to determine the international trajectory of the law in the relevant area. In other words, as judges in the United States often do in deciding open questions of the law by looking to the judicial trend of other courts, on issues of cross-border significance policymakers should look for trends in comparative law. For example, in the case of the death penalty, the decided international momentum is toward abolition. Similarly, the strict U.S. drinking age runs against the global grain, as only a smattering of countries have the same rigid limit and in most countries the legal age is 18. Many countries, too, are moving toward legalization of some or all narcotics.

Another factor to consider in lawmaking that affects border crossing is protection of human rights and of vulnerable populations. Child sex trafficking clearly imperils Mexican youth. Although potentially illegal in Mexico, as discussed above inadequate enforcement invites child sex tourism south of the border. For such legal subjects with decidedly harmful effects on a vulnerable population, the two countries should impede cross-border traffic that aims to exploit differences in law or its enforcement. Here, the two countries should consider how to share enforcement resources and intelligence. Also, as was done for sex with youth under the age of 18, U.S. citizens who travel to Mexico to commit certain crimes ought to be subject to prosecution in the United States when their crime, as with child exploitation, is not victimless.[3]

Under this harm reduction analysis, prostitution should be legalized where it does not entail involuntary sexual servitude. Mexico's longtime approach of licensing prostitutes in border town regions and requiring regular health exams suggests an approach that protects the prostitute's health far better than the current prohibitions in most every U.S. city that drive street prostitutes into the dangerous hands of pimps and prevent the creation of educative and support networks among prostitutes. Instructive here is the emerging international trend to decriminalize prostitution, as reflected by The Netherlands (2000), Germany (2002), and New Zealand (2003).[4]

Abortion is among the most difficult subjects to address from a cross-border perspective given the strong Roman Catholic influence prevailing in Mexico. Although in 2007, abortion was made legal in Mexico City during the first 12 weeks of pregnancy, most Mexican states prohibit or significantly restrict the procedure. The reality that Mexican women of means are able to cross into the United States (or head to Mexico City) for a safe abortion should prompt the Mexican government and these restrictive Mexican states to consider whether their prohibitory stance discriminates against poor Mexican women, a decidedly vulnerable population. For these women, the back-alley abortion, wherever conducted, poses grave threats to health. But backlash against the allowance of legal abortions in Mexico City is pulling most Mexican states toward prohibition, with some 17 of Mexico's 31 states passing constitutional amendments in the last few years declaring that life begins at conception.[5] Given the strong religious influences and constitutional status of this issue on both sides of the border, abortion may be one policy area that defies cross-border coordination of law.

With significant immigration crossing both directions between the United States and Mexico, a related subject is legal differences between the two countries that, although not prompting migration, nonetheless may surprise new arrivals with their criminal consequences. For Mexican immigrants, who are often male workers, most likely this takes the form of differences between the United States and Mexico on the age of sexual consent. Although Mexico's age of consent is complicated and varies by state, it can be as low as the federal floor of 12, which is younger than any U.S. jurisdiction. By comparison, Spain's age of consent is 13, which is representative of lower ages of consent in Europe than in the United States. Because it is impractical for a country to specify different legal standards for its residents depending on their country of origin, the United States and Mexico should consider the culture shock effect of these laws. At minimum, efforts to better communicate a warning of the differences in such laws should be undertaken in the appropriate language of the migrant group. This can be challenging when the target audience is one of undocumented immigrants who disdain contact with officials. Still, with the prospect of reform of immigration laws to eliminate or reduce undocumented passage by broadening legal means of entry, the potential for communicating such cross-border legal differences improves.

Conclusion

Predicting the future of border crossing is risky business, but demographics and history seem to point to several trends. In the southbound direction, as the U.S. Anglo population grows older,[1] and as the U.S. economy swings wildly as it has in the last decade, no doubt U.S. retirees will continue to flock to the border seeking a cheaper retirement on the warm shores of some Mexican beach.[2] The escalating drug war in Mexico may imperil this migration, but if violence crosses the border north, economics may nonetheless hold sway in the choice of locale for retirement. Moreover, regardless of location, the preference of U.S. retirees for the sterility and security of gate-guarded communities will mute any war outside the walls.

Heading in the other direction, immigrant labor pipelines to the United States arguably may slow considerably, even in the face of rising U.S. labor demand. Supporting this prediction is the decline of the Mexican birthrate—from 6.1 children per Mexican woman in 1974 to just 2.3 children on average by 2009.[3] U.S. labor relies on the youngest members of the Mexican labor force, luring workers in their youth into stressful, dangerous labor that the participants likely cannot endure for more than a few years. As the Mexican population itself begins to age, some observers predict that the labor pool will shrink. Still, should a U.S. labor shortage ensue, younger Mexican workers may prove vulnerable to depart from Mexico for the enhanced salaries that a shortage presumably would spur. Others point to the longstanding history and culture of Mexican immigration into the Southwest and the rest of the United States and suggest there will always be occasion for considerable Mexican migration, even if it consists of older Mexicans joining relatives in the United States for retirement. Some researchers also have forecast mass migration from Mexico prompted by global warming that devastates crop yields and further weakens Mexico's reeling agricultural industry.[4]

Myself, I envision a future with the possibility of signs at the U.S.-Mexico border quite different from the 1990s highway billboard an anti-immigrant group erected inside the California border near the Arizona state line that warned: "Welcome to California—The Illegal Immigration State. Don't Let This Happen to Your State!" Rather, a couple of decades from now the billboard, placed just inside the Mexican border in border towns such as Tijuana, might read: "Empleadores estadounidenses le ruegan que se una a sus compatriotas que han encontrado nuevas opportunidades y un brillante porvenir en los Estados Unidos. Para más información llame al 1-800-SI VENGA." (United States employers urge you to join your fellow country-men and women who have found new opportunity and bright futures in the United States. Call 1-800-Come Now for further information.)

Elsewhere I predicted a continuation of the gradual blending over time of U.S. and Mexican cultures—language, music, food, history, architecture, and more.[5] Our economies and futures, too, are increasingly tied together. About 80 percent of Mexican exports head to the United States, and U.S. employers depend on Mexican labor as they have for at least the last century. Tourist destinations in both countries rely on border-crossing visitors, with the reciprocity of the United States as the primary destination for Mexican tourists and Mexico as the country most visited by U.S. residents.[6] As friendly neighbors, cultural blending and economic interdependence will promote cross-border travel to the point that the international line between the two countries may eventually fade to something akin to a state boundary. U.S. retirees might escape to the sunny beaches of Mexico as they often do now to landlocked Arizona. Mexican immigrants will migrate as needed for job opportunities. Mexican-grown marijuana might come north through lawful distributors as Corona beer does now. Differences in law will fade some with the intermingling of people and cultures. Perhaps, eventually, the border will become less of the open wound that Gloria Anzaldúa wrote of where "the Third World grates against the first and bleeds."[7] Rather than a horizontal gnashing, the border might become a cultural waterway, navigable with ease as local economies, cultures, and priorities dictate.

As they ignore state lines within their own countries, U.S. and Mexican residents will continue crossing the U.S-Mexico border as they have for decades in the pursuit of vice and virtue. Especially in the interest of human survival, no border wall or impediment to entry will succeed in overcoming the human spirit, nor should it.

Notes

INTRODUCTION

1. Elizabeth McCormick and Patrick McCormick, "Hospitality: How a Biblical Virtue Could Transform United States Immigration Policy," *University of Detroit Mercy Law Review* 83 (2006): 857, 891 (explaining that in addition to per-country limits on entry through family reunification and other grounds, only 5,000 immigrant visas each year aim to accommodate the entire demand for low-skilled workers in U.S. jobs such as construction, factory workers, housekeeping, and landscaping).

PART I

1. Country singer Johnny Rodriguez's "Run for the Border" (1993) is true to its title when the narrator escapes a jealous husband wielding a knife.

2. Andrew Selee, David Shirk, and Eric Olson, "Five Myths About Mexico's Drug War," *Washington Post*, http://www.washingtonpost.com/wp-dyn/content/article/2010/03/26/AR2010032602226.html (March 28, 2010, last visited November 22, 2010).

CHAPTER 1

1. http://www.manishchawley.com/pages/4_calvin-hobbes.php?nav=panel&row=148 (last visited September 14, 2010).

2. Steven W. Bender, *Greasers and Gringos: Latinos, Law, and the American Imagination* (New York: New York University Press, 2003), 32–35.

3. Allen L. Woll, "Hollywood Bandits, 1910–1981," in *Bandidos: The Varieties of Latin American Banditry*, ed. Richard W. Slatta (Westport, CT: Greenwood Press, 1987), 171, 172.

4. Carroll Graham, *Border Town* (New York: Dell Publishing, paperback ed., 1934). A voluntary Hollywood-industry censoring organization, the Production Code Administration, led filmmakers to fire the author Graham as scriptwriter and recast the story with a fiery-tempered ex-lawyer who heads south of the border to pursue his business ambitions rather than as a fugitive from justice. Steven W. Bender, "Savage Fronteras and Tribal Boundaries: Chasing Success in Hollywood's Bordertown," in *Screening Justice*, ed. Teree E. Foster, Rennard Strickland, and Taunya Banks (Buffalo, NY: William S. Hein & Company, 2006), 13.

5. Graham, *Border Town*, 15.

6. Karl Jacoby, "Between North and South: The Alternative Borderlands of William H. Ellis and the African American Colony of 1895," in *Continental Crossroads: Remapping*

U.S.-Mexico Borderlands History, ed. Samuel Truett and Elliott Young (Durham, NC: Duke University Press, 2004), 217.

7. "Fugitive Slaves," *Texas State Gazette*, December 12, 1857, 2.

8. Devin C. McNulty, "The Changing Face of Extraditions Between Mexico and the United States," *Champion* 31 (April 2007): 32, 33.

9. Bruce Zagaris and Julia Padierna Peralta, "Mexico-United States Extradition and Alternatives: From Fugitive Slaves to Drug Traffickers—150 Years and Beyond the Rio Grande's Winding Courses," *American University Journal of International Law and Policy* 12 (1997): 519, 524.

10. See W. C. Nunn, *Escape from Reconstruction* (Fort Worth: Texas Christian University Press, 1956); Andrew F. Rolle, *The Lost Cause: The Confederate Exodus to Mexico* (Norman: University of Oklahoma Press, 1965).

11. Nunn, *Escape from Reconstruction*, 50.

12. Rolle, *Lost Cause*, 188.

13. See chapter 3 for discussion of the anti–foreign investment climate sparked by the Mexican Revolution.

14. Thomas Cottam Romney, *The Mormon Colonies in Mexico* (Salt Lake City: University of Utah Press, 2005), 216; John Mason Hart, *Empire and Revolution: The Americans in Mexico since the Civil War* (Berkeley: University of California Press, 2002), 238–43.

15. Zagaris and Peralta, "Mexico–United States Extradition," 525.

16. Alfredo Mirandé, *Gringo Justice* (Notre Dame: University of Notre Dame Press, 1987), 17.

17. Ibid., 74–75.

18. Américo Paredes, *"With His Pistol in His Hand:" A Border Ballad and Its Hero* (Austin: University of Texas Press, 1958), 93.

19. Thomas Torrans, *The Magic Curtain: The Mexican–American Border in Fiction, Film, and Song* (Fort Worth: Texas Christian University Press, 2002), 58.

20. Steven W. Bender, "Sight, Sound, and Stereotype: The War on Terrorism and Its Consequences for Latina/os," *Oregon Law Review* 81 (2002): 1153, 1157 n.14 (noting the discrepancy in accounts of the number of U.S. residents killed, with some reports of 17 and others of 18 killed).

21. Ollie Reed Jr., "Villa the Terrorist?" *Albuquerque Tribune*, February 28, 2002, A1.

22. See also Chris Frazer, *Bandit Nation: A History of Outlaws and Cultural Struggle in Mexico, 1810–1920* (Lincoln: University of Nebraska Press, 2006), 198 (suggesting other possible motives, including that Villa may have been attempting to spark war with the United States); Raul A. Fernandez, *The Mexican–American Border Region: Issues and Trends* (Notre Dame: University of Notre Dame Press, 1989), 29 (mentioning the speculation by some that Germany backed Villa to distract the United States from World War I).

23. Fernandez, *Mexican–American Border*, 28.

24. Thomas Torrans, *Forging the Tortilla Curtain: Cultural Drift and Change Along the United States–Mexico Border From the Spanish Era to the Present* (Fort Worth: Texas Christian University Press, 2002), 219.

25. Ibid., 220.

26. Robert F. Castro, "Busting the Bandito Boyz: Militarism, Masculinity, and the Hunting of Undocumented Persons in the U.S.–Mexico Borderlands," *Journal of Hate Studies* 6 (2007/2008): 7, 10.

27. Brian DeLay, "Independent Indians and the U.S.–Mexican War," *American Historical Review* 112 (February 2007), http://www.historycooperative.org/journals/ahr/112.1/delay.html (last visited December 11, 2009).

28. Ibid.

29. See, for example, Shelley Bowen Hatfield, *Chasing Shadows: Indians Along the United States–Mexico Border 1876–1911* (Albuquerque: University of New Mexico, 1998), 15 (describing land-grabbing practices of Mexican and U.S. governments, including removal of Yaquis).

30. Oscar J. Martínez, *Troublesome Border* (Tucson: University of Arizona Press, rev. ed. 2006), 50.

31. DeLay, "Independent Indians."

32. Treaty of Guadalupe Hidalgo, art. XI.

33. Ibid., available at http://bartleby.com/43/31.html (last visited December 3, 2009).

34. Gadsden Purchase Treaty, art. II.

35. DeLay, "Independent Indians;" Hatfield, *Chasing Shadows*.

36. Zagaris and Peralta, "Mexico–United States Extradition," 526.

37. Paul Ganster and David E. Lorey, *The U.S.–Mexican Border into the Twenty-First Century* (Lanham, MD: Rowman & Littlefield, 2d ed., 2008), 196.

38. Angus MacLean, *Legends of the California Bandidos* (Fresno, CA: Pioneer Publishing, 1977), 60 (pointing out that not all crimes of the era were committed by south-of-the-border bandidos, given that European settlers of all backgrounds, as well as the Chinese, Arabs, Hindus, and others, were prone to heinous crimes).

39. Louis Sahagun, "Brazen Rail Bandits on the Border," *Los Angeles Times*, July 23, 1995, 1.

40. "Captured Marine Provoked Curiosity in Mexico," http://newsofcyber.blogspot.com/2008/04/captured–marine–provoked–curiosity–in.html (April 11, 2008; last visited December 11, 2009).

41. "Ángel Maturino Reséndiz," http://en.wikipedia.org/wiki/Ángel_Maturino_Reséndiz (last visited November 16, 2010).

42. For discussion on the convoluted issue of the legality within the United States of abductions in Mexico and other foreign countries by bounty hunters, see Andrew Berenson, "Comment, An Examination of the Rights of American Bounty Hunters to Engage in Extraterritorial Abductions in Mexico," *University of Miami Inter-American Law Review* 30 (1998): 461; Ryan M. Porcello, "International Bounty Hunter Ride-Along: Should U.K. Thrillseekers Be Permitted to Pay to Experience a Week in the Life of a U.S. Bounty Hunter," *Vanderbilt Journal of Transactional Law* 35 (2002): 953 (contending the U.S. Supreme Court's decision in *Reese v. United States*, 76 U.S. (9 Wall.) 13 (1869) prohibits such foreign capture but explaining how this ruling is undercut by decisions allowing courts to exercise jurisdiction over such captured defendants).

43. Duane "Dog" Chapman with Laura Morton, *You Can Run, But You Can't Hide* (New York: Hyperion, 2007), 279.

44. Kenn Abaygo, *Advanced Fugitive: Running, Hiding, Surviving, and Thriving Forever* (Boulder, CO: Paladin Press, 1997).

45. Tracy Wilkinson, "Mexico Under Siege," *Los Angeles Times*, December 5, 2008, 3.

46. Ibid. (Then-Mexico President Vicente Fox remarked on signing the law that "Mexico shares the opinion that capital punishment is a violation of human rights.")

47. Marion Lloyd, "Mexico: Death Penalty Gaining Support," http://www.huffington-post.com/2009/01/14/mexico-death-penalty-gain_n_157868.html (January 14, 2009; last visited December 11, 2009).

48. "Death Penalty in Mexico is Step Backwards in Human Rights, Catholic Lawyers Warn," http://www.catholicnewsagency.com/new.php?n=13497 (August 12, 2008; last visited December 11, 2009).

49. See "List of United States Supreme Court Decisions on Capital Punishment," http://en.wikipedia.org/wiki/List_of_United_States_Supreme_Court_decisions_on_capital_punishment (last visited October 14, 2009) (detailing history of constraints mostly imposed under Eighth Amendment prohibition of cruel and unusual punishment to encompass execution of the mentally retarded and crimes against the person that do not result in death).

50. http://www.deathwatchinternational.org/the_facts.php (last visited December 2, 2009) (suggesting the actual China figures might far exceed this estimated total).

51. "New Mexico Governor Signs Bill to Repeal Death Penalty," http://www.deathpenaltyinfo.org/documents/richardsonstatement.pdf (March 18, 2009; last visited December 11, 2009).

52. United States–Mexico Extradition Treaty of 1978, art. 8.

53. Letter from Dianne Feinstein to Honorable Vicente Fox, July 29, 2003.

54. Ginger Thompson, "High Court Overturns Extraditions Ban," *New York Times*, November 30, 2005, A14.

55. Query whether such a strategy by the prosecutor would violate the defendant's due process rights, particularly if the defendant was privy to the negotiations.

56. Parul Joshi, "Cesar Laurean Pleads Not Guilty," http://www2.wnct.com/nct/news/local/article/cesar_laurean_pleads_not_guilty/38358/ (June 8, 2009; last visited October 21, 2009).

57. "Escape to Mexico Blocks Death Penalty," *USA Today*, http://www.usatoday.com/news/nation/2008-01-17-Extradition_N.htm (January 17, 2008; last visited January 8, 2010).

58. John Ross, "Mexico Ends the Death Penalty," http://www.counterpunch.org/ross12232005.html (December 23, 2005; last visited December 11, 2009) (discussing how the Mexican government, if timely contacted, can supply legal assistance in criminal and capital cases). José Ernesto Medellín, a Mexican national convicted of a gang-related killing of two young girls in 1993, was one of the death row inmates affected by the decision, but Texas moved forward with plans to execute him while ignoring the World Court's ruling. Although the Bush administration eventually supported the ruling and called for its enforcement, the U.S. Supreme Court refused to bind Texas to these presidential efforts to enforce a World Court ruling against it. *Medellin v. Texas*, 129 S. Ct. 360 (2008). Rebuffing the efforts of the World Court to stay the execution as having no standing in the state of Texas, Texas executed Medellín in August 2008. A similar drama and outcome accompanied the execution by Texas in 2011 of Mexican national Humberto Leal.

59. Carlton Smith, *Love, Daddy* (New York: St. Martin's Paperbacks, 2003), 69.

60. Ibid., 174–76.

61. *State v. Longo*, 341 Or. 580, 148 P.3d 382 (2006) (on direct review of the trial, Oregon Supreme Court finds no basis for challenge under extradition treaty or Vienna Convention under these circumstances; court also rejects Longo's convoluted argument in the penalty phase of the trial that he didn't know of Mexico's treatment of death penalty

extraditions, and thus his failure to gain such knowledge before fleeing to Mexico should be viewed as an absence of premeditation in committing the murders). Longo regained the spotlight in 2011 when the *New York Times* published his op-ed urging the Oregon prison to allow him and other inmates to donate their organs, in return for which he would forego his remaining appeals. Christian Longo, "Giving Life after Death Row," *New York Times*, March 5, 2011. In November 2011, Oregon's governor issued a moratorium on executions during his term in office.

62. http://www.internationaljusticeproject.org/nationalsJMedinaMexNationals.cfm (last visited October 14, 2009) (describing efforts of Mexican consulate that succeeded when Texas prosecutors offered the men guilty pleas the two accepted that spared their lives).

63. The kidnap and felony murder charge was unusual—the Mexican doctor was accused of prolonging the life of a federal drug agent so that others could continue torturing and interrogating the agent. A U.S. trial judge ultimately acquitted him.

64. United States–Mexico Extradition Treaty of 1978, art. 9.

65. *United States v. Alvarez-Machain*, 504 U.S. 655 (1992). Another case of the same era authored by Chief Justice Rehnquist considered the rights of a Mexican citizen under the U.S. Constitution. Here, Mexican police cooperated and escorted the drug suspect to the U.S. border. U.S. officials later searched his Mexican residences in concert with Mexican police without obtaining a warrant. The Court answered in the negative whether "the Fourth Amendment applies to the search and seizure by United States agents of property that is owned by a nonresident alien and located in a foreign country," thereby upholding the warrantless search. *United States v. Verdugo-Urquidez*, 494 U.S. 259 (1990).

66. Zagaris and Peralta, "Mexico–United States Extradition," 581.

67. McNulty, "Changing Face of Extraditions" (detailing reasons for the loosening of extraditions); Zagaris and Peralta, "Mexico–United States Extradition," 606–12. Still, extradition requests are conditioned on a showing of evidence sufficient to the requested country to justify a criminal trial or, if the fugitive is an escapee already convicted, proof that he is the convict. United States–Mexico Extradition Treaty of 1978, art. 3.

68. Zagaris and Peralta, "Mexico–United States Extradition," 532 (providing statistics from 1996 in which 91 extradition requests were pending in Mexico, 52 of them drug trafficking–related).

69. Vicente Fox and Rob Allyn, *Revolution of Hope: The Life, Faith, and Dreams of a Mexican President* (New York: Viking 2007), 324.

70. See Nicholas Riccardi, "Both Sides in Arizona's Immigration Debate Use Crime Argument," *Los Angeles Times*, May 3, 2010, http://articles.latimes.com/2010/may/03/nation/la-na-arizona-crime-20100503 (last visited November 10, 2010) (debunking claims of anti–immigrant groups that vastly overstate the responsibility of undocumented immigrants for U.S. crime).

PART II

1. Bill Ong Hing, *Deporting Our Souls: Values, Morality, and Immigration Policy* (New York: Cambridge University Press, 2006), 125–34 (detailing the economic benefits of immigration); Tyler Cowen, "How Immigrants Create More Jobs," *New York Times*, October 30, 2010, 6.

2. Jorge Ramos, *A Country for All: An Immigrant Manifesto* (New York: Vintage Books, 2010), 44 (citing a study by a UCLA professor for the William C. Velasquez Institute con-

cluding that immigration reform could generate between 4.5 and 5.4 billion in additional tax revenue, and create between 750,000 and 900,000 jobs); see also Giovanni Peri, "The Effects of Immigrants on U.S. Employment and Productivity," *Federal Reserve Bank of San Francisco Economic Letter* 2010–26 (August 30, 2010), http://www.frbsf.org/publications/economics/letter/2010/el2010-26.html (last visited November 16, 2010) (arguing that immigration boosts U.S. worker income).

3. Jorge I. Domínguez and Rafael Fernández de Castro, *The United States and Mexico: Between Partnership and Conflict* (New York: Routledge, 2001), 152.

4. "Mexico's President Speaks Out About the Safety of Retirees and Tourists in His Country," http://www.aarp.org/about-aarp/press-center/info-03-2011/mexico_president_speaks_out_about_the_safety_of_retirees_and_tourists.html (posted March 1, 2011; last visited May 1, 2011).

5. Tim Rutten, "Missing the Whitman Story," *Los Angeles Times*, October 2, 2010, http://articles.latimes.com/2010/oct/02/opinion/la-oe-1002-rutten-20101002 (last visited November 2, 2010).

CHAPTER 2

1. http://www.tomdispatch.com/post/122537/mike_davis_on_manifest_destiny_the_sequel (September 19, 2006; last visited December 20, 2010).

2. Les Christie, "Retire in Style South of the Border," www.cnn.com (February 14, 2006; last visited October 9, 2009).

3. Les Christie, "The Rush to a Mexican Retirement is On," www.cnn.com (April 12, 2005; last visited August 20, 2009).

4. http://www.zillow.com/.

5. Jenalia Moreno, "American Invasion," *Houston Chronicle*, December 28, 2004, 1.

6. Ibid.

7. See Barry Golson, *Gringos in Paradise: An American Couple Builds Their Retirement Dream House in a Seaside Village in Mexico* (New York: Scribner, 2006), 241 (describing how the couple furnished their two-unit home, with two living rooms and kitchens, and a combined four bedrooms, with hand-crafted Mexican furniture for under $7,000, the cost of a New York friend's couch); see also Robert Nelson, *Boomers in Paradise: Living in Puerto Vallarta* (BookSurge Publishing, 2008) (detailing experiences of U.S. transplants in Puerto Vallarta).

8. Fernando Romero, *Hyper-Border: The Contemporary U.S-Mexico Border and Its Future* (New York: Princeton Architectural Press, 2008), 262.

9. http://www.mexconnect.com/articles/1883-mexico-s-a-breeze (last visited January 12, 2010) (detailing procedure for obtaining pre-approval of inventory list from Mexican consulate before bringing the items across the border).

10. Mike Davis, "The Baby Boomer Border Invasion," Tomdispatch.com (September 26, 2006; last visited December 11, 2009).

11. "Mexican Immigration and Retirement Information," http://www.pacificcoasttravelinfo.com/mexicoimmigration.asp (last visited October 19, 2009).

12. Kevin Brass, "Case for Retirement Visa in United States May Gain New Traction," *New York Times*, http://raisingtheroof.blogs.nytimes.com/2008/11/26/case-for-retirement-visa-in-united-states-may-gain-new--traction/ (November 26, 2008; last visited November 24, 2010).

13. Jack Smith, *God and Mr. Gomez* (New York: Reader's Digest Press, 1974).

14. http://www.mexperience.com/liveandwork/immigration.htm (last visited January 20, 2010).

15. Christie, "Retire in Style."

16. Christine Harrell, "Owning Retirement Property in Mexico: How to Finance Your Dreams," http://www.streetdirectory.com/travel_guide/150563/retirement/owning_retirement_property_in_mexico__how_to_finance_the_dream.html (last visited August 30, 2009).

17. Melissa M. Kellogg, "South of the Border," *Mortgage Banking* (November 2009): 34.

18. Larry Olmstead, "Sleepy-Resort Feel with Laid-Back Price," *USA Today*, February 6, 2009, 10B.

19. Les Christie, "Retire to Mexico–The Price is Right," http://money.cnn.com/2010/04/28/real_estate/Mexican_housing_bust/index.htm (April 28, 2010; last visited August 1, 2010).

20. Translation derived from John De La Vega, *Mexican Real Estate: Laws and Practices Affecting Private U.S. Ownership* (Tucson: University of Arizona Press, 1976).

21. Michael T. Madison, Jeffry R. Dwyer, and Steven W. Bender, *The Law of Real Estate Financing* (Eagan, MN: West, rev. ed. 2010), 2:78.

22. NAFTA, art. 1110.

23. Corrie M. Anders, "Real Estate Reforms Make Mexico a Good Place for Second Home, Investment," http://www.escapehomes.com/articles/Real_estate_reforms_make_Mexico_a_good_place_for_second_home_investment_.htm (last visited October 20, 2009). One source reported interest rates in mid-2008 between 7% and 9%. http://www.liveloreto.com/market-considerations (last visited September 4, 2010).

24. Joseph Contreras, *In the Shadow of the Giant: The Americanization of Mexico* (New Brunswick, NJ: Rutgers University Press, 2009), 141.

25. Davis, "Baby Boomer."

26. Ramón Eduardo Ruiz, *On the Rim of Mexico: Encounters of the Rich and Poor* (Boulder, CO: Westview Press, 1998), 17–18; see also Ronald L. Mize and Alicia C. S. Swords, *Consuming Mexican Labor: From the Bracero Program to NAFTA* (Ontario: University of Toronto Press, 2011), 207; Roberto Lovato, "Dispatch from Cancún: Developing Paradise in the Suicide Capital," http://www.huffingtonpost.com/roberto-lovato/dispatch-from-cancn-devel_b_791723.html (posted December 3, 2010; last visited May 2, 2011) (detailing the isolation and high suicide incidence among tourism workers).

27. Steven W. Bender, *Tierra y Libertad: Land, Liberty, and Latino Housing* (New York: New York University Press, 2010).

CHAPTER 3

1. Hart, *Empire and Revolution*, 122.

2. Ibid., 123.

3. Justin Akers Chacón and Mike Davis, *No One Is Illegal: Fighting Violence and State Repression on the U.S.–Mexico Border* (Chicago: Haymarket Books, 2006), 104.

4. Hart, *Empire and Revolution*, 167.

5. Domínguez and Castro, *The United States and Mexico*, 38.

6. John J. Dwyer, *The Agrarian Dispute: The Expropriation of American-Owned Rural Land in Postrevolutionary Mexico* (Durham, NC: Duke University Press, 2008), 1, 159, 161, 258–59 (also discussing how some of the land was expropriated without compensation).

7. Gregory C. Shaffer, "Note, An Alternative to Unilateral Immigration Controls: Toward a Coordinated U.S.–Mexico Binational Approach," *Stanford Law Review* 41 (1988): 187, 197. Compare Alan Weisman, *La Frontera: The United States Border with Mexico* (San Diego: Harcourt Brace Jovanovich, 1986), 88 (stating that the restriction against majority foreign ownership was in place at least since the 1930s).

8. Domínguez and Castro, *The United States and Mexico*, 138.

9. Shaffer, "Alternative to Unilateral Immigration," 202.

10. Ganster and Lorey, *U.S.–Mexican Border*, 100.

11. Although initially restricted to the northern border area and certain zones in Baja and Western Sonora, Mexican law now allows the establishment of maquiladoras anywhere in Mexico. Jorge A. Vargas, *Mexican Law for the American Lawyer* (Durham, NC: Carolina Academic Press, 2009), 271.

12. Joan B. Anderson and James Gerber, *Fifty Years of Change on the U.S.–Mexico Border: Growth, Development, and Quality of Life* (Austin: University of Texas Press, 2008), 81. Japanese-owned maquiladoras employed an estimated 30 percent of Tijuana's maquiladora work force in the mid-1980s. Brian O'Reilly, "Business Makes a Run for the Border," *Fortune* (August 18, 1986).

13. Domínguez and Castro, *The United States and Mexico*, 138.

14. Ruiz, *Rim of Mexico*, 66.

15. Hart, *Empire and Revolution*, 449.

16. Ibid.

17. Charles Bowden, *Down by the River: Drugs, Money, Murder, and Family* (New York: Simon & Schuster, 2002), 15.

18. Hart, *Empire and Revolution*, 450.

19. See Elvia R. Arriola, "Voices from the Barbed Wires of Despair: Women in the Maquiladoras, Latina Critical Legal Theory, and Gender at the U.S.–Mexico Border," *DePaul Law Review* 49 (2000): 729, 813 (Table A).

20. Hart, *Empire and Revolution*, 448.

21. Sam Quinones, "The Dead Women of Juárez," in *Puro Border: Dispatches, Snapshots & Graffiti from La Frontera*, ed. Luis Humberto Crosthwaite, John William Byrd, and Bobby Byrd (El Paso, TX: Cinco Puntos Press, 2003), 139, 141–42.

22. Michael Joseph McGuinness, "The Politics of Labor Regulation in North America: A Reconsideration of Labor Law Enforcement in Mexico," *University of Pennsylvania Journal of International Economic Law* 21 (2000): 1, 18.

23. Kathleen Staudt and Irasema Coronado, *Fronteras No Más: Toward Social Justice at the U.S.–Mexico Border* (New York: Palgrave Macmillan, 2002); Chacón and Davis, *No One Is Illegal*, 119.

24. See Mark J. Russo, "NAALC: A Tex-Mex Requiem for Labor Protection," *University of Miami Inter-American Law Review* 34 (2002): 51, 87 (specifying that Mexican labor law, derived from its 1917 Constitution, prohibits employment of children under 14 and those between 14 and 16 must not exceed six hours daily). Compare Staudt and Coronado, *Fronteras No Más*, 109 (stating Mexican law bans labor by those under 15, which appears to incorrectly summarize the Constitution).

25. Elvia R. Arriola, "Accountability for Murder in the Maquiladoras: Linking Corporate Indifference to Gender Violence at the U.S.–Mexico Border," *Seattle Journal for Social Justice* 5 (2007), 603, 617.

26. David Bacon, *The Children of NAFTA: Labor Wars on the U.S./Mexico Border* (Berkeley: University of California Press, 2004), 63 (observing that such wage penalties are common practice despite their illegality under Mexico labor law).

27. McGuinness, "Politics of Labor Regulation," 18 (citing commentators).

28. *Maquilapolis: City of Factories* (2006).

29. Bacon, *Children of NAFTA*, 167 ("In practice, there is no respect for the law . . . because our government's policy is to attract foreign investment by maintaining conditions which the companies want, like low wages, few regulations, and no unions"; remarks of Benedicto Martínez).

30. Ruiz, *Rim of Mexico*, 66.

31. Arriola, "Accountability for Murder in the Maquiladoras," 610–11 (discussing work of feminist researcher Norma Iglesias Prieto); see also Alicia Schmidt Camacho, *Migrant Imaginaries: Latino Cultural Politics in the U.S.–Mexico Borderlands* (New York: New York University Press, 2008), 246–47; Ruiz, *Rim of Mexico*, 80 (explaining employer preference for young, single women); *Maquilapolis: City of Factories* (documentary of Tijuana maquiladora workers explaining preference for female workers "because we had agile hands and would be cheap and docile").

32. Teresa Rodriguez, *The Daughters of Juárez: A True Story of Serial Murder South of the Border* (New York: Atria Books, 2007) (describing how one maquiladora worker, barred from entry to her work because she arrived four minutes late for her shift, disappeared on her way home, presumably on foot). Rodriguez surveys the various theories behind the widespread murders, implicating gang members, drug traffickers, serial killers from the United States, and even local police officers). Femicide in Juárez has a long history. See H. Gordon Frost, *The Gentlemen's Club: The Story of Prostitution in El Paso* (El Paso, TX: Mangan Books, 1983), 288 (describing atrocities many decades ago when some U.S.-based prostitutes set up shop in Juárez and were found brutally beaten and murdered in the desert).

33. Arriola, "Accountability for Murder in the Maquiladoras," 607.

34. Chacón and Davis, *No One Is Illegal*, 118 (interview of Enrique Davalos).

35. Ruiz, *Rim of Mexico*, 91 (discussing inequitable distribution of water to maquiladoras).

36. Kori Westbrook, "The North American Free Trade Agreement's Effects on Mexico's Environment," *Currents: International Trade Law Journal* 10 (2001): 86, 90.

37. Janice Shields, "'Social Dumping' in Mexico Under NAFTA," http://www.multi-nationalmonitor.org/hyper/issues/1995/04/mm0495_08.html (last visited November 5, 2009).

38. Westbrook, "North American Free Trade," 89.

39. Ibid., 90; *Maquilapolis* (vividly illustrating the health impacts of maquiladoras).

40. Shields, "Social Dumping."

41. Anderson and Gerber, *Fifty Years of Change*, 110.

42. Hart, *Empire and Revolution*, 482; Ruiz, *Rim of Mexico*, 211 (explaining how maquiladora managers illegally dispose of hazardous wastes).

43. Hart, *Empire and Revolution*, 481.

44. But see Kevin P. Gallagher, *Free Trade and the Environment: Mexico, NAFTA, and Beyond* (Stanford: Stanford University Press, 2004), 2–3 (contending that from 1985 to 1999 there had been no mass migration of heavy polluting firms to Mexico and suggesting that means environmental costs of compliance may not be so overwhelming they cause corporations to relocate; Gallagher then suggests developing countries might use this experience to enact appropriate environmental standards, knowing these shouldn't scare away foreign investment).

45. Nicholas Peters, "NAFTA and Environmental Regulation in Mexico," *Law and Business Review of the Americas* 12 (2006): 119; Senator Eliot Shapleigh, *Texas Borderlands: Frontier of the Future* (El Paso, TX, February 2009) http://shapleigh.org/reporting_to_you, (last visited November 20, 2010), 200 (stating that "[s]ince NAFTA, spending on the environment in Mexico has fallen 45 percent in real terms and plant-level environmental inspections declined at a similar rate"). NAFTA tried to address the race to the bottom issue by providing "it is inappropriate to encourage investment by relaxing domestic health, safety, or environmental measures." NAFTA, art. 1114.

46. Bill Ong Hing, *Ethical Borders: NAFTA, Globalization, and Mexican Migration* (Philadelphia: Temple University Press, 2010), 55.

47. Ruiz, *Rim of Mexico*, 229.

48. See generally Ross Perot and Pat Choate, *Save Your Job, Save Our Country: Why NAFTA Must Be Stopped—Now!* (New York, Hyperion, 1993) (describing the absence of legal protections in Mexico for laborers and the environment).

49. Domínguez and Castro, *The United States and Mexico*, 140 (these changes in the duty structure were phased in; also noting that NAFTA eclipsed the limited maquiladora structure with the flexibility to use Mexican raw materials and ship those assembled goods duty-free across the border, or to sell the maquiladora assembled goods in Mexican markets rather than return them assembled to the United States). Factories registered as maquiladoras were previously restricted from selling their finished products in Mexican markets.

50. Lila J. Truett and Dale B. Truett, "NAFTA and the Maquiladoras: Boon or Bane?" *Contemporary Economic Policy* 25 (February 22, 2007): 374 (describing previous procedure by which component parts from places like Japan could enter the United States and be shipped along with other U.S. parts to Mexico for assembly without duty); Gary Clyde Hufbauer and Jeffrey J. Schott, *NAFTA Revisited: Achievements and Challenges* (Washington, DC: Institute for International Economics, October 2005), 49 (reporting that some Asian-owned electronics maquiladoras chose to shut down rather than bear the production cost hike on maquiladora imports of non-NAFTA components).

51. See William C. Gruben and Sherry L. Kiser, "NAFTA and Maquiladoras: Is the Growth Connected?" http://www.dallasfed.org/research/border/tbe_gruben.html (last visited January 30, 2010) (discrediting those who attributed the initial post–NAFTA maquiladora growth to NAFTA).

52. Domínguez and Castro, *The United States and Mexico*, 140. Congress approved NAFTA in 1993, to take effect January 1, 1994.

53. Hufbauer and Schott, *NAFTA Revisited*, 104.

54. Ibid., 48–49 (detailing these and other contributing factors); see also Anderson and Gerber, *Fifty Years of Change*, 90 (raising additional factors).

55. Hing, *Ethical Borders*, 19 (Mexico's wages, while less than 10 percent of U.S. manufacturing wages, were thus undercut, causing the loss of 200,000 jobs between 2002 and 2003).

56. Ganster and Lorey, *U.S.–Mexican Border*, 100.

57. Louis R. Sadler, "The Historical Dynamics of Smuggling in the U.S.–Mexican Border Region, 1550–1998," in *Organized Crime and Democratic Governability: Mexico and the U.S. Mexican Borderlands*, ed. John Bailey and Roy Godson (Pittsburgh: University of Pittsburgh Press, 2000), 161, 165.

58. Ibid., 172.

59. Peter Andreas, *Border Games: Policing the U.S.–Mexico Divide* (Ithaca, NY: Cornell University Press, 2000), 31.

60. Ruiz, *Rim of Mexico*, 16; see also Chad Richardson and Rosalva Resendiz, *On the Edge of the Law: Culture, Labor and Deviance on the South Texas Border* (Austin: University of Texas Press, 2006), 201–13 (describing practices of trafficking of stolen cars into Mexico).

61. Ruiz, *Rim of Mexico*, 11 (stating the effect of the early 1990s peso devaluation as causing a 72 percent drop in sales in downtown Brownsville, Texas).

62. Dennis Wagner, "Drop in Legal Mexican Visitors Hurts Southern Arizona," *USA Today*, August 6, 2010, http://www.usatoday.com/news/nation/2010-08-06-fewerlegals06_ST_N.htm (last visited August 21, 2010).

63. "2009 Investment Climate Statement, Bureau of Economic, Energy, and Business Affairs" (February 2009), http://www.state.gov/e/eeb/rls/othr/ics/2009/117350.htm (last visited December 7, 2009).

64. Contreras, *Shadow of the Giant*, 7.

65. http://corporate.homedepot.com/wps/portal/THD_Mexico (last visited October 19, 2009).

66. Anheuser-Busch, however, did not control a majority of Modelo's voting shares. In the corporate world of dog-eat-dog, Belgian brewer InBev ultimately acquired Anheuser-Busch in 2008.

67. Ganster and Lorey, *U.S.–Mexican Border*, 193.

68. Leo R. Chavez, *The Latino Threat: Constructing Immigrants, Citizens, and the Nation* (Stanford: Stanford University Press, 2008), 34. See also Contreras, *Shadow of the Giant*, 94 (arguing that NAFTA was not entirely or even primarily at fault for the influx of Mexican immigrants, placing blame on the Mexican peso crisis among other possibilities).

69. Thomas L. Friedman, "What's That Sound?" *New York Times*, April 1, 2004, A23.

70. "Fleeing the Drug War Torn City," http://www.borderlandbeat.com/2010/02/fleeing-drug-war-torn-city.html (February 21, 2010; last visited August 10, 2010).

71. Jason Lange and Krista Hughes, "U.S. Warns Mexican Drug War Curbing Investment," http://www.reuters.com/article/idUSTRE6A35F620101104 (November 4, 2010, last visited November 22, 2010).

72. Tom Miller, "The Borderblasters," in *U.S.–Mexico Borderlands: Historical and Contemporary Perspectives*, ed. Oscar J. Martínez (Wilmington, DE: SR Books, 1996), 228.

73. Ibid., 229.

74. Gene Fowler and Bill Crawford, *Border Radio: Quacks, Yodelers, Pitchmen, Psychics, and Other Amazing Broadcasters of the American Airwaves* (Austin: University of Texas Press, 2002), 266.

75. Ibid., 13, 270.

76. Peter Laufer, *Wetback Nation: The Case for Opening the Mexican–American Border* (Chicago: Ivan R. Dee, 2004), 157.

77. Fowler and Crawford, *Border Radio*, 267.

78. Ibid., 266.

79. Ibid., 224 (describing how Mexico law effective in 1937 did require that radio programs contain at least 25 percent Mexican music).

80. Miller, "Borderblasters," 235.

81. Ibid., 231.

PART III

1. By illicit I mean the particular aim is unlawful in the country of departure at the time of the border crossing. Generally I do not opine as to the morality of the illicit act that spurs the crossing.

2. Ruiz, *Rim of Mexico*, 218.

3. John M. McCardell Jr., "Commentary, Drinking Age of 21 Doesn't Work," www.cnn.com (posted September 16, 2009; last visited September 16, 2009).

CHAPTER 4

1. See John A. Price, *Tijuana: Urbanization in a Border Culture* (Notre Dame: University of Notre Dame Press, 1973), 50 (stating San Francisco did so in 1917). See chapter 5 for discussion of the flourishing prostitution industry that took hold in Mexico.

2. Ruiz, *Rim of Mexico*, 45. Compare Milo Kearney and Anthony Knopp, *Border Cuates: A History of the U.S.–Mexican Twin Cities* (Austin, TX: Eakin Press, 1995), 199 (stating California prohibited horse betting in 1911).

3. T. D. Proffitt III, *Tijuana: The History of a Mexican Metropolis* (San Diego: San Diego State University Press, 1994), 186 (tracing the development of Tijuana tourism from spas in the 1880s to horse racing, boxing matches, and bull fights in the 1890s).

4. Lawrence A. Herzog, *Where North Meets South: Cities, Space, and Politics on the U.S.–Mexico Border* (Austin: Center for Mexican American Studies, University of Texas at Austin, 1990), 97.

5. The Eighteenth Amendment to the U.S. Constitution became law in 1919, but it was not enforced until the Volstead Act took effect in January 1920.

6. Dominique Ahedo et al. "Prohibition Stimulated Economies of El Paso, Juárez," *Borderlands* 19 (2000–2001): 16, http://www.epcc.edu/nwlibrary/borderlands (last visited September 21, 2009) (presumably these statistics encompass just the El Paso/Ciudad Juárez region that is the focus of its discussion). For other border regions, reports that on July 4, 1920, 65,000 U.S. residents crossed into Tijuana suggest the overall border traffic during Prohibition years was staggering. An alternate explanation for the Prohibition-era statistics is that advances in U.S. border management enabled a better accounting of what might have been large or larger numbers of crossers pre-Prohibition than reported.

7. Price, *Tijuana*, 49.

8. Kearney and Knopp, *Border Cuates*, 200 (noting the growth would have been greater had most laborers not chosen to live on the U.S. side of the border to avoid the higher cost of U.S. goods in Mexico).

9. Ruiz, *Rim of Mexico*, 46.

10. Ganster and Lorey, *U.S.–Mexican Border*, 46.

11. Ibid.; Ovid Demaris, *Poso del Mundo: Inside the Mexican–American Border, from Tijuana to Matamoros* (Boston: Little, Brown, 1970), 164.

12. Kearney and Knopp, *Border Cuates*, 198.

13. Oscar J. Martínez, "Prohibition and Depression in Ciudad Juárez–El Paso," in *U.S.–Mexico Borderlands: Historical and Contemporary Perspectives*, ed. Oscar J. Martínez (Wilmington, DE: SR Books, 1996), 151, 152.

14. See Eric Michael Schantz, "All Night at the Owl: The Social and Political Relations of Mexicali's Red–Light District, 1909–1925," in *On the Border: Society and Culture Between the United States and Mexico*, ed. Andrew Grant Wood (Lanham, MD: SR Books, 2001), 91, 119.

15. Torrans, *Forging the Tortilla Curtain*, 15.

16. Bender, "Savage Fronteras and Tribal Boundaries."

17. Graham, *Border Town*.

18. Edward Lonnie Langston, *The Impact of Prohibition on the Mexican–United States Border: The El Paso–Ciudad Juarez Case* (Dissertation, Texas Tech University, May 1974), 131.

19. Martínez, "Prohibition and Depression," 151.

20. Langston, *Impact of Prohibition*, 120–22 (describing factors leading to the closure of the horsetrack for almost ten years starting in 1917).

21. Oscar J. Martínez, *Border Boom Town: Ciudad Juárez since 1848* (Austin: University of Texas Press, 1978), 52 (remarks of writer Edward L. Langston).

22. Ahedo et al., "Prohibition Stimulated Economies."

23. Martínez, *Troublesome Border*, 108.

24. Ganster and Lorey, *U.S.–Mexican Border*, 46. But see Demaris, *Poso del Mundo*, 165 (listing the same three U.S. resident owners along with a Mexican general as the creators of Agua Caliente).

25. Ruiz, *Rim of Mexico*, 50–51.

26. Herzog, *North Meets South*, 97–98; Martínez, *Border Boom Town*, 66 (noting the early closure lasted for two years).

27. Vincent Cabeza de Baca and Juan Cabeza de Baca, "The 'Shame Suicides' and Tijuana," in *On the Border: Society and Culture Between the United States and Mexico*, ed. Andrew Grant Wood (Lanham, MD: SR Books, 2001), 145, 169 (President Roosevelt lifted the curfew in 1933).

28. Martínez, "Prohibition and Depression," 158.

29. Langston, *Impact of Prohibition*, 239.

30. Ibid., 132.

31. Demaris, *Poso del Mundo*, 168.

32. Martínez, "Prohibition and Depression," 158 (quoting from *Herald Post* newspaper).

33. Hiram Soto, "Revamped Caliente Gets Back in the Game," *San Diego Union-Tribune*, May 14, 2008, B1.

34. See Barbara G. Brents, Crystal A. Jackson, and Kathryn Hausbeck, *The State of Sex: Tourism, Sex, and Sin in the New American Heartland* (New York: Routledge, 2010), 8 (reporting approximately 36 licensed brothels in Nevada, with some 25 to 30 operating).

35. Ruiz, *Rim of Mexico*, 53 (discussing that Texas no longer prohibits sale of liquor by the drink at taverns, having passed legislation in 1971 to give counties the option to allow liquor, which El Paso County exercised).

36. Kearney and Knopp, *Border Cuates*, 217.

37. Price, *Tijuana*, 41.

38. Hart, *Empire and Revolution*, 367.

39. "Respectable Tijuana," *Time* (August 28, 1972).

40. Ibid. (describing advertisement).

41. José David Saldívar, *Border Matters: Remapping American Cultural Studies* (Berkeley: University of California Press, 1997), 32.

42. Fernando Romero, "TJ Night Life: U.S. Youths Pack Discos and Bars," *San Diego Union-Tribune*, April 22, 1986, E1.

43. James E. Lange, Robert B. Voas, and Mark B. Johnson, "South of the Border: A Legal Haven for Underage Drinking," *Addiction* 97 (2002): 1195, 1202; James E. Lange and Robert B. Voas, "Youth Escaping Limits on Drinking: Binging in Mexico," *Addiction* 95 (2000): 521 (finding an even higher rate of drunkenness for those aged 21–25, and suggesting the lure and the acceptability of the party scene, rather than the accessibility of drinking, was responsible for drawing these legal age drinkers south of the border; also finding in more limited testing that 35.5 percent of all pedestrian crossers back into El Paso were above the legal blood alcohol content for driving).

44. Saldívar, *Border Matters*, 132.

45. Daniel D. Arreola and James R. Curtis, "Tourist Landscapes," in *U.S.-Mexico Borderlands: Historical and Contemporary Perspectives*, ed. Oscar J. Martínez (Wilmington, DE: SR Books, 1996), 236, 240.

46. Nancy Cleeland, "Wild in the Streets of TJ," *San Diego Union*, November 7, 1988, C1.

47. Arreola and Curtis, "Tourist Landscapes," 242.

48. James E. Garcia, "Texas Teens Drawn to Mexican Bars," *Austin American-Statesman*, September 10, 1989, A1.

49. Ibid.

50. Scott J. Shelley, "Note, Border Crossing, Club-Hopping, and Underage 'Possession' of Alcohol: An Analysis of the Law Enforcement Response to the Problem of Cross-Border Underage Drinking in Southern Arizona," *Arizona Law Review* 43 (2001): 709, 710.

51. Marc Lacey, "The Mexican Border's Lost World," http://www.nytimes.com/2010/08/01/weekinreview/01lacey.html?_r=1&ref=marc_lacey (July 31, 2010; last visited August 10, 2010).

52. John Howells and Don Merwin, *Choose Mexico for Retirement: Information for Travel, Retirement, Investment, and Affordable Living* (Guilford, CT: Globe Pequot Press, 10th ed., 2007), 160.

53. "Alcohol and Spring Break," http://www.traumaf.org/featured/3-14-02springbreak.shtml (last visited December 24, 2009).

54. Ibid.

55. Ibid.

56. Contreras, *Shadow of the Giant*, 158.

57. "After Terror, Cancun Spring Break Still Booms," http://www.latinamericanstudies.org/mexico/cancun.htm (March 8, 2002; last visited December 10, 2009).

58. "Hidden Camera: Cancun Trips Dangerous for Students," http://www.click2houston.com/news/4504602/detail.html (May 18, 2005; last visited June 7, 2009).

59. "Warning for Parents of Teens Traveling to Cancun," http://www.epinions.com/content_1740480644 (June 26, 2001; last visited December 10, 2009).

60. Tara Kelley-Baker et al., "A Night in Tijuana: Female Victimization in a High-Risk Environment," *Journal of Alcohol and Drug Education* 52(3) (2008): 46.

61. Contreras, *Shadow of the Giant*, 156.

62. "Bill O'Reilly Wrong on Mexico," http://www.latinbusinesschronicle.com/app/article.aspx?id=3189 (March 4, 2009; last visited September 22, 2009).

63. William M. Welch, "Tijuana Off-Limits to U.S. Marines," *USA Today*, January 22, 2009, 3A.

64. Kellogg, "South of the Border," 32, 34.

65. "O'Reilly Wrong on Mexico."

66. Kellogg, "South of the Border," 34.

67. Catherine E. Shoichet, "Mexico City Woos Same-Sex Honeymooners," http://articles.cnn.com/2010-08-31/travel/mexico.same.sex.honeymoon_1_gay-marriage-law-gay-couples-gay-travelers?_s=PM:TRAVEL (last visited September 6, 2010).

68. Fiamma Montezemolo, René Peralta, and Heriberto Yepez, *Here Is Tijuana* (London: Black Dog Publishing, 2006), 121 (some Tijuana nightclub owners reside in San Diego).

69. Contreras, *Shadow of the Giant*, 151.

70. Ibid., 152.

71. Mize and Swords, *Consuming Mexican Labor*, 207–8.

72. Lovato, "Dispatch from Cancún."

CHAPTER 5

1. Christmas "special" of two hours for $160 with 18-year-old escort available for "Lesbian Shows and Private Orgies" as advertised in English on Tijuana escort service website, http://www.adultbaja.com/abvip008/profile-008.htm.

2. Bender, *Greasers and Gringos*, 64–81.

3. James A. Sandos, "Prostitution and Drugs: The United States Army on the Mexican–American Border, 1916–1917," *Pacific Historical Review* 49 (November 1980): 621, 645. At the same time, federal laws were enacted addressing the immigration or interstate transport of prostitutes—the Alien Prostitution Importation Act of 1875 aimed primarily at excluding Chinese prostitutes, the 1910 Mann Act, and the Immigration Act of 1917 that allowed the exclusion of prostitutes. See generally Kevin R. Johnson, *The "Huddled Masses" Myth: Immigration and Civil Rights* (Philadelphia: Temple University Press, 2004), 126–28.

4. Frost, *The Gentlemen's Club*, 22.

5. Ibid., 198.

6. Schantz, "All Night at the Owl," 106.

7. Ruiz, *Rim of Mexico*, 55 (discussing the 500 registered prostitutes in Tijuana in 1932).

8. Colonel Edwin E. "Buzz" Aldrin, Jr., with Wayne Warga, *Return to Earth* (New York: Random House, 1973), 116.

9. Ruiz, *Rim of Mexico*, 53.

10. Ibid., 54.

11. Jack Kerouac, *On the Road* (New York: Penguin Books, 1991 ed.), 288.

12. Brents, Jackson, and Hausbeck, *The State of Sex*, 36.

13. Ruiz, *Rim of Mexico*, 54.

14. Montezemolo, Peralta, and Yepez, *Here Is Tijuana*, 84.

15. Frost, *The Gentlemen's Club*, 296.

16. http://www.adelitabar.com/ (last visited September 28, 2009).

17. http://www.tijuanafaq.com/hobbyingbars–5.php (last visited September 28, 2009).

18. David J. Bellis, *Hotel Ritz—Comparing Mexican and U.S. Street Prostitutes: Factors in HIV/AIDS Transmission* (Binghamton, NY: Haworth Press, 2003), 59.

19. Michael Hemmingson, *Zona Norte: The Post-Structural Body of Erotic Dancers and Sex Workers in Tijuana, San Diego, and Los Angeles: An Auto/ethnography of Desire and Addiction* (Newcastle upon Tyne, UK: Cambridge Scholars Publishing, 2008), 28–29. Although Craigslist succumbed to pressure from authorities in the United States to remove its adult services listings, its Tijuana site still offers erotic service listings. Dennis Romero, "Craigslist's Defunct 'Erotic Services' Ads Live on in Tijuana," http://blogs. laweekly.com/informer/2010/09/craigslist_sex_ads_tijuana.php (September 22, 2010; last visited October 29, 2010).

20. Paige Lauren Diener and Blake Schmidt, "In Mexico, Many Prostitutes are Single Mothers," *Sun* (Yuma, AZ), May 10, 2006, 1.

21. http://health.ucsd.edu/news/2009/7–10–hiv+infection.htm (last visited September 28, 2009).

22. Bellis, *Hotel Ritz*, 70.

23. Ibid., 85.

24. Robert J. Stevenson, *A Mexican Border Prostitution Community During the Late Vietnam Era: La Zona* (Lewiston, NY: Edward Mellen Press, 2005), 28–29.

25. For example, the Optional Protocol to the UN Convention on the Rights of the Child on the Sale of Children, Child Prostitution, and Child Pornography, http://www. un–documents.net/opcrcsc.htm (last visited September 29, 2009).

26. Schantz, "All Night at the Owl," 112.

27. Hemmingson, *Zona Norte*, 89–90.

28. Catherine Bremer, "Child Sex Industry Thrives Despite Acapulco Arrests," http:// groups.yahoo.com/group/FAMILYCOURTREFORM/message/16455 (March 19, 2004; last visited November 26, 2010).

29. Laurence Iliff and Brendan M. Case, "Child Sex, Cancún a Troubling Mix," *Dallas Morning News*, March 26, 2004, 1A.

30. Sowmia Nair, U.S. Department of Justice, "Child Sex Tourism," http:// www.usdoj. gov/criminal/ceos/sextour.html (last visited September 14, 2009) (quoting U.S. retired schoolteacher).

31. Montezemolo, Peralta, and Yepez, *Here Is Tijuana*, 85.

32. Sebastian Rotella, *Twilight on the Line: Underworlds and Politics at the U.S.–Mexico Border* (New York: W.W. Norton, 1998), 67.

33. Peter Landesman, "The Girls Next Door," *New York Times*, January 25, 2004, § 6, 30.

34. Ibid.

35. Ibid.

36. Julian Sher, "What It's Like to Be 17 and Having Sex for Money," http://www.alter-net.org/story/149228/what_it%27s_like_to_be_17_and_having_sex_for_money?page=1 (December 16, 2010; last visited December 21, 2010).

37. Landesman, "Girls Next Door."

38. Diana Washington Valdez, "Child-Sex Tourism Growing in Border Cities like Juárez," *El Paso Times,* June 20, 2009, 7B.

39. Proffitt, *Tijuana,* 259.

40. Luis Alberto Urrea, *The Devil's Highway* (New York: Little, Brown, 2004), 208.

CHAPTER 6

1. "Divorce Across the Border," *Time* (July 23, 1965).

2. A. C. Sanders, "Divorce Mexican Style," *El Paso Magazine,* http://epmediagroup.com/features/474–divorce–mexican–style (February 1, 2008; last visited October 8, 2009).

3. Ibid.

4. Ibid. (this source states more than half a million couples flocked to the border in that time period; because many divorces were by proxy, in which only one spouse actually crossed into Mexico, it is unclear whether and how this source counted those proxy crossers).

5. Demaris, *Poso del Mundo,* 34.

6. "The Perils of Mexican Divorce," *Time* (December 27, 1963).

7. Sanders, "Divorce Mexican Style;" Kearney and Knopp, *Border Cuates,* 228.

8. "Comment, New York-Approved Mexican Divorces: Are They Valid in Other States?" *University of Pennsylvania Law Review* 114 (1966): 771 (collecting case law).

9. *Rosenstiel v. Rosenstiel,* 16 N.Y.2d 64, 209 N.E.2d 709, 262 N.Y.S.2d 86 (1965).

10. See *Warrender v. Warrender,* 79 N.J. Super. 114, 190 A.2d 684 (App. Div. 1963), aff'd per curiam, 42 N.J. 287, 200 A.2d 123 (1964); *Golden v. Golden,* 41 N.M. 356, 68 P.2d 928 (1937); *Bobala v. Bobala,* 68 Ohio App. 63, 33 N.E.2d 845 (1940).

11. "Perils of Mexican Divorce" (suggesting Mexican federal law required foreigners to obtain divorces under the laws of Mexico City, which did not permit divorces by mutual consent).

12. Martínez, *Border Boom Town,* 126.

13. http://www.cowboycupid.biz/ (last visited August 1, 2010). Among other options, the Mexican women would be eligible for a so-called fiancé visa that allows U.S. entry for a 90-day period pending marriage. However, there may be a considerable wait in procuring that visa, delaying the entry and marriage in the United States.

14. Stephen Zamora, José Ramón Cossío, Leonel Pereznieto, José Roldán-Xopa, and David Lopez, *Mexican Law* (Oxford: Oxford University Press, 2004), 468.

15. Ivan Barrera, "New Abortion Clinic Opens in San Ysidro," http://www.sdnews-notes.com/ed/articles/1998/0298ib.htm (last visited December 10, 2009).

16. Demaris, *Poso del Mundo,* 31.

17. Richard Brautigan, *The Abortion: An Historical Romance 1966* (New York: Simon & Schuster, 1970) (detailing the fictional journey by plane and bus from San Francisco to Tijuana).

18. Demaris, *Poso del Mundo,* 32 (observing the bail for those caught giving or receiving an abortion in Mexico ranged from $800 to $2,000 and landed several U.S. residents in the Tijuana jail).

19. Veronica Angulo and Sylvia Guendelman, "Crossing the Border for Abortion Services: The Tijuana-San Diego Connection," *Health Care for Women International* 23 (2002): 642, 651.

20. Emanuella Grinberg, "Promise of Holistic Healing Draws Cancer Patients to Mexico Clinics," http://www.cnn.com/2009/HEALTH/06/18/hauser.alternative.cancer.treatment/index.html (June 18, 2009; last visited June 20, 2009) (discussing 13-year-old cancer victim whose mother fled a Minnesota court order requiring resumption of chemotherapy and headed toward Mexico until an arrest warrant was issued).

21. Department of Health and Human Services, "Prescription Drug Use Within Nevada," http://mhds.nv.gov/dmdocuments/SAPrescriptionDrugFactSheetDec08.pdf (last visited November 2, 2010).

22. Donald E. de Kieffer, "The Mexican Drug Connection: How Trade in Pharmaceuticals Has Wrecked the FDA," *Southwestern Journal of Law and Trade in the Americas* 9 (2002–2003): 321, 322.

23. Montezemolo, Peralta, and Yepez, *Here Is Tijuana*, 125.

24. Ibid.

25. Juan Villoro, "Nothing to Declare: Welcome to Tijuana," in *Puro Border: Dispatches, Snapshots & Graffiti from La Frontera*, ed. Luis Humberto Crosthwaite, John William Byrd, and Bobby Byrd (El Paso, TX: Cinco Puntos Press, 2003), 197, 200.

26. Michele L. Creech, "Comment, Make a Run for the Border: Why the United States Government is Looking to the International Market for Affordable Prescription Drugs," *Emory International Law Review* 15 (2001): 593 (explaining why pharmaceutical prices are so high in the United States).

27. A. Rafik Mohamed and Erik D. Fritsvold, *Dorm Room Dealers: Drugs and the Privileges of Race and Class* (Boulder, CO: Lynne Rienner, 2010), 83, 94 (describing how mostly white U.S. college drug dealers head to Tijuana to tap black market dealers for OxyContin and Vicodin, meeting suppliers in bars and strip joints and then walking across the border with the bounty of pills: "[U.S. border agents] seemed so preoccupied with terrorism, undocumented aliens, and street drugs that they could not care less about a rich college kid coming through customs with a few hundred OxyContin pills in his pockets").

28. Stan Grossfeld, "Border Shopping for Steroids Fast and Easy," *Boston Globe*, April 28, 2005, C9.

29. Laura Tillman, "Desperate U.S. Women Forced to Go to Mexico to Take Care of Unwanted Pregnancies," www.alternet.org/story/148015/ (August 29, 2010, last visited September 6, 2010).

PART IV

1. Jeffrey S. Passel and D'Vera Cohn, *U.S. Unauthorized Immigration Flows Are Down Sharply Since Mid–Decade* (Pew Hispanic Center, September 1, 2010), fig. A1, http://pewhispanic.org/files/reports/126.pdf (last visited September 1, 2010).

2. Douglas S. Massey, Jorge Durand, and Nolan J. Malone, *Beyond Smoke and Mirrors: Mexican Immigration in an Era of Economic Integration* (New York: Russell Sage Foundation, 2002), 7.

3. "2009 Investment Climate Statement."

4. Andreas, *Border Games*.

5. Peter Reuter and David Ronfeldt, *Quest for Integrity: The Mexican–U.S. Drug Issue in the 1980s* (Santa Monica: RAND Corporation, 1991), 10.

6. "Ask Mexico to Send Draft Dodgers Back," *New York Times*, June 7, 1920, 9.

7. Hart, *Empire and Revolution*, 239–43.

8. Andreas, *Border Games*, 32.

9. Bill Long, "Mexico Bars 200 Hippies at Border," *San Diego Union*, February 4, 1968, B5; Aurelio Garcia II, "Trip to Mexico Out for Hippies," *San Diego Union*, February 2, 1968, B1.

10. Lee Grant, "Mexicans Bar Long-Haired Men," *San Diego Union*, March 25, 1970, B1.

CHAPTER 7

1. Graham, *Border Town*, 107.

2. Proffitt, *Tijuana*, 263.

3. Frank Mangan, *Bordertown Revisited* (El Paso, TX: Guynes Press, 1973), 130.

4. Langston, *Impact of Prohibition*, 251, 253.

5. Demaris, *Poso del Mundo*, 28 (remarks of retired U.S. customs agent).

6. Langston, *Impact of Prohibition*, 245.

7. Gabriela A. Recio, "Drugs and Alcohol: U.S. Prohibition and the Origins of the Drug Trade in Mexico, 1910–1930," *Journal of Latin American Studies* 34 (2002): 21, 33.

8. Ruiz, *Rim of Mexico*, 48.

9. Ahedo et al., "Prohibition Stimulated Economies."

10. Mangan, *Bordertown Revisited*, 130.

11. Langston, *Impact of Prohibition*, 245–46.

12. Ibid., 322; see also Martínez, "Prohibition and Depression," 152 (reporting that during the five-year period between 1928 and 1933, "seventeen U.S. lawmen were killed along the Texas–New Mexico–Arizona portion of the border, seven in the El Paso area").

13. Langston, *Impact of Prohibition*, 314.

14. Ibid., 254.

15. Mangan, *Bordertown Revisited*, 131.

16. Langston, *Impact of Prohibition*, 222–24.

17. Ruiz, *Rim of Mexico*, 44.

18. Langston, *Impact of Prohibition*, 226–27.

19. Recio, "Drugs and Alcohol," 31–32.

20. Andrew Sinclair, *Era of Excess: A Social History of the Prohibition Movement* (New York: Harper & Row, 1964), 198.

CHAPTER 8

1. Paul Butler, *Let's Get Free: A Hip-Hop Theory of Justice* (New York: New Press, 2009), 44.

2. Sandos, "Prostitution and Drugs," 638.

3. Frost, *The Gentlemen's Club*, 31.

4. Mária Celia Toro, *Mexico's "War" on Drugs: Causes and Consequences* (Boulder, CO: Lynne Rienner, 1995), 8 (by decree of Mexican President Calles); Andreas, *Border Games*, 40 (detailing motives for Mexico's drug enforcement laws in the early 1900s).

5. Elias Castillo and Peter Unsinger, "Mexican Drug Syndicates in California," in *Organized Crime and Democratic Governability: Mexico and the U.S. Mexican Borderlands*, ed. John Bailey and Roy Godson (Pittsburgh: University of Pittsburgh Press, 2000), 199, 200.

6. Ruiz, *Rim of Mexico*, 181.

7. Letizia Paoli, Victoria A. Greenfield, and Peter Reuter, *The World Heroin Market: Can Supply Be Cut?* (New York: Oxford University Press, 2009), 292.

8. *Hooked: Illegal Drugs and How They Got That Way* (A & E Television Network, 2000).

9. "Nonmedical Drug Use in the United States," in *Drugs in the Western Hemisphere: An Odyssey of Cultures in Conflict*, ed. William O. Walker III (Wilmington, DE: Scholarly Resources, 1996), 41, 45.

10. *Hooked: Illegal Drugs.*

11. Butler, *Let's Get Free*, 45.

12. "Nonmedical Drug Use," 45.

13. *Hooked: Illegal Drugs*; see also Peter Schrag, *Not Fit for Our Society: Immigration and Nativism in America* (Berkeley: University of California Press, 2010), 135 (describing publisher William Randolph Hearst's anti–Mexican motivations in whipping up "reefer-madness hysteria").

14. Martínez, *Troublesome Border*, 139.

15. Toro, *Mexico's "War" on Drugs*, 8.

16. Richard B. Craig, "Mexico's Antidrug Campaign in the 1970s," in *Drugs in the Western Hemisphere: An Odyssey of Cultures in Conflict*, ed. William O. Walker III (Wilmington, DE: Scholarly Resources, 1996), 174, 175.

17. Ganster and Lorey, *U.S.–Mexican Border*, 176.

18. Ceci Connolly, "The Inside Woman," *Washington Post*, September 12, 2010, A1.

19. Butler, *Let's Get Free*, 44.

20. Gabriela D. Lemus, "U.S.–Mexican Border Drug Control: Operation Alliance as a Case Study," in *Drug Trafficking in the Americas*, ed. Bruce M. Bagley and William O. Walker III (New Brunswick, NJ: Transaction, 1994), 423, 429.

21. Toro, *Mexico's "War" on Drugs*, 15.

22. David Crary, "Vast US Illegal Drug Market Fuels Mexican Cartels," http://abcnews.go.com/US/wireStory?id=7680279 (May 26, 2009; last visited November 9, 2009).

23. Carrie Kahn, "Meth Production Moves to Mexico," http://www.npr.org/templates/story/story.php?storyId=9307871 (April 3, 2009; last visited November 9, 2009).

24. The Meth Epidemic, http://www.pbs.org/wgbh/pages/frontline/meth/etc/upd-mexico.html (February 14, 2006; last visited December 10, 2009). After Mexico's ban on trade in pseudoephedrine, it appears the production of meth is starting to shift back to the United States, particularly in states that do not rigidly regulate this core ingredient of potent meth.

25. "The Mexican Campaign Against Growers, 1962," in *Drugs in the Western Hemisphere: An Odyssey of Cultures in Conflict*, ed. William O. Walker III (Wilmington, DE: Scholarly Resources, 1996), 172.

26. Bender, *Greasers and Gringos*, 47.

27. Andreas, *Border Games*, 67.

28. Ibid., 78–79.

29. Daniel Mejía and Carlos Esteban Posada, "Cocaine Production and Trafficking: What Do We Know?" in *Innocent Bystanders: Developing Countries and the War on Drugs*, ed. Philip Keefer and Norman Loayza (Washington, DC: World Bank, 2010), 253, 290; Paoli, Greenfield, and Reuter, *World Heroin Market*, 64–65 (detailing failure of eradication efforts).

30. Andreas, *Border Games*, 52–53.

31. Elaine Shannon, *Desperados: Latin Drug Lords, U.S. Lawmen, and the War America Can't Win* (New York: Viking, 1988), 47.

32. Ibid., 52 (discussing the eventual failure of Operation Cooperation); see also Martínez, *Troublesome Border*, 140 (discussing a brief reinstitution of the strict border enforcement strategy for several weeks in 1985 in response to the murder of a U.S. drug agent).

33. Andreas, *Border Games*, 42.

34. Ruiz, *Rim of Mexico*, 188 (reporting estimates that some 33,000 acres in Mexico are planted in opium poppies).

35. Toro, *Mexico's "War" on Drugs*, 39.

36. Tony Payan, *The Three U.S.–Mexico Border Wars: Drugs, Immigration, and Homeland Security* (Westport, CT: Praeger Security International, 2006), 25.

37. Bowden, *Down by the River*, 2.

38. Ganster and Lorey, *U.S.–Mexican Border*, 176.

39. Payan, *Three U.S.–Mexico Border Wars*, 25.

40. "Mexico Cartels Turning Into Full–Scale Mafias," http://www.msnbc.msn.com/id/32437386/ (last visited November 2, 2010).

41. Ruiz, *Rim of Mexico*, 172.

42. Bender, *Greasers and Gringos*, 45.

43. Romero, *Hyper-Border*, 142.

44. Jorge Chabat, "Drug Trafficking in U.S.–Mexican Relations: What You See Is What You Get," in *Drug Trafficking in the Americas*, ed. Bruce M. Bagley and William O. Walker III (New Brunswick, NJ: Transaction, 1994), 373, 377.

45. Elijah Wald, *Narcocorrido: A Journey into the Music of Drugs, Guns, and Guerrillas* (New York: HarperCollins, 2001), 50.

46. Fox and Allyn, *Revolution of Hope*, 323.

47. Julie Watson, "Mexico's Lax Drug Laws Worry US Police," *Milwaukee Journal and Sentinel*, August 27, 2009, 3A.

48. Fox and Allyn, *Revolution of Hope*, 328.

49. Richardson and Resendiz, *On the Edge of the Law*, 188 (DEA reported a kilo of cocaine costing between $31,000 and $45,000 in 1987 was down to between $14,000 and $24,000 in 2003).

50. William O. Walker III, "After Camarena," in *Drug Trafficking in the Americas*, ed. Bruce M. Bagley and William O. Walker III (New Brunswick, NJ: Transaction, 1994), 395, 401.

51. http://www.drugpolicy.org/library/factsheets/drugtreatmen/index.cfm (last visited January 12, 2010).

52. http://www.bts.gov/publications/national_transportation_statistics/pdf/entire.pdf (last visited December 1, 2010).

53. Andreas, *Border Games*, 75.

54. "743 Pounds of Marijuana Found in Septic Tank Truck, Arizona Police Say," http://www.cnn.com/2010/CRIME/01/29/arizona.marijuana.bust/index.html?hpt=T2 (January 29, 2010; last visited January 29, 2010).

55. http://www.ktla.com/news/nationworld/sns-c-border-busts-pictures,0,5014646.photogallery (last visited August 21, 2010).

56. Ibid., 80.

57. Payan, *Three U.S.–Mexico Border Wars*, 33.

58. Gary "Rusty" Fleming, *Drug Wars: Narco Warfare in the Twenty-First Century* (BookSurge Publishing, 2008), 117.

59. Payan, *Three U.S.–Mexico Border Wars*, 33.

60. Ibid., 34.

61. Connolly, "Inside Woman."

62. Martínez, *Troublesome Border*, 145.

63. Payan, *Three U.S.–Mexico Border Wars*, 32.

64. Willem van Schendel, "Spaces of Engagement: How Borderlands, Illegal Flows, and Territorial States Interlock," in *Illicit Flows and Criminal Things: States, Borders, and the Other Side of Globalization*, ed. Willem van Schendel and Itty Abraham (Bloomington: Indiana University Press, 2005), 38, 53.

65. Here, fiction mirrors reality, as a Southern California seizure revealed dog cages made of fiberglass mixed with cocaine, intended to be melted into cocaine once safely within the United States. See Judge James P. Gray, *Why Our Drug Laws Have Failed and What We Can Do About It: A Judicial Indictment of the War on Drugs* (Philadelphia: Temple University Press, 2001), 60.

66. See Dave Demerijan, "Mexican Drug Smugglers Try Flying the Unfriendly Skies," http://www.wired.com/autopia/2009/03/drug-smugglers/ (March 18, 2009; last visited November 4, 2009); Emily Bazar, "Ultralight Aircraft Emerging Trend in Drug Trafficking," http://www.freerepublic.com/focus/f-news/2201326/posts (March 6, 2009; last visited November 4, 2009).

67. Jackie Castillo, "Elaborate Drug Tunnel Found Along Mexico Border," www.cnn.com (June 11, 2009; last visited June 11, 2009). Season four of the Showtime comedy series *Weeds* featured a drug tunnel connecting a Tijuana nightclub to a San Ysidro maternity store.

68. Payan, *Three U.S.–Mexico Border Wars*, 36.

69. Matea Gold, "Tunnel Under Border May be 20 Years Old," *Los Angeles Times*, May 19, 2002, 9.

70. Sandy Huffaker, "As U.S. Tightens Mexico Border, Smugglers are Taking to the Sea," *New York Times*, July 18, 2009, A11.

71. Tim Golden, "Tons of Cocaine Reaching Mexico in Old Jets," *New York Times*, January 10, 1995, 1 (also describing how smugglers of Colombian cocaine are using old passenger jets with the seats ripped out to fly enormous quantities of cocaine into Mexico for trafficking to the United States).

72. "Colombia Captures Drug Smuggling Submarine Capable of Transporting 8 Tons," Fox News Latino, February 15, 2011, http://latino.foxnews.com/latino/news/2011/02/15/colombia-captures-drug-smuggling-submarine-capable-traveling-mexico/ (last visited April 16, 2011).

73. Huffaker, "U.S. Tightens Mexico Border."

74. Richardson and Resendiz, *On the Edge of the Law*, 171.

75. Bryan Denson, "Mexican Pot, Oregon's Problem," *Oregonian*, September 29, 2009, 1.

76. Huffaker, "U.S. Tightens Mexico Border."

77. Arthur Brice, "Deadliest Year in Mexico's War on Drugs," http://www.cnn.com/2009/WORLD/americas/12/31/mexico.violence/index.html (January 1, 2010; last

visited January 20, 2010) (2009 statistic); 2010 Drug War Death Toll in Ciudad Juarez Topped 3,100, http://www.kwtx.com/home/headlines/2010_Drug_War_Death_Toll_In_Ciudad_Juarez_Topped_3100__112773939.html (January 2, 2011; last visited January 16, 2011) (2010 statistic).

78. Marc Lacey, "In Mexican City, Drug War Ills Slip into Shadows," *New York Times*, June 13, 2009, A1 (describing the military takeover of the corrupt police force in Nuevo Laredo).

79. Ed Hornick, "Obama Heads to Mexico Amid Escalating Drug Violence," http://www.cnn.com/2009/POLITICS/04/15/obama.mexico/index.html (April 15, 2009; last visited December 10, 2009).

80. Fox and Allyn, *Revolution of Hope*, 321.

81. Marc Lacey, "In an Escalating Drug War, Mexico Fights the Cartels, and Itself," *New York Times*, March 30, 2009, A1.

82. Ibid.

83. Tomas Kellner and Francesco Pipitone, "Inside Mexico's Drug War," *World Policy Journal* 27 (Spring 2010): 21 (describing the brazen murder by a drug cartel of a Mexican trucking executive who resisted the cartel's efforts to smuggle narcotics in his trucks).

84. Ruben Navarrette Jr., "Commentary: What Mexico's Drug War Means for U.S.," http://www.cnn.com/2009/POLITICS/02/27/navarrette.mexico/index.html (February 27, 2009; last visited December 10, 2009).

85. Ken Ellingwood, "Mexico Takes Different Tack on Juarez Violence," *Los Angeles Times*, July 12, 2010, http://articles.latimes.com/2010/jul/12/world/la-fg-mexico-juarez-20100713 (last visited August 21, 2010).

86. Dan Glaister, "Mexico and the US: As Guns Go South, Drugs—and Violence—Go North," http://www.truthout.org/031109C (March 9, 2009; last visited May 28, 2009).

87. Hornick, "Obama Heads to Mexico."

88. Glaister, "Mexico and the US."

89. James C. McKinley Jr., "U.S. Stymied as Guns Flow to Mexican Cartels," *New York Times*, April 15, 2009, A1.

90. Ibid.

91. "Remarks by Secretary Napolitano at the Border Security Conference," http://www.dhs.gov/ynews/speeches/sp_1250028863008.shtm (August 11, 2009; last visited November 9, 2009). The U.S. Bureau of Alcohol, Tobacco, Firearms, and Explosives was embroiled in cross-border controversy in the summer of 2011 when its undercover operation came to light that allowed Mexican drug cartels to buy large quantities of assault weapons in the hope of tracking the arsenals and building a case against the purchasers.

92. Ioan Grillo, "Mexico's Attorney General Calls on U.S. to Stop Guns and Drug Money from Heading South," http://legacy.signonsandiego.com/news/mexico/20070328-2057-mexico-usguns.html (March 28, 2007; last visited December 1, 2010).

93. Payan, *Three U.S.–Mexico Border Wars*, 47.

94. Toro, *Mexico's "War" on Drugs*, 53.

95. Ken Stier, "Foreign Tax Cheats Find U.S. Banks a Safe Haven," http://www.time.com/time/business/article/0,8599,1933288,00.html (October 29, 2009; last visited August 2, 2010) ("If you are a Mexican drug lord, you can put as much money as you want in U.S. banks. We ain't going to tax it, and the Mexicans can't tax it because they are never going to know about it"; remarks of international tax publisher).

96. Grillo, "Mexico's Attorney General."

97. "Mexican Ex-President's Drug Proposal Stirs Debate," http://www.aolnews.com/world/article/mexican-ex-presidents-call-to-legalize-drugs-stirs-debate/19588481 (last visited August 22, 2010).

CHAPTER 9

1. In contrast to drug enforcement, for undocumented immigration there is little or no effort at interdiction within Mexico as there is little ability, aside from perhaps identifying migrants in transit from Central American countries or those contracting with known coyotes, to determine who is an emigrant before their crossing.

2. Jim Gilchrist and Jerome R. Corsi, *Minutemen: The Battle to Secure America's Borders* (Los Angeles: World Ahead Publishing, 2006), 4.

3. Tom Tancredo, *In Mortal Danger: The Battle for America's Border and Security* (Nashville: Cumberland House Publishing, 2006), 177.

4. *Plyler v. Doe*, 457 U.S. 202 (1982). In some border towns, children residing in Mexico allegedly have attended school on the U.S. side. When a Texas school district cracked down on the practice in 2009, it was revealed that some of the children, while living in Mexico, had been born in the United States and were thus U.S. citizens. School officials, however, take the position that only residents of the local U.S. community are entitled to admission in local schools. Mayra Cuevas-Nazario, "Texas School District Turns Away Students From Mexico," www.cnn.com (September 11, 2009; last visited September 11, 2009).

5. Johnson, *Huddled Masses*, 160.

6. Steven W. Bender, Raquel Aldana, Gilbert Paul Carrasco, and Joaquin G. Avila, *Everyday Law for Latino/as* (Boulder, CO: Paradigm Publishers, 2008), 205.

7. On family reunification, see generally Evelyn Cruz, "Because You're Mine, I Walk the Line: The Trials and Tribulations of the Family Visa Program," *Fordham Urban Law Journal* 38 (2011): 155.

8. Bender et al., *Everyday Law for Latino/as*, 179–80 (describing exception for children born of "alien enemies in hostile occupation").

9. Patrick J. Buchanan, *State of Emergency: The Third World Invasion and Conquest of America* (New York: St. Martin's Press, 2006), 259.

10. Bender et al., *Everyday Law for Latino/as*, 185–89.

11. Bob Christie and Paul J. Weber, "'Birth Tourism' A Tiny Portion of Immigrant Babies," http://www.boston.com/news/nation/articles/2010/09/03/birth_tourism_a_tiny_portion_of_immigrant_babies/ (September 3, 2010, last visited May 9, 2011).

12. Chavez, *Latino Threat*, 77–78.

13. http://blogs.suntimes.com/sweet/2009/12/rep_luis_gutierrez_renewing_pu.html (December 13, 2009, last visited November 23, 2010) (comment posted on *Chicago-Sun Times* website in response to story on the federal immigration reform bill).

14. Ruiz, *Rim of Mexico*, 140; Richardson and Resendiz, *On the Edge of the Law*, 121 (detailing survey findings that most undocumented Mexicans reported economic reasons for their migration to the United States).

15. Wayne A. Cornelius, *The Future of Mexican Immigrants in California: A New Perspective for Public Policy* (La Jolla: University of California, San Diego Press, 1981), 47.

16. Kevin R. Johnson, *Opening the Floodgates: Why America Needs to Rethink Its Borders and Immigration Laws* (New York: New York University Press, 2007), 201.

17. Bender, *Tierra y Libertad*, 24.

18. Bill Ong Hing, *Defining America Through Immigration Policy* (Philadelphia, PA: Temple University Press, 2004), 38 (the Exclusion Act did permit entry of teachers, students, and merchants, but with small quotas). Chinese immigrants remained excluded until 1943.

19. Grace Peña Delgado, "At Exclusion's Southern Gate: Changing Categories of Race and Class among Chinese Fronterizos, 1882–1904," in *Continental Crossroads: Remapping U.S.–Mexico Borderlands History*, ed. Samuel Truett and Elliott Young (Durham, NC: Duke University Press, 2004), 198.

20. Laufer, *Wetback Nation*, 71–72.

21. See generally David G. Gutiérrez, *Walls and Mirrors: Mexican Americans, Mexican Immigrants, and the Politics of Ethnicity* (Berkeley: University of California Press, 1995), 52.

22. Joseph Nevins, *Operation Gatekeeper: The Rise of the "Illegal Alien" and the Making of the U.S.–Mexico Boundary* (New York: Routledge, 2002), 27.

23. Kitty Calavita, *U.S. Immigration Law and the Control of Labor: 1820–1924* (Orlando, FL: Academic Press, 1984), 135 (these exemptions were extended through 1920 under pressure from Southwestern sugar beet growers); Mark Reisler, *By the Sweat of Their Brow: Mexican Immigrant Labor in the United States, 1900–1940* (Westport, CT: Greenwood Press, 1976), 27–33 (discussing the department order issued May 23, 1917 by the Secretary of Labor, applicable initially to just agricultural workers and conditioned upon remaining in the United States for no more than six months but later extended for work lasting the duration of the war and to other specified fields of employment). Scholars disagree as to how long the exemptions for Mexican immigrants were kept in place. For example, Acuña contends the head tax and literacy exemptions lasted until 1921. Rodolfo Acuña, *Occupied America: A History of Chicanos* (New York: HarperCollins, 3d ed. 1988), 160. Compare Nevins, *Operation Gatekeeper*, 33 (stating that for the first time in August 1928 the United States ordered consular officials to enforce the restrictions on illiteracy against Mexicans, as well as to enforce the head tax).

24. Reisler, *Sweat of Their Brow*, 59.

25. Hing, *Defining America*, 121.

26. Ibid., 124.

27. See Mae M. Ngai, *Impossible Subjects: Illegal Aliens and the Making of Modern America* (Princeton, NJ: Princeton University Press, 2004), 70–71 (describing how many Mexicans, perhaps 20 to 30 percent, entered during the 1920s and 1930s as "temporary visitors" rather than as immigrants under this entry category that allowed them to stay up to a year and work in U.S. industries, such as during an agricultural season, upon payment of a refundable head tax).

28. Nevins, *Operation Gatekeeper*, 28.

29. Ibid., 29.

30. Acuña, *Occupied America*, 185.

31. Mirandé, *Gringo Justice*, 105.

32. Ibid., 107.

33. Bill Ong Hing, "Immigration Policy: Thinking Outside the (Big) Box," *Connecticut Law Review* 39 (2007): 1401, 1421. See also Calavita, *U.S. Immigration Law*, 160 (stating that

in September 1930, the U.S. president "advised consular officials to interpret strictly the public charge clause in order to reduce immigration during the Great Depression").

34. Gilbert Paul Carrasco, "Latinos in the United States: Invitation and Exile," in *Immigrants Out! The New Nativism and the Anti-Immigrant Impulse in the United States*, ed. Juan F. Perea (New York: New York University Press, 1997), 190, 193.

35. Acuña, *Occupied America*, 202–3.

36. Bender, *Greasers and Gringos*, 134.

37. Ngai, *Impossible Subjects*, 75.

38. Steven W. Bender, *One Night in America: Robert Kennedy, César Chávez, and the Dream of Dignity* (Boulder, CO: Paradigm, 2008), 66.

39. Chacón and Davis, *No One Is Illegal*, 140.

40. Ibid.

41. Ngai, *Impossible Subjects*, 139.

42. Chacón and Davis, *No One Is Illegal*, 140.

43. These monies, representing a 10 percent withholding, were ostensibly paid by the U.S. government to Mexico, yet some bracero workers never received these funds. A class action lawsuit against the Mexican government, which was settled in 2008, authorized payments to those who worked during World War II from 1942 through 1946 or (more likely) their surviving family members who live in the United States.

44. Mirandé, *Gringo Justice*, 121.

45. Acuña, *Occupied America*, 263.

46. Ibid.

47. Chacón and Davis, *No One Is Illegal*, 145

48. Ibid., 143.

49. Ibid., 146.

50. Ibid.

51. Ibid.

52. Acuña, *Occupied America*, 264.

53. Ibid., 265.

54. Chacón and Davis, *No One Is Illegal*, 144; Ngai, *Impossible Subjects*, 154 (supplying a photograph of this procedure known condescendingly as "drying out the wetbacks").

55. Bender, *One Night in America*, 111.

56. Ibid., 102.

57. Mirandé, *Gringo Justice*, 125.

58. Carrasco, "Latinos in the United States," 197.

59. See generally Ngai, *Impossible Subjects*, 256 (detailing concerns of Latin American immigration sparked by reports of population growth in Latin America and the Caribbean).

60. Johnson, *Huddled Masses*, 25. In addition to the restrictions on numbers, Western Hemisphere entrants were allowed to cross the border conditioned on a showing they would not displace U.S. workers.

61. Douglas S. Massey, "Only by Addressing the Realities of North American Economic Integration Can We Solve the Problem," *Boston Review* (May/June 2009).

62. Bender, *One Night in America*, 107.

63. Ibid.

64. Kevin R. Johnson and Bernard Trujillo, *Immigration Law and the U.S.-Mexico Border: ¿Sí se puede?* (manuscript in preparation, on file with author).

65. Ngai, *Impossible Subjects*, 261.

66. Johnson and Trujillo, *Immigration Law*.

67. McCormick and McCormick, "Hospitality." The so-called diversity lottery visas that authorize another 50,000 visas annually for permanent residency are of little help to Mexican residents, as the lottery is only open to applicants from countries with immigration below a specified threshold in the previous five years, thus excluding Mexico and several other Latin countries.

68. Ngai, *Impossible Subjects*, 266.

69. Nevins, *Operation Gatekeeper*, 68.

70. Compare Ngai, *Impossible Subjects*, 266 (2.7 million) with Samuel Huntington, *Who Are We? The Challenges to America's National Identity* (New York: Simon & Schuster, 2004), 225 (3.1 million).

71. Bender, *One Night in America*, 112.

72. Nevins, *Operation Gatekeeper*, 35.

73. Mirandé, *Gringo Justice*, 143–44.

74. Andreas, *Border Games*, 96.

75. David Bacon, "The Brutal Side of Obama's 'Softer' Immigration Enforcement," www.alternet.org (December 16, 2009; last visited December 16, 2009).

76. Jorge A. Bustamante, "Undocumented Immigration: Research Findings and Policy Options," in *Mexico and the United States: Managing the Relationship*, ed. Riordan Roett (Boulder, CO: Westview Press, 1988), 109, 113.

77. Bender, *Greasers and Gringos*, 117; Massey, Durand, and Malone, *Beyond Smoke and Mirrors*, 88.

78. Bender, *Greasers and Gringos*, 122.

79. Johnson, *Opening the Floodgates*, 112.

80. Ibid., 173 (citing 2002 report from Public Policy Institute of California).

81. Bacon, *Children of NAFTA*, 48.

82. See Randy Shaw, "BP Oil Spill Submerges Concerns for Immigrants," http://www.beyondchron.org/articles/BP_Oil_Spill_Submerges_Concern_for_Immigrants_8220.html (June 15, 2010; last visited July 9, 2010).

83. http://www.aclu.org/immigrants-rights/us-mexico-border-crossing-deaths-are-humanitarian-crisis-according-report-aclu-and (last visited November 27, 2009).

84. The tragic journey of these migrants in 2001 is told in Urrea, *Devil's Highway*.

85. Bender, *Greasers and Gringos*, 124.

86. Jorge Ramos, *Dying to Cross: The Worst Immigration Tragedy in American History* (New York: HarperCollins, 2005) (reporting that 16 of the 19 dead were Mexican; on average those transported had paid between $1,000 and $1,500 to travel from the Mexican border to Houston. Most had crossed the border to reach the U.S. safe house by a variety of means, including by floating down a river on inner tubes and tires supplied by the coyotes).

87. For background on the tragedy, see Ruben Martinez, *Crossing Over: A Mexican Family on the Migrant Trail* (New York: Henry Holt, 2001).

88. Maria Jimenez, "Humanitarian Crisis: Migrant Deaths at the U.S.–Mexico Border," http://www.aclu.org/immigrants-rights/humanitarian-crisis-migrant-deaths-us-mexico-border (October 1, 2009; last visited December 5, 2009): 26.

89. Rudy Adler, Victoria Criado, and Brett Huneycutt, *Border Film Project: Photos by Migrants and Minutemen on the U.S.–Mexico Border* (New York: Harry N. Abrams, 2007).

90. Erlinda V. Gonzales-Berry and Marcela Mendoza, *Mexicanos in Oregon: Their Stories, Their Lives* (Corvallis: Oregon State University Press, 2010), 112.

91. E. Eduardo Castillo, "Mexican Migrants Massacre: Drug Cartel Suspected in Killing of 72," http://www.huffingtonpost.com/2010/08/26/mexico–migrants–massacre–_n_695299.html (last visited October 24, 2010).

92. Stephen Lendman, "Modern Slavery in America," http://baltimorechronicle.com/2009/030609Lendman.shtml (last visited October 24, 2010).

93. John Bowe, *Nobodies: Modern American Slave Labor and the Dark Side of the New Global Economy* (New York: Random House, 2007), 17–19.

94. Ibid., 102.

95. Francisco Vásquez Mendoza, "The Shadow of the Polleros," in *Puro Border: Dispatches, Snapshots and Graffiti from La Frontera*, ed. Luis Humberto Crosthwaite, John William Byrd, and Bobby Byrd (El Paso, TX: Cinco Puntos Press, 2003), 50.

96. Montezemolo, Peralta, and Yepez, *Here Is Tijuana*, 11.

97. Buchanan, *State of Emergency*, 254.

98. Margaret Regan, *The Death of Josseline: Immigration Stories from the Arizona Borderlands* (Boston: Beacon Press, 2010), 122, 175–76.

99. Ibid., 72 (two million were pedestrians).

100. Pew Hispanic Center, "Modes of Entry for the Unauthorized Migrant Population," http://pewhispanic.org/factsheets/factsheet.php?FactsheetID=19 (May 22, 2006; last visited December 10, 2009). In order to receive a border-crossing visa, the applicant must establish funds sufficient to cover expenses in the United States, compelling social and economic ties to a home country, and a residence outside the United States, all designed to ensure a return to the home country after the visit. See http://travel.state.gov/visa/temp/types/types_1262.html (last visited February 6, 2010).

101. Lawrence A. Herzog, "Border Commuter Workers and Transfrontier Metropolitan Structure along the U.S.–Mexico Border," in *U.S.–Mexico Borderlands: Historical and Contemporary Perspectives*, ed. Oscar J. Martínez (Wilmington, DE: SR Books, 1996), 176, 184–85. Cf. Michael Quintanilla and Peter Copeland, "Mexican Maids: El Paso's Worst-kept Secret," in *U.S.–Mexico Borderlands*, 213 (describing the low-wage employment sector in El Paso of undocumented and commuter Mexican maids with homes in Juárez).

102. Payan, *Three U.S.–Mexico Border Wars*, 71.

103. John B. Roberts II, "Close Mexican Border to Terrorists," *Washington Times*, March 1, 2005, A1.

104. Gilchrist and Corsi, *Minutemen*, 162–67.

105. Peter Beinart, "The Wrong Place to Stop Terrorists," *Washington Post*, May 4, 2006, A25.

106. Montezemolo, Peralta, and Yepez, *Here Is Tijuana*, 12.

107. Fox and Allyn, *Revolution of Hope*, 323.

108. Johnson, *Opening the Floodgates*, 185.

109. Passel and Cohn, *Unauthorized Immigration*.

110. Luis Alberto Urrea, "A Wild Calm at the Edge of the Abyss," *Playboy* (October 2009): 104. See also Julia Preston, "Sharp Drop in Border Arrests Is Tied to Recession, Experts Say," *New York Times*, November 26, 2009, A20 (noting the Obama administration claimed that improvements in border security led to the decreased migrant flow, but that researchers attribute the slowdown to the deep U.S. recession).

111. Marcus Stern, "U.S. Changes Approach to Deportation," *USA Today*, September 10, 2010, 8A (discussing changes in deportation policy to better target immigrants who have committed serious crimes).

112. Taylor Barnes, "Mexicans Create Jobs in the U.S.," http://abcnews.go.com/Business/mexicans-create-jobs-us/story?id=10023810 (last visited August 1, 2010). Those without considerable financial resources are seeking asylum in the United States from drug violence, but in 2009 the ceiling for refugees from all of Latin America and the Caribbean was only 5,000. Paola Reyes, "E-2 Visas Provide Immigration Opportunities to Wealthy Mexicans Fleeing Violence," http://latindispatch.com/2010/02/04/e-2-visas-provide-immigration-opportunities-to-wealthy-mexicans-fleeing-violence/ (February 4, 2010; last visited August 10, 2010). Should violence continue and reach into the lower classes, the exodus might compare to migration during the Central American upheaval in the 1980s and 1990s. See Kevin R. Johnson, "The Intersection of Race and Class in U.S. Immigration Law and Enforcement," *Law and Contemporary Problems* 72 (2009): 1, 22 (discussing that the U.S. government routinely classified those fleeing civil war in Central America and Haiti as economic refugees subject to deportation, rather than as eligible for asylum).

113. Ana Campoy, "Mexicans Fleeing Violence Spur a Boom in El Paso," http://online.wsj.com/article/NA_WSJ_PUB:SB125651480451107029.html (October 26, 2009; last visited August 10, 2010) (statistics from El Paso Hispanic Chamber of Commerce for 12 months ending July 31, 2009).

114. Adler, Criado, and Huneycutt, *Border Film Project*.

PART V

1. Human trafficking of laborers won't be as big a problem after expanded legalization lowers the cost of migration, although there is still potential for abuse that may result in involuntary servitude given lack of migrant money for housing deposits, transport within the country, and other costs in the United States.

2. The Mexican government ignited a firestorm of controversy in late 2004 when it published a 32-page guide for Mexican migrants that covered dangers of crossing as an undocumented immigrant.

CHAPTER 10

1. Bender, *Greasers and Gringos*, 133.

2. Kim Murphy, "Olympic Hospitality an Irony for Utah Latinos," *Los Angeles Times*, February 8, 2002, A1.

3. Bender, "Sight, Sound and Stereotype," 1155.

4. William K. Rashbaum, "United States Attorney Plans Drug-Terror Unit," *New York Times*, January 18, 2010, A16.

5. Joshua Holland, "Michelle Malkin and Michael Savage Use Swine Flu Crisis to Peddle Their Xenophobia," www.alternet.org. (April 29, 2009; last visited April 29, 2009).

6. Al Giordano, "How 'The NAFTA Flu' Exploded," http://www.narconews.com/Issue57/article3512.html (April 29, 2009; last visited December 15, 2009).

7. Bender, *Greasers and Gringos*, 46.

8. Johnson, *Opening the Floodgates*, 176–177.

9. Jason Beaubien, "As the Drug War Rages On, Will Mexico Surrender?" http://www.npr.org/templates/story/story.php?storyId=129009629 (August 6, 2010; last visited August 6, 2010).

10. "Mexico's President Speaks Out."

11. See Earl Shorris, *Latinos: A Biography of the People* (New York: W.W. Norton, 1992) (describing the demeaning views of Mexican Americans, referred to as pochos, within Mexico). Of late, perhaps due to reliance on the remittance economy and the virulent attacks on Mexicans within the United States from media, politicians, voters, and residents, these negative views have shifted to support the Mexican immigrant.

12. Michèle Alexandre, "Sex, Drugs, Rock & Roll and the Moral Dirigisme: Toward a Reformation of Drug and Prostitution Regulations," *University of Missouri, Kansas City Law Review* 78 (2009): 101, 110.

13. See Jennifer M. Chacón, "Misery and Myopia: Understanding the Failures of U.S. Efforts to Stop Human Trafficking," *Fordham Law Review* 74 (2006): 2977 (describing the shortcomings of the Victims of Trafficking and Violence Protection Act of 2000 and blaming border interdiction strategies, among other U.S. policies, for facilitating trafficking).

14. Contreras, *Shadow of the Giant*, 179.

15. Kevin R. Johnson, "Legal Immigration in the 21st Century," in *Blueprints for An Ideal Legal Immigration Policy*, ed. Richard D. Lamm and Alan Simpson (Washington, DC: Center for Immigration Studies, March 2001), 37, 38. Although NAFTA does include some provisions on the temporary entry of professional business workers, it otherwise fails to address migration. One explanation for the failure is the reluctance of some in Congress to abdicate, in their view, the immigration power to the executive. See Joel P. Trachtman, *The International Law Economic Migration: Toward the Fourth Freedom* (Kalamazoo, MI: W.E. Upjohn Institute for Employment Research, 2009), 223–24 (discussing position of Congressman James Sensenbrenner, who opposes inclusion of immigration law provisions in free trade agreements as contrary to the constitutional provision exclusively enumerating immigration as a power of Congress, but pointing out Sensenbrenner's omission that Congress must nonetheless approve trade agreements so presumably this constitutional provision is not sidestepped).

16. http://mexidata.info/id858.html (last visited January 12, 2010).

17. Treaty of Guadalupe Hidalgo, art. 21.

18. http://www.ice.gov/about/offices/enforcement-removal-operations/secure-communities/index.htm (last visited November 29, 2010).

19. Payan, *Three U.S.–Mexico Border Wars*, 26.

20. Laufer, *Wetback Nation*, 205.

21. Richardson and Resendiz, *On the Edge of the Law*, 7.

22. Bender, *One Night in America*, 169 (describing the 1960s Alliance for Progress championed by the Kennedys that would have established U.S. responsibility for political, economic, and social development in Latin America).

23. See Shaffer, "Alternative to Unilateral Immigration" (criticizing U.S. immigration laws for focusing only on migration controls without the other half of the equation needed to curb immigration—bolstering Mexico's economy).

24. Hing, *Ethical Borders*, 5, 46 (also noting that under NAFTA the Mexican government drastically cut subsidies to its own farmers, with 85 percent of remaining subsidies going toward larger Mexican farms).

25. Ibid., 14.

26. Ibid., 133–43.

27. Ibid., 171; see also Johnson, *Opening the Floodgates*, 128–29 (making the case that the United States owes a moral obligation to Mexican nationals based on our contribution to the disparity in wealth between the two countries, which justifies loosening of migration policies).

28. Regan, *Death of Josseline*, 39–43 (describing fruits of micro-credit in Mexico).

29. See generally Stephen D. Morris, *Political Corruption in Mexico: The Impact of Democratization* (Boulder, CO: Lynne Rienner, 2009), 1 (noting that Mexico devotes an estimated 9–12 percent of its gross domestic product to bribes).

CHAPTER 11

1. Regan, *Death of Josseline*, xxviii.

2. Yet that return to prior law must be without the regulatory ploys the United States used, as discussed in chapter 9, to restrict Mexican immigration as it desired. Economic downturns in the United States are sufficient to stem Mexican immigration without coercion, as Mexican laborers are sensitive to the call of U.S. employers.

3. Johnson, *Opening the Floodgates*, 43–44, 129 (proposing an expansion of NAFTA to encompass a free flow of people as a second best solution to a broad open borders policy).

4. Stephen Zamora, "A Proposed North American Regional Development Fund: The Next Phase of North American Integration Under NAFTA," *Loyola University Chicago Law Journal* 40 (2008): 93, 125–26 (detailing the relative paucity of U.S. development aid to Mexico in 2004, with half the $93 million of Official Development Assistance going toward narcotics control and military/security).

5. http://ec.europa.eu/justice/policies/citizenship/docs/guide_free_movement_low.pdf (last visited May 3, 2011); Emily Gibbs, Comment, "Free Movement of Labor in North America: Using the European Union as a Model for the Creation of North American Citizenship," *University of San Francisco Law Review* 45 (2010): 265, 278; Hing, *Ethical Borders*, 81–82 (explaining the initial ability of EU countries to phase-in free movement of labor, which expired in 2011).

6. Catherine Dauvergne, *Making People Illegal: What Globalization Means for Migration and Law* (New York: Cambridge University Press, 2008), 147 (explaining that in 2006 only 2 percent of Europeans of working age were living in a country outside their nationality); Johnson, *Opening the Floodgates*, 28 (discounting fears that Mexicans would overrun the United States under an open borders regime by looking to the European Union experience, where EU members Bulgaria and Romania have a lower per capita GDP than Mexico); see also Kevin R. Johnson, "Protecting National Security Through More Liberal Admission of Immigrants," *University of Chicago Legal Forum* 2007 (2007): 157, 177 (observing the ease of travel between U.S. states has not resulted in mass migration from poorer to richer states).

7. It would be realistic for government to impose some minimum residency standard on the receipt of benefits if based on U.S. (rather than purely local) residency, and if the period is reasonably short and cognizant of labor seasons, such as six months of residency over the preceding two-year period.

8. Some threshold number of employees would trigger the tax contribution, in order to shield very small businesses from the requirements. One of the challenges of such a taxation system is that many needed services delivered to local immigrant populations are supplied through local rather than federal governments, and some attention would need to be paid in any taxing structure of immigrant labor to ensure that the relevant authority received the tax revenue. Another challenge is that employers might pass along the tax to vulnerable immigrant workers in the form of a wage cut. The tax should be operative only for workers governed by federal minimum wage protections.

9. Anna Gorman, "UCLA Study Says Legalizing Workers Would Aid Economy," *Los Angeles Times*, January 7, 2010, A4.

10. Shapleigh, *Texas Borderlands*, 399.

11. Opening immigration to Western Hemisphere residents may not completely eliminate undocumented immigration through Mexico if there is a return to the days of Asian immigrants entering through our southern border. But the obvious focus of our current immigration enforcement spending is Mexicans and other Latinos/as, as evidenced by recent deportation rates comprised almost entirely of Latinos/as despite undocumented immigration from other regions.

CHAPTER 12

1. Langston, *Impact of Prohibition*, 327 (quoting editorial writer for *El Paso Times* circa 1927).

2. Butler, *Let's Get Free*, 53.

3. See generally Gray, *Why Our Drug Laws Have Failed* (detailing these and other options of drug treatment and education). Here, I refer to decriminalization and legalization interchangeably, preferring the former term to retain the potential for some government oversight of decriminalized narcotics, such as through abuse treatment programs and regulated quantities of sale.

4. Tony Newman, "Marijuana in America: More Mainstream Than Ever, More Arrests Than Ever," www.alternet.org (September 30, 2009; last visited October 1, 2009).

5. Ibid.

6. Bender, *Greasers and Gringos*, 51.

7. Congress did act in 2010 to reduce the disparity in criminal sentencing between possessing crack and powder cocaine from 100:1 to 18:1.

8. *United States v. Brignoni–Ponce*, 422 U.S. 873, 884 (1975) ("Except at the border and its functional equivalents, officers on roving patrol may stop vehicles only if they are aware of specific articulable facts, together with rational inferences from those facts, that reasonably warrant suspicion that the vehicles contain aliens who may be illegally in the country"; therefore, at the border, officials need not have particularized suspicion in their searches). See also *United States v. Flores-Montano*, 541 U.S. 149, 152 (2004) ("The government's interest in preventing entry of unwanted persons and effects is at its zenith at the international border"). The courts limit the discretionless border search to so-called routine searches, in contrast to non-routine searches: "'In order to conduct a search that goes beyond the routine, an inspector must have reasonable suspicion,' and the 'critical factor' in determining whether a search is 'routine' is the 'degree of intrusiveness.'" Ibid.

For search purposes, the border includes the area extending 100 miles inland from the border. 8 C.F.R. § 287.1 (a)(1–3).

9. Mohamed and Fritsvold, *Dorm Room Dealers* (a study of about 50 dealers at Southern California colleges, who were Caucasian aside from a handful of minority dealers).

10. Professor Roberto Rodriguez suggested this approach, mindful that the Sheriff Joes of the legal community would never undertake it, as there are different rules in the criminal enforcement arena for white U.S. residents than for minorities and especially Mexican undocumented immigrants. Roberto Rodriguez, "Arizona's SB 1070: A Crack Law by any Other Name," http://www.commondreams.org/view/2010/07/11-0 (July 11, 2010; last visited November 17, 2010).

11. Tony Newman, "10 Signs the Failed Drug War is Finally Ending," www.alternet.org (December 4, 2009; last visited December 7, 2009).

12. Moreover, drinking laws fail to discourage minors anyway, and minors should be sold licenses to drink on completion of alcohol training courses in the same way they are tested and licensed to drive.

13. http://www.drugpolicy.org/library/factsheets/drugtreatmen/index.cfm (last visited January 13, 2010) (citing study finding that dollar for dollar providing treatment to cocaine users was ten times as effective as interdiction efforts in reducing drug abuse); Mohamed and Fritsvold, *Dorm Room Dealers*, 129 (observing the staggering cost of interdiction has done little to curtail drug use).

14. Steven B. Duke, "Drugs: To Legalize or Not," *Wall Street Journal*, April 25, 2009, W1.

15. Watson, "Mexico's New Drug Law."

16. Ibid. (discussing decriminalization efforts in Argentina, Brazil, Colombia, and Uruguay).

17. Bud Foster, Mexico Decriminalizes Drugs in Small Amounts, http://www.mpp.org/states/arizona/news/mexico-decriminalizes-drugs.html (August 24, 2009; last visited January 13, 2010).

18. Watson, "Mexico's New Drug Law."

19. Newman, "10 Signs."

20. Steve Fox, Paul Armentano, and Mason Tvert, *Marijuana Is Safer: So Why Are We Driving People to Drink?* (White River Junction, VT: Chelsea Green Publishing, 2009) (detailing harmful externalities and health risks of alcohol in comparison to marijuana).

21. Steve Fox, "Lies About Marijuana Drive People to a Much More Harmful Drug," www.alternet.org (November 9, 2009; last visited November 9, 2009). Legalization and regulation of marijuana might facilitate further testing on the question of whether lung cancer results from smoking the drug, together with the dissemination of warnings and suggestions for alternate forms of ingestion.

22. For example, contaminated heroin was tied in early 2010 to the deaths of several users in Scotland from the disease of anthrax.

23. Paul Armentano, "Pot Versus Alcohol: Experts Say Booze is the Greater Danger," http://www.alternet.org/drugs/147392/pot_versus_alcohol%3A_experts_say_booze_is_the_bigger_danger/ (last visited August 1, 2010).

24. "Study: Alcohol 'Most Harmful Drug,' Followed by Crack and Heroin," http://www.cnn.com/2010/HEALTH/11/01/alcohol.harm/index.html?hpt=C2 (last visited November 1, 2010).

25. Paul Armentano, "Are U.S. Pot Laws the Root Cause of Mexican Drug Violence," http://blogs.alternet.org/speakeasy/2010/03/17/are-u-s-pot-laws-the-root-cause-of-mexican-drug-violence/ (last visited August 1, 2010).

26. Samuel I. del Villar, "The Illicit U.S.–Mexico Drug Market: Failure of Policy and an Alternative," in *Mexico and the United States: Managing the Relationship*, ed. Riordan Roett (Boulder, CO: Westview Press, 1988), 191, 203 (stating that opium poppy production is essentially restricted to the mountainous Northwestern region of Mexico).

27. Adam Tschorn, "Marijuana's New High Life," *Los Angeles Times*, August 30, 2009, Image Sec., 1.

28. http://blogs.alternet.org/speakeasy/2010/10/29/gallup-record-number-of-americans-now-say-they-support-marijuana-legalization/ (last visited November 12, 2010).

29. Andy Dworkin, "Kids Use Fewer Illegal Drugs," *Oregonian*, December 15, 2009, 1A.

30. Ryan Grim, "Arnold: Time to Talk About Legalizing Pot," http://www.huffingtonpost.com/2009/05/05/arnold-time-to-talk-about_n_197244.html (May 5, 2009; last visited September 13, 2010).

31. Steven Wishnia, "Pot is More Mainstream Than Ever, So Why is Legalization Still Taboo?" www.alternet.org (October 29, 2009; last visited October 29, 2009).

32. See Jason Beaubien, "As the Drug War Rages On, Will Mexico Surrender?" http://www.borderlandbeat.com/2010/08/as–drug–war–rages–on–will–mexico_07.html (last visited August 21, 2010) (detailing the resurgence of the PRI in Mexico which long ruled the country while keeping the drug trade in bounds with bribes in exchange for tacit government tolerance).

33. During the regime of Vicente Fox, the Mexican Congress had approved legalization of user quantities of drugs, but Fox killed that legislation after U.S. officials raised alarm. Lacey, "Escalating Drug War."

34. Convened by former presidents of Mexico, Colombia, and Brazil, the Latin American Commission on Drugs and Democracy issued a report in 2009 (Drugs and Democracy: Toward a Paradigm Shift, http://www.drogasedemocracia.org/Arquivos/declaracao_ingles_site.pdf ; last visited August 21, 2010) urging a dialogue between the U.S. government and Latin America to develop such alternatives to the failed war on drugs. In the same vein, considerable immigration from countries such as Guatemala through Mexico into the United States compels hemispheric dialogue on the immigration front. Indeed, ill treatment of Central American migrants discovered in Mexico rivals or exceeds the bounds of U.S. immigration policing. See Chris Hawley, "Activists Blast Mexico's Immigration Law," *USA Today*, http://www.usatoday.com/news/world/2010-05-25-mexico-migrants_N.htm (May 25, 2010; last visited November 25, 2010).

CHAPTER 13

1. Steven W. Bender, *Comprende? The Significance of Spanish in English-Only Times* (Mountain View, CA: Floricanto Press, 2008).

2. Laura Carlsen, "Obama and NAFTA," http://www.commondreams.org/view/2009/01/10-8 (last visited May 1, 2011). Alternatively, eliminating U.S. farm subsidies, or restoring Mexican farm subsidies, might address the imbalance of trade and support for agricultural staples. See Hing, *Ethical Borders*, 46 (detailing how the Mexican government under NAFTA drastically reduced farm subsidies from $2 billion in 1994 to $500

million in 2000, with most of the remaining subsidies going to larger Mexican farming operations).

3. Hing, *Ethical Borders,* 51 (suggesting that Mexican President Calderón has insisted he will not renegotiate and will address the concerns of Mexican farmers through other means).

4. Ruiz, *Rim of Mexico,* 60.

5. Ramos, *A Country for All,* 73.

6. Marcela Sánchez, "Remittances as a Source of Productivity," *Poder Hispanic* (July 2010): 15; see generally Ezra Rosser, "Immigrant Remittances," *Connecticut Law Review* 41 (2008): 1.

CHAPTER 14

1. http://www.avert.org/age-of-consent.htm (last visited December 17, 2009) (noting for some states a lesser age is specified, for example, when the age gap between the two parties is small).

2. Duke, "Drugs: To Legalize or Not" (suggesting further that the cartels already are heavily armed and weapons do not wear out quickly, minimizing the impact of U.S. gun reform on the drug war).

3. 18 U.S.C. § 2423(b) (persons who travel in foreign commerce for purpose of engaging in sex with a person under 18 may be imprisoned for up to 30 years). The child pornography industry is another area ripe for enforcement.

4. Brents, Jackson, and Hausbeck, *The State of Sex,* 231; Alexandre, "Sex, Drugs, Rock & Roll," 125.

5. Elisabeth Malkin, "Many States in Mexico Crack Down on Abortion," http://www.nytimes.com/2010/09/23/world/americas/23mexico.html (September 22, 2010; last visited October 29, 2010). Mexico's Supreme Court in 2011 let stand Baja California's state constitution provision on conception that effectively bars elective abortions. Sources differ on the number of Mexican states with such provisions, variously listing 16, 17, and 18 states.

CONCLUSION

1. Bill Ong Hing, "NAFTA, Globalization, and Mexican Immigrants," *Journal of Law, Economics & Policy* 5 (2009): 87, 134–35 (reporting projections that by 2030 one in five U.S. residents will be a senior citizen, and that the U.S. fertility rate will fall below replacement level by 2015 to 2020, at the same time that job growth is projected in lower-skilled occupations).

2. Some Anglos are hostile toward the Mexican culture, but given the growth of the Mexican population in the United States, presumably they realize that living in a Mexican beach enclave designed and intended for U.S. residents is little different, apart from its cheaper costs, from a Southern California gated community in which some Anglos currently seek haven from encroaching minorities.

3. Frank D. Bean and B. Lindsay Lowell, "NAFTA and Mexican Migration to the United States," in *NAFTA's Impact on North America: The First Decade,* ed. Sidney Weintraub (Washington, DC: Center for Strategic and International Studies, 2004), 263, 278 (1974 figure); https://www.cia.gov/library/publications/the-world-factbook/geos/mx.html (2009 estimate).

4. "Climate Change Will Increase Mexico–US Migration," July 27, 2010, http://www.bbc.co.uk/news/world-us-canada-10770674 (last visited August 2, 2010) (describing study by Princeton researchers predicting that global warming may bring between 1.4 and 6.7 million Mexicans to the United States by 2080). In the bigger picture, that number is relatively small and likely will not offset the U.S. labor needs in that time period.

5. Bender, *Comprende?*

6. Romero, *Hyper-Border*, 113.

7. Gloria Anzaldúa, *Borderlands/La Frontera: The New Mestiza* (San Francisco: Aunt Lute Books, 2d ed., 1999), 25.

Index

About the Author

STEVEN W. BENDER is Professor of Law at Seattle University School of Law. He is the author of *Tierra y Libertad: Land, Liberty, and Latino Housing* (NYU Press, 2010), *Greasers and Gringos: Latinos, Law, and the American Imagination* (NYU Press, 2003), and *One Night in America: Robert Kennedy, César Chávez, and the Dream of Dignity* (Paradigm Publishers, 2008).